# NEW WORLD OF WINE FROM THE CAPE OF GOOD HOPE

*The Definitive Guide to the South African Wine Industry*

# New World of Wine from the Cape of Good Hope

## The Definitive Guide to the South African Wine Industry

Phyllis Hands
Dave Hughes

*Photography and design by Keith Phillips*

Nederburg manor house

*Editor:*
Harry J. Stephan Ph.D.

*Photography, design and layout:*
Keith Phillips

*Subeditor:*
Abigail R. Collins

*Layout:*
Nicholas H. Stephan

*Illustrator:*
Dedré Fouquet

*Proofreader:*
Leni Martin

*Reproduction:*
Mega Digital, Cape Town

*Printed and bound:*
Tien Wah Press (Pte) Ltd, Singapore

New World of Wine from the Cape of Good Hope © 2001
Stephan Phillips (Pty) Ltd

Maps and graphics © 2001
Stephan Phillips (Pty) Ltd

Text © 2001
Phyllis Hands and Dave Hughes

Text Chapter 5 Virtuosi © 2001
Stephan Phillips (Pty) Ltd

Reg. No. 96/16989/07

ISBN 0-9584247-2-1

Stephan Phillips (Pty) Ltd
P O Box 1230
Somerset West 7129
South Africa

www.stephanphillips.com

STEPHAN PHILLIPS

Rural Stellenbosch

# CONTENTS

Riebeek kloof

# FOREWORD

The rich experience and collective wisdom of Phyllis Hands and Dave Hughes, so apparent in this finely crafted book, allows them to reflect the unique qualities of the South African wine and brandy industry.

The largest, most spectacular concentration of flowers and plants found anywhere on Earth, the Cape Floral Kingdom, is in the Western Cape. The whole of Europe has only one tenth of the number of plant species and South America with its incredible diversity of bird life, less than a quarter. This diversity of plant life is evidence of a great diversity of soils and micro-climates so necessary for producing wines and brandies with a style and quality to capture the imagination. Nowhere else in the world does the biodiversity of a region, cultural richness and a wine and brandy heritage combine to find expression in such a unique way.

Over 300 years of wine and brandy experience enriched by cultural influences accumulated from all over Europe, North America, Africa and the East and blended in an environment that has become a benchmark for diversity is only now starting to realise its full potential for the production of wines and brandies of distinction, capable of offering the world a unique experience.

The book beautifully captures the character of South Africa's wines and brandies and makes a special contribution to communicating these qualities to the rest of the world.

Dr Anton E. Rupert

*Soil preparation at Kanonkop near Stellenbosch.*

# Acknowledgements

We thank Harry and Hope Stephan who have continued to support our endeavours. We would also like to thank the following:

Bennie Howard and his team at the Nederburg International Auction.

Cristine Rudman, principal/director of the Cape Wine Academy.

Harry Hands for his hours of typing.

Laura Bamber, Dirk van der Westhuizen, Martin Koen, Patricia LoSciuto, Ja-neen Gilliatt, Sean Heydenrych and the team at Mega Digital.

Peet Engelbrecht, Leon Pienaar, Wendy Jonker and the employees at the Wine and Spirit Board and the Plant, Health and Quality Division of the Department of Agriculture who work so tirelessly for the industry.

Yvette van der Merwe and Debbie Wait at the South African Wine Industry Information and Systems for supplying statistics on the wine industry.

Simon Barlow for historic material on the Cape winelands.

Johan Pienaar and Paul Wallace for reviewing our work on viticulture. Mark Carmichael-Green and Jean Daneel who assisted us with our research on wine making.

Debra Savage at Rupert and Rothschild for her patience and good humour.

Dr Johan Steenkamp and Danie van Schalkwyk at Nietvoorbij for their invaluable assistance on grape varieties.

Marius le Roux for permission to photograph at the Stellenbosch Museum.

Leon Wolmarans, manager for GIS and Photography at the Council of Geoscience in Pretoria, for supplying maps.

Ian Scott of BDO Spencer Steward for his assistance.

John Young of Film and TV Lighting who assisted us with lights on demand.

Diane Heyns at Fairview for her help styling our food shots.

Fernando Neto at Vilamoura who provided such a perfect ambience while we photographed his delicious seafood.

Table mountain

Dedicated to those who enjoy good food, fine wine and the celebration of life.

Vilamoura restaurant

# Introduction

The Cape of Good Hope, symbol of Africa, destination of dreams, magical and mysterious, lies at the foot of a rocky peninsula that hangs precariously off the southern shores of Africa. Named by Portuguese navigator Bartolomeu Dias, the first explorer to round the Cape in 1488, this promontory extends 50 kilometres into the cold waters where the Atlantic and Indian oceans meet.

Dias named this Cape 'Cabo da Boa Esperança' after finding the sea route to the East Indies. Since his initial discovery, Cape Town has remained the 'Tavern of the Seas', attracting mariners from all points of the compass with its unbelievable charm.

In 1580, Sir Francis Drake wrote on arrival, 'This Cape is the most stately thing and the fairest cape we saw in the whole circumference of the earth.'

Cape Town still remains the tavern of the seas, a destination that heralds good food, great wine, fine summer weather and a special brand of hospitality that is unique to this city at the foot of Africa.

*(old documents from top) Original Rustenberg deed, early map of the Cape, VOC parchment, early painting of Cape Dutch building with Table Mountain behind.* COURTESY SIMON BARLOW.

*(background) Cape Point from a mariner's perspective.*

Vines were originally introduced to South Africa by Jan van Riebeeck who understood that wine would help in the battle against scurvy on Dutch sailing vessels. Scurvy is caused primarily by a lack of vitamin C, and wine certainly helped alleviate this problem. One should not underestimate the value of Van Riebeeck's contribution, as scurvy often decimated nearly half of a ship's complement during the voyage around the Cape to the East.

In 1655 Van Riebeeck planted his first vines in the Dutch East India Company's garden, and then extended planting to Bosheuwel, an area of just over 100 hectares along the Amstel River, now called the Liesbeek. In 1659 the first wine in the Cape was made from these plantings.

Vines and wine arrived at Africa's most southern shores because of trade, and not as in many other New World countries, for the religious purpose of using wine as a sacrament. As a result, the wine industry developed early in the Cape Colony, and of all the New World wine-making countries, the wines of the Cape were the first to become famous. In the late 18th and early 19th centuries, Constantia wine, a sweet dessert wine, was a great favourite in the royal courts of Europe and was venerated by writers of that time. Napoleon Bonaparte reputedly requested a bottle of Constantia on his deathbed. If his wish had been granted, he no doubt would have died a satisfied man.

In modern times the wine industry did not come into its own until the end of the Second World War. One of the most important contributing factors was the perfecting of cold fermentation techniques for white wines in the late 1950s. These techniques have now been introduced in cellars in a great number of the hotter wine-making regions of the world. Until the early 1960s spirits, and particularly brandy, were the most consumed alcoholic beverages other than beer.

The early days of wine making at the Cape were not without extreme hardship. The pioneers found the peninsula teeming with game and virtually uninhabited. Prior to colonisation, the Western Cape was inhabited for at least 40 000 years by two closely related Stone Age pastoral nomadic tribes, the Khoikhoi and the San (Bushmen).

The original homes of the settlers were generally simple and basic. After the wine trade boomed with England in the 18th and 19th centuries, farmers enlarged their homes and in many instances decorated their buildings with beautiful Cape Dutch gables. The majestic beauty of the Cape winelands, with its stark and imposing mountain ranges and gracious Cape Dutch homesteads nestling in the shade of giant oaks in vine-covered valleys, has become a definitive tourist attraction. In 1922 Jan Smuts commented on these historic buildings: 'The old Dutch homesteads of South Africa deserve to be better known than they are. In a country where, as a rule, Nature is everything and Art literally nowhere, our old Dutch houses form an exception to the rule. A very important contribution to architecture was made by the Dutch in South Africa. It is

evident that this noble architecture could only have arisen in times of comparative quiet and leisure. People hurried and urged by violent competition have not the time to consider the artistic effect of their houses, or to plan gardens in which to enjoy leisure. Such are usually found in what are called older countries. South Africa has a great heritage, a fine tradition which has come down to the present day.'

Certainly Capetonians have a proud heritage which they will continue to treasure and share with all who visit the Cape, and a mood of confident anticipation prevails in the winelands as we celebrate the new millennium.

(far left) An old bottle of the famous early sweet wine from Constantia.

(left) Old farm kitchen, Stellenbosch. Courtesy Stellenbosch Museum.

(top) Manor house at L'Ormarins.

(above) Historic manor house and vineyards at Groot Constantia.

(right) Vergelegen manor house framed by 300-year-old camphor trees.

# HISTORY

1488  The Portuguese mariner, Bartolomeu Dias, rounds the southern tip of Africa. Portugal's King Henry names it Cabo de Boa Esperanca, the Cape of Good Hope.

1580  Sir Francis Drake rounds the Cape on his circumnavigation of the world and writes in his diary: 'This Cape is the most stately thing and the fairest cape we saw in the whole circumference of the earth.'

1652  Jan van Riebeeck arrives in Table Bay on the *Drommedaris*. He establishes a settlement to provide Dutch East India Company merchantmen with fresh produce, water and wine for their long voyages to the East Indies.

1655  Van Riebeeck successfully plants grapevines in the Company's Garden.

1657  In February, the Dutch East India Company releases 49 officers, who become South Africa's first free burghers. Each is given a small land grant of under 50 hectares to farm along the Amstel River near the Company's headquarters. These new Dutch farmers have no knowledge of viticulture, and it is only when they see Van Riebeeck's promising vineyards that they realise that vines are easier to grow than wheat. The settlement is now joined by a number of Germans, several of whom move to the fertile valleys of Rondebosch and Constantia.

1659  On February 2, Van Riebeeck writes in his diary: 'Today, praise be to God, wine was made for the first time from Cape grapes.'

1679  Simon van der Stel is appointed governor, and establishes the town of Stellenbosch, 60 kilometres east of Cape Town.

1680  Simon van der Stel plants 100 000 vines in the Constantia valley. He later develops Constantia as a model wine and fruit farm.

1688  France's King Louis XIV revokes the Edict of Nantes. As a result, 150 French Huguenots emigrate to the Cape, followed by 50 more the following year. The new immigrants are given land grants primarily in the Franschhoek valley.

1699  Simon van der Stel is succeeded as governor by his son, Willem Adriaan, who as a competent farmer not only improves the quality of the farms in the Cape, but also leaves as his legacy a most comprehensive Garden Calendar.

1761  Constantia exports wine to Europe. By 1778 Constantia wines win acclaim throughout Europe.

1795  The first British occupation of the Cape Colony.

1803  The end of the first British occupation.

1806  The second occupation by the British begins.

1814  The Congress of Vienna formally gives Great Britain control of the Cape Colony.

1825  Cape wine exports boom after Great Britain places heavy tariffs on French wines. Farmers increase their vineyards dramatically.

1861  Great Britain lowers tariffs on French wine imports. South African wine exports drop dramatically.

1885  The phylloxera louse appears in the Cape winelands and devastates the vineyards.

1904  Vineyards are re-established, as vines are grafted onto phylloxera-resistant rootstocks imported from the United States of America.

1906  In response to the depression in the wine and spirit industry, the first South African wine co-operatives are formed. Ten million vines are uprooted in the drier areas of Robertson and Oudtshoorn in order to plant lucerne to feed ostriches whose feathers are much prized around the world.

1918  As over-production has become a severe problem, the chairman of the Cape Wine Farmers & Wine Merchants Association, Dr Charles Kohler, calls on all farmers to sell exclusively through co-operatives. De Ko-öperatiewe Wijnbouwers Vereniging van Zuid Afrika Beperkt (KWV) is formed to stabilise wine prices and ensure members a suitable return on their grapes.

1924  An American doctor, William Charles Winshaw, who had arrived in the Cape in 1899, joins Oude Libertas' owner Gideon Krige, and begins producing natural wine. The KWV is empowered by the Smuts government, through the Wine and Spirit Control Act No. 5, to set minimum prices for wine for distillation. The Act also initiates a process of legal control over the industry that is expanded over the following decades. Wine merchants who cannot negotiate favourable terms go out of business.

1925  Professor Perold of Stellenbosch University successfully cross-pollinates Pinot Noir of Burgundy with Cinsaut of the Rhône (known as Hermitage in the Cape), creating Pinotage, a grape variety that is unique to South Africa's vineyards.

1935  SFW becomes a public company.

1937  Nederburg is bought by Johann Graue, one of the innovators of cold fermentation for white wines.

1940  Wine and Spirit Control Act No. 23 empowers the KWV to set minimum grape and wine prices and decrees that wine can be purchased only with the organisation's permission.

1945  Distillers Corporation is formed by Dr Anton Rupert.

1950  W & A Gilbey open a distillery in Natal.

1957  Due to over-production, the KWV institutes a quota system limiting the number of vines a farmer may plant.

1959  SFW launches Lieberstein, a semi-sweet white wine. In five years sales rise from 30 000 to 31 million litres.

1961  SFW markets the first Pinotage under the Lanzerac label.

1962  Gilbeys acquires R. Santhagens Cape Limited, one of the country's oldest brandy producers and leading wine merchants.

1971  The Stellenbosch Wine Route is launched.

1973  The Wine of Origin legislation is implemented.

1975  The first Nederburg Auction of Rare Cape Wines is held at Nederburg.

1979  The Cape Wine Academy is founded under the auspices of SFW.

1983  The government rejects recommendations for a less monopolistic structure for the wine industry.

1990 The gold Superior Wine of Origin Seal is discontinued.

1991 Union Wine and Douglas Green amalgamate to form Douglas Green Bellingham. The Veritas Awards are introduced for bottled wines.

1992 President de Klerk implements changes that will eventually lead to majority rule. The United States and other countries begin to lift economic sanctions and South Africa once again exports wines. The KWV suspends the quota system. The Cape Wine Academy and KWV wine courses merge.

1993 A new, simplified Wine of Origin seal is introduced.

1995 For the first time wine estates are allowed to buy in grapes for wine making. The amount bought in is not to exceed 45 per cent of the estate's production, and the wine has to be bottled under a second label.

1996 The minimum pricing for the purchase of grapes is abolished.

1997 KWV registers as a private company on December 1st. ARC Infruitec-Nietvoorbij is founded.

1998 New Liquor Bill is approved by Parliament (3-tier system).

1999 New Liquor Bill is rejected as unconstitutional and referred back to Parliament for amendment.

2000 Chenin Blanc Association is formed in May.

2001 Distell becomes a public company in March. New Liquor Bill remains under discussion.

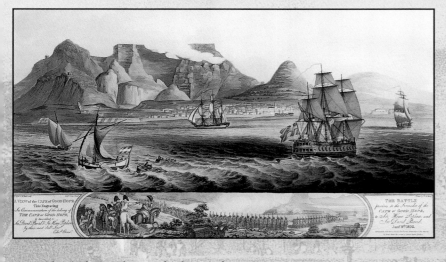

*(above) The British arrive for the second occupation.* COURTESY SIMON BARLOW.

*(background) Lutheran Church, Cape Town.* COURTESY SIMON BARLOW.

*(right) La Concorde, KWV's headquarters.*

Since President Nelson Mandela walked to freedom, the South African wine industry has gone through a number of major changes. Under the old apartheid regime, the industry was as stultified as the government that controlled it. Quota systems regulated where farmers could plant their grapes and technical innovations together with the importation of new plant material were severely restricted. The new breeze that blew through a democratic South Africa brought international contact and much-needed capital. Wineries that had long been dormant blossomed with new varieties and styles. These new wineries, however, were in the main quite large and had their own corporate cultures. Only in the recent past has the industry seen the development of true artisan wineries. This explosion of some 150 additional wineries has begun not only because new buyers have bought small parcels of land, but more importantly because a number of the Cape's premier winemakers have left the corporate wineries to produce their own labels. The list of these artisan winemakers is impressive and they are offering wines of unique character and distinction. Moreover, viticulturists like Michel Rolland and Dr Phil Freeze are regular visitors to South Africa's shores, proof positive that innovation is attracting the finest consultants that the world has to offer. The current debates on the best use of South Africa's *terroir*, especially with regard to planting distances, canopy management, rootstocks, clones and techniques to ensure optimum ripeness have certainly improved the quality of grapes that enter the cellars. These improvements in the vineyards have been captured in the bottle and South African wines are winning new converts both at home and abroad.

South African wines have featured at a number of prestigious wine events. In 1999 Kanonkop Estate won the Pichon Longueville Comtesse de Lalande Trophy for the best blended red wine at the International Wine and Spirit Competition (IWSC) with its Paul Sauer 1995. In 2000, at the same event, Kanonkop added to its impressive array of awards by winning the Perold Trophy for the best Pinotage. South African wines have also won accolades at the International Wine Challenge in London, the Challenge International du Vin Vinexpo and Chardonnay du Monde in France and the Monde Selection Concours Internationale des Vins de Bruxelles in Belgium. Klein Constantia's Vin de Constance has recaptured the glory days of South African sweet wines. This extraordinary wine, made from Muscat de Frontignan clones brought to South Africa by Jan van Riebeeck in 1656, graces the tables of Le Gavroche, Che and Mirrabelle in London. *Decanter* rated Villiera's Pinotage 1997 as one of the premier wines of the year, while *Wine Spectator* placed Neil Ellis' Sauvignon Blanc in the top five worldwide.

# EXPORTS

When export figures are taken into consideration, growth in South Africa's traditional markets like the United Kingdom, The Netherlands, Scandinavia and Germany is impressive. The figures in emerging export markets also demonstrate that South Africa's wine industry has developed a solid beachhead and these sales bode well for the new millennium. This success is remarkable as South African wineries have only been able to compete on an international scale since the recent transition to democracy, a few short years ago. What is even more remarkable is the change within the industry. The byword within South Africa has been 'transformation' and the wine industry is no exception. Gone are the days of excessive control as the industry has developed many artisan wineries that are dedicated to quality.

Regulation within the industry has also undergone innovative change. The Liquor Products Act of 1989 created the Wine and Spirit Board, which is appointed by the Minister of Agriculture. The Board certifies all wine that is destined for export. This certification not only entails a sensory evaluation of bottled wine, but also includes on site inspections at the premises of each and every winemaker. More importantly, the Board is responsible for the guidelines that form the Scheme for the Integrated Production of Wine (IPW) including standards for integrated pest management. One of the most important principles of IPW is that production should proceed in harmony with nature. As such, the industry as a whole is becoming far more cognisant of the environment and the working relationship between the Board and producers is reducing the injudicious use of chemical and mechanical practices which in turn influences disease susceptibility, ripening and grape quality.

In the years since sanctions were lifted, South African exports have climbed in the aggregate from 855 000 cases in 1990 to 15.4 million cases in 2000 (fig. 1.1). These figures are case equivalent, however, and include bulk wine. This is an incredible 1 700 per cent increase, but the trend does reflect that growth has slowed over the past five years.

### Total Exports 1991 to 2000
### Million Case Equivalents
FIG. 1.1

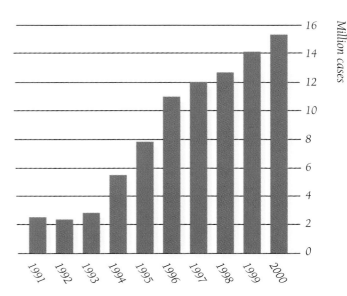

*Vaughan Johnson's Wine & Cigar Shop at the Victoria and Alfred Waterfront, Cape Town.*

The pie chart and graphs, reflecting growth to individual countries, are compiled from figures taken from South African Wine Industry Information and Systems. These figures only represent export volumes of bottled wine. The latest data available are the 2000 figures. The pie chart (fig. 1.2) simply reflects the breakdown of total exports by country. For example, Great Britain imported 4.932 million cases in 2000 and this represents 48.13 per cent of the total. The Netherlands lies in second place with 21.03 per cent, followed closely by Scandinavia and Germany. The United States and the Far East have increased their positions, importing 2.25 and 2.01 per cent respectively. Canada has always been a traditional market for South African wines and imports 1.62 per cent. In terms of South Africa's overall growth, it has dropped from 5 per cent of the total exports in 1995. Africa only takes off 0.77 per cent of total exports, down from 4 per cent in 1995.

The change in percentage to these countries is proportionate to the huge growth that has taken place in imports to the United Kingdom, The Netherlands and Scandinavia.

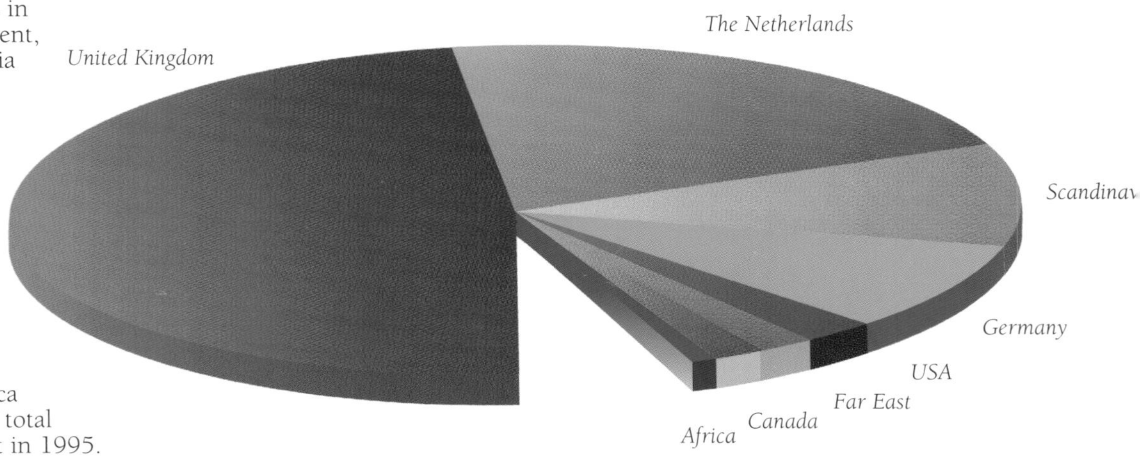

The growth patterns run for four consecutive years from 1997 to 2000 (fig. 1.3). Once again the numbers indicate that the largest growth between 1997 and 2000 has been to Great Britain. Exports have jumped by almost 70 per cent, and if the trend continues Great Britain will soon account for more than 50 per cent of total South African exports. The trends in The Netherlands, Scandinavia and Germany have also shown reasonable increases, but from a much smaller base than in Great Britain. The trend line in the United States remains fairly static for a market of its size, and there has been a decline in sales to Canada, as well as to the Far East. Growth to the African markets remained static between 1997 and 1998, but there has been a marked drop in the 1999 and 2000 figures.

### Total Exports by Country in 2000
### Million Cases

FIG. 1.2

The Netherlands

United Kingdom

Scandinavia

Germany

USA

Far East

Africa    Canada

### Export Comparison 1997 to 2000
### Million Cases

FIG. 1.3

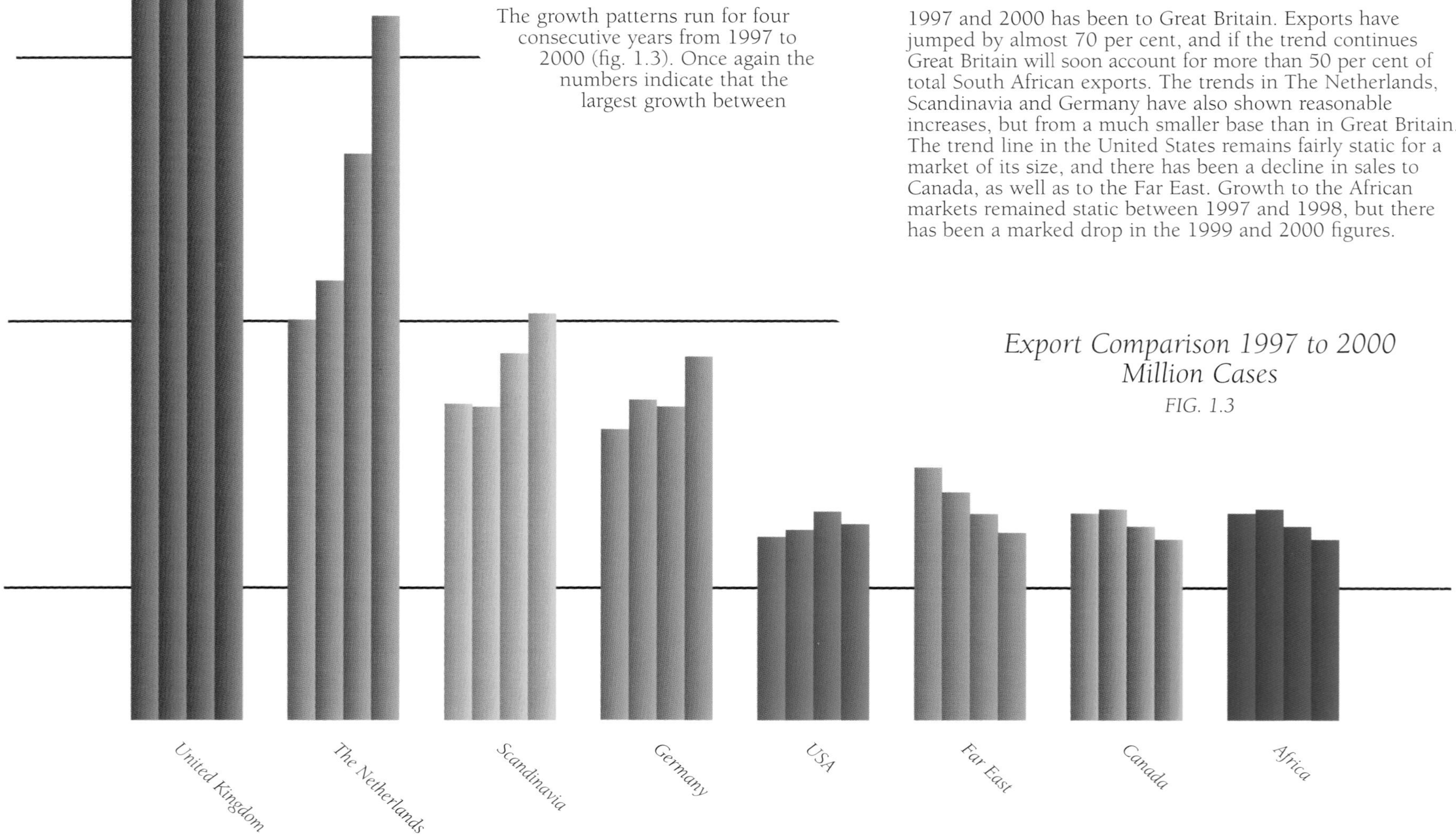

United Kingdom    The Netherlands    Scandinavia    Germany    USA    Far East    Canada    Africa

*Spier Wine Shop.*

# Area and Production

The story of South African wine begins in the vineyards. The total area under vines has increased marginally, but what the figures really demonstrate is how the face of the industry is changing from predominantly white to red wines. Where South Africa concentrated on white wines in the past, 75 per cent of new plantings are red varieties and of these, Cabernet Sauvignon and Shiraz predominate. Certainly the climate in South Africa is conducive to Rhône-style wines and we can expect that South Africa will plant more of these varieties in addition to the traditional Bordeaux mix. Red varieties, however, still account for only 15 per cent of South Africa's total grape crop, up from 10 per cent in 1995.

In global terms, South Africa's wine industry is small compared to that of France or Italy. The latest available figures (1998) demonstrate that South Africa is among the top 20 producer nations of the world, with a total area under vines of 111 000 hectares (see fig. 1.4). This represents 1.4 per cent of the world's total vineyard area. Spain has the largest area under vines: a planted area of just on 1.2 million hectares, which represents 15.1 per cent of the global figure. France and Italy represent 11.7 and 11.5 per cent respectively, while the United States of America has planted 4.7 per cent and Australia about 1.3 per cent of the world's total area under vines.

The extent of the various plantings does not correspond with wine production. While South Africa only rates in the top 20 in terms of planted area, it is among the top 10, in seventh place with 3.2 per cent, with regard to its contribution to the world's total wine production (see fig. 1.5). In this category Italy and France have 20.9 per cent and 20.4 per cent respectively, producing 5.4 billion and 5.3 billion cases; Spain has increased production markedly to 11.7 per cent and the USA follows with 7.9 per cent. Argentina produces 4.9 per cent, followed by Australia with 2.9 per cent.

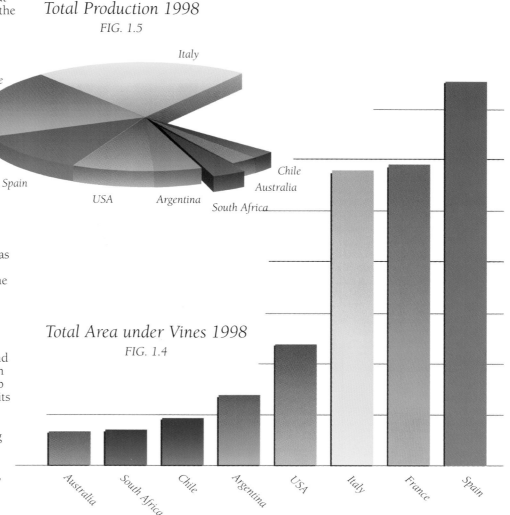

*Total Production 1998*
FIG. 1.5

Italy
France
Spain
USA
Argentina
South Africa
Chile
Australia

*Total Area under Vines 1998*
FIG. 1.4

Australia · South Africa · Chile · Argentina · USA · Italy · France · Spain

# NEDERBURG AUCTION

The Nederburg International Auction is the premier event on the South African wine calendar. Over the past 26 years it has developed into an international event, with major local and overseas wine buyers bidding for a stringently selected range of the finest wines produced by the Cape's premier estates and wineries.

The auction was established with three main objectives in mind: to serve as an incentive to higher wine standards in South Africa; to develop an awareness of South African wines; and to ensure a fair distribution of rare wines. The selection of a winemaker's wine for the auction has been a benchmark of quality, and labels bearing the words 'Sold at the Nederburg Auction' are regarded as seals of approval by both licensees and their customers.

The main auction hall.

Over the years the Nederberg International Auction has developed into one of the best of its kind in the world and ranks with the Hospice de Beaune, Kloster Eberbach and Napa Valley auctions. Auctioneer Patrick Grubb, previously of Sotheby's wine division in London, has wielded the hammer since 1975. At the last auction he knocked down 144 items (8 696 cases) entered by 70 participants for a total value of R6.4 million. The average price for red wine was R1 156.59 per 9-litre case and for white R712.13 per 9-litre case.

Auctioneer Patrick Grubb.

The auction is a great social occasion for the wine world. The permanent auction hall, built in 1980, is named after Johann Graue, a previous owner of Nederburg, in recognition of his extensive contribution to quality wine production in South Africa. In 1998, the Nederburg Auction Centre was completed and this venue can accommodate 2000 guests. Guest speakers who have graced the podium at the Nederburg Auction include Allan Shoup, president and CEO of Stimson Lane Vineyards and Estates; the late Professor Maynard Amerine, Marimar Torres and Robert Mondavi from the Napa Valley, and Professor Alejandro Hernãndez, president of the OIV, Chile. Also from the New World were Philip Gregan, CEO of the Wine Institute of New Zealand and Robin Day of the Orlando Wyndham Group of Australia. Representatives from the Old World number Christian Bizot of Bollinger, Robert Drouhin of Maison Joseph Drouhin, Paul Pontallier of Château Margaux, Jean Hugel, Paul Bouchard, Dr Hans Ambrosi and Ľubomir Vitek, general director and chairman of Slovakia's Malokarpatsky Vinársky Podnik. To mark the 25th anniversary of the Nederburg Auction in 1999, the guest speaker was Günter Brözel, doyen of the South African wine industry and former Nederburg cellarmaster for 33 years. Shin Torii, president of Suntory International, celebrated the millennium auction in 2000 and Ms Zelma Long from California held the floor in 2001.

Guests at the Nederburg Auction.

The Nederburg Auction is not all business, however, as guests are treated to a festive gourmet luncheon under gaily coloured flags while 20 of South Africa's top couturiers present their season's creations.

(right) Nederburg Auction Millennium Cap Classique.

(far right) The annual fashion show at the Auction.

(opposite page) Historic Nederburg manor house.

# 2 Viticulture

Ask a Frenchman about grapes and he will immediately talk terroir. Terroir is a concept that covers location, soil and climate. In Bordeaux, for example, winemakers constantly experience problems with rain late in the growing season. This dilutes the extracts in the grapes as the berries swell.

In South Africa, winemakers experience quite the opposite. Harvest time is normally warm to hot. As a consequence, sugars can rise rapidly, and aromas and flavours can be detrimentally affected. Thus, winemakers have to adapt their farming practices to terroir and this is done primarily by managing the vineyard correctly.

Devon valley near Stellenbosch

# SOIL

Until the late 1940s, planting vineyards in the Cape was a haphazard affair. Farmers usually planted where it was easiest to cultivate and did not necessarily consider the best site for a specific variety. As with most agricultural ventures today, establishing a vineyard has become a scientific exercise. Before planting, South African grape growers now undertake a thorough physical and chemical analysis of their soils, and if necessary rectify any imbalances before establishing a vineyard.

Generally the climate in the Western Cape is temperate and mirrors Mediterranean conditions. Most of the rainfall occurs in winter when the vines are dormant. Moreover, Cape farmers do not suffer the consequences of the extreme cold, severe frost and considerable rainfall during the harvest that some of their European counterparts experience. Instead, many of the inland wine regions in the Cape encounter too much sunshine and heat, which produces more everyday drinking wines. Artisan winemakers, however, are now planting in new areas along the coast such as Walker Bay and Darling Hills. Here they enjoy cooler temperatures and create wines similar to the premium quality wines produced in Stellenbosch, Paarl and Franschhoek.

South African soils are not always fertile, but this is not necessarily a disadvantage. Rich soils often produce over-vigorous vines which in turn produce grapes with little complexity or character.

Soil classification is an intricate and specialised subject. The basic criteria are organised according to the colour of the topsoil and subsoil; the presence and order of various layers in the soil; and the clay content and sand fraction. Names are given to soils in areas or locations where they were first described. Within these soil types, variations can occur and they are referred to as a 'series' within a soil type.

Good drainage can be recognised in soils that are red, yellow or light brown whereas dark colours, ranging from blue-black to dark brown, indicate poor to average drainage, possibly with a high water table for most of the year. In these soils, 'rust spots' or white spotting are further signs that the soil is waterlogged. White colours demonstrate too much drainage and can be seen predominantly in sandy soils where nutrients and chemical compounds have leached away.

Water retention capacity is a term that refers to the amount of water stored by the soil. This factor is key to the overall vegetative growth and fruiting capacity of South Africa's vines.

The depth that is accessible to root penetration is called the effective depth of the soil. Barriers or restrictions, such as water retention capacity and plant nutrients within the soil, determine the effective depth of root growth. Soil depth is classified as deep (90 centimetres or more); medium (60 to 90 centimetres); or shallow (less than 60 centimetres).

In South Africa three basic parent materials produce the following soil types:

| | Parent materials | Soil types |
|---|---|---|
| 1. | Granite | Tukulu; Hutton; Clovelly |
| 2. | Shale | Swartland; Glenrosa |
| 3. | Sandstone | Longlands; Fernwood; Estcourt |

*Soil at autumn preparation.*

# Terroir and location

The French word *terroir* describes not only the position of a vineyard, but also other factors such as soil type and climatic conditions. *Terroir* is of prime importance in producing quality wine and when determining the best grape variety and rootstock for a particular vineyard site.

On a larger scale, 'location' indicates either a district classification, such as Stellenbosch, Paarl or Worcester, or a specific ward within a district, such as Simonsberg, Nuy, Bonnievale or Helderberg. Location is used to identify a position in the landscape, a terrain or topographical unit within a specific area. Each terrain unit comprises a number of soil types, and the position of each terrain unit allows for the influence of prevailing climatic conditions. For example, a terrain unit that lies on a hilltop or slope would typically consist of deep, well-drained Tukulu or Glenrosa soils. Lower slopes and plains would consist of medium-deep to shallow, duplex soils comprised of a sand layer covering a heavy, structured clay. On the valley floor, soils are often deep to medium-deep, wet or layered alluvial Longlands soils.

## The Vine

There is a close relationship between the biological functions of the vine's different parts above and below the ground. To understand the fascinating annual cycle of the vine and the performance of the plant as a whole, one should have a basic knowledge of the relationship between its various organs.

## Chemical properties

The chemical properties of soils are related to the nutrients and other chemical compounds found in the soil. A high content of any chemical compound could act as a restriction to root growth or have a negative effect on plant growth. Chemical properties in the soil are typically identified by the following terms:

pH: refers to the degree of acidity or alkalinity on a scale of 1 (very acid) to 14 (very alkaline). A pH of 7 is neutral.

Free lime: too much results in high pH values; compacted layers of free lime can inhibit root growth.

Salinity: denotes an excess of salts such as sodium or magnesium, resulting in brackish conditions. Excess salts are typically found in soils derived from shale or in low-lying wet soils, and they restrict root and plant growth. Artificial drainage and the application of gypsum alleviate the problem.

*L'Ormarins vineyard below the Groot Drakenstein mountain.*

## The vine above the ground

### Trunk

The trunk is the main, permanent and undivided stem of the vine. It increases in diameter every year and forms the connecting link between the roots and the arms or main branches.

### Arms

The arms, or branches, of the trunk carry canes or spurs, which are pruned to produce the grape crop.

### Shoots and canes

Each year the vine produces buds which develop into succulent shoots. These shoots bear flowers and fruit and later mature into woody canes. At maturation, they succumb to the pruning shears in preparation for the next harvest.

### Shoot system

Buds are most easily seen on a dormant vine in winter. The succulent growth that develops from each bud in spring is called a shoot. During spring the shoots flower and bear fruit. When a shoot matures, normally by autumn, it turns brown and woody and is called a cane. The best canes form from year-old wood that has grown steadily since the beginning of the season. Regular growth is shown by canes with internodes of normal length for the variety.

The growing tip refers to the end of the shoot where growth takes place and is usually about 15 centimetres long. At relatively regular intervals along the shoot, buds develop and leaves arise where there are nodes.

Lateral shoots are not of primary importance. Those that remain short and never become woody are called temporary laterals. Their main function is to increase the leaf surface of the vine.

What appears sometimes to be a single bud is really a well-developed central bud with a secondary bud on either side. If the main compound bud is destroyed, one of the secondary buds will take its place to make certain that grapes will be borne.

(far left, behind) Shoot system.

(left, behind) Pre-berry bunch.

(left) Fourty-year-old Pinotage vine.

(right) Budding sequence of a compound bud.

31

## Tendrils

Tendrils perform the important role of supporting the vine by attaching themselves to stakes or wires in the vineyard. If no support of this kind is available, tendrils attach to other parts of the same vine. The tips move away from the light until they meet some kind of support. Tendrils protect shoots from wind damage, hold them in position to provide shade for developing bunches of grapes, and help keep fruit off the ground.

## Flowers

Although seldom used for propagation, flowers and fruit are the reproductive parts of the vine. Flower clusters are formed in the compound buds during the preceding summer. After the shoots begin to grow in the late spring of the next season they bloom for approximately 10 days, depending on the grape variety. Most *vinifera* have hermaphroditic flowers and therefore are self-pollinating. When flowering, the pollen grains fall on the stigma of nearby flowers and fertilisation occurs.

## Berries or fruit

Each berry or fruit consists of a husk (skin), flesh (pulp) and pips (seeds). There can be as many as four pips in each berry, depending on the variety. A thin wax-like layer on the skin, called the bloom, prevents evaporation and contains microscopic yeast cells and bacteria. The skin contains colour pigments, tannin, fruit acid, and aromatic and flavouring substances (aldehydes and esters).

The proportion of the skin to pulp ratio is higher in smaller berries than in larger ones. The result is more colour and flavour in smaller berry varieties, such as Cabernet Sauvignon, compared to Cinsaut, which has larger berries.

The flesh of most grapes is clear and virtually colourless. Mostly made up of water (70 to 80 per cent), the flesh also comprises carbohydrates in the form of sugars; pips containing tannin and oil; traces of proteins; vitamins A, B and C, and traces of other vitamins.

## Bunch or grape cluster

The vine's flowers are borne in a bunch on a central column, called the rachis. Branches arise from the rachis at different intervals and divide to form the pedicels, or cap stems, which bear the individual flowers. The region of the rachis that extends from the shoot to its first branch is called the peduncle or stem.

Depending on the grape variety, the bunch or cluster has a different shape, as does the berry.

## Leaves

Ampelography is a fascinating and complex study of describing and identifying vine species and varieties. This is often done by examining the shapes of the vine leaves. As a shoot increases in length, leaves are arranged in two vertical rows along the shoot and develop at the growing tip. A leaf has three defined parts: the stalk or petiole; the stipules or bracts which have short-lived, broad scales that drop off early in the growing season; and the blade, or flat part of the leaf, which is usually divided into five lobes. The spaces between the lobes are called sinuses. Small pores called stomata, mainly positioned on the underside of the leaf blade, allow oxygen, carbon dioxide and water vapour to enter or exit the leaf.

A leaf's main veins develop from a single point on the stalk, in different sizes and shapes, and the whole leaf has a network of veins that are all interconnected.

*(above right) New growth.*
*(right) Shapes of grape bunches. Clockwise from far left: conical; cylindrical; twin-bunched; branched; kidney-shaped; shouldered.*

*Shoot*

*Pre-flowering*

*Node*

The chief function of veins is to transmit minerals, water and other important nutritious substances to and from the leaf. Veins also give mechanical support to the leaf's tissue. The cells of this tissue are especially adapted for the production of carbohydrates and require sunlight for photosynthesis.

## The vine below the ground

### Roots

The root system is a major component of the vine in terms of both bulk and function, making up about one third of the vine's entire dry weight. In South Africa, most of the roots are usually located in the upper 60 centimetres of the soil, with deeper roots penetrating to 1.5 metres. In the Bordeaux district of Haut-Médoc, home of the world-famous Margaux wines, roots can penetrate to more than 7.6 metres in the coarse sands or gravelly soils.

Root depth may be limited by the occurrence of a water table, hardpan (a soil zone impervious to root growth), shallow soils, acidic subsoils, or by a zone of toxic materials in the soil. Compacted soils invariably impede roots. Therefore, roots are best developed in soils that do not have any physical or chemical restrictions.

Deep soil tillage is necessary to promote a root system that is capable of using the full water potential of the soil during dry periods. Soil depth, however, is not necessarily the only measure of efficiency. The right chemical balance is also of great importance.

Roots play an important role in accumulating nutrient reserves during autumn. Early in the following spring, the soil temperature is too low for root growth and activity. Since perennial plants require more nutrients during this period than the roots can absorb, the vine depends on these stored nutrients for budburst and initial growth.

Root growth is seriously impeded by an acid soil with a pH below 4.5. In contrast, root growth can be increased considerably by adding agricultural lime (calcitic lime or dolomitic lime) to the soil during vineyard preparation. This can increase the pH to an optimum level between 5.5 and 6.0. Root growth, as well as the growth rate of the whole vine, also depends on nutrients from the soil. The essential macro-elements required for satisfactory growth are nitrogen, phosphorus and potassium. Smaller amounts of magnesium and zinc are also essential, as are various minor trace elements such as boron and copper.

---

The following are the most commonly used rootstocks in South African vineyards:

*Richter 99:* the increased popularity of this rootstock over the past two decades can be attributed to its vigour and high production potential in a variety of soils. Richter 99 also performs extremely well when excessive soil moisture is a problem. Its affinity to different grape varieties is exceptionally good, and satisfactory results are often obtained with both bench and aerial grafting.
*Richter 110:* compares well with Richter 99 and is used in heavy, fertile soils.
*Mgt 101-14:* favours gravelly, shallow and sandy soils.
*Ramsey:* is used in poor sandy soils under irrigation.
*Jacquez:* prefers deep, sandy, virgin soils.
*Ruggeri 140:* is very resistant to drought.
*3306, 3309* and *420A:* are new dwarfing rootstocks designed to limit vigorous vegetative growth.

---

*The author, Phyllis Hands, preparing to plant new rootstock in her vineyard.*

# ROOTSTOCKS

In the mid-1880s an onslaught of microscopic insects, called *Phylloxera vastatrix*, nearly destroyed the Cape's vineyards. Fortunately, by the time the epidemic reached South Africa, Europe had already found a means of controlling the pest. This was done by grafting local vine cuttings onto phylloxera-resistant rootstock from the United States.

Finding the right rootstock, however, is not the whole story of successful vine growing. Without an affinity between the vine cutting (or scion) and the rootstock, vines will perish.

'Affinity' is used to describe the success of a graft combination over the longer term. Although a rootstock and scion appear to be compatible, poor affinity can cause a deterioration of the graft combination after a few years and lead to eventual failure.

This situation arose in South Africa during the 1920s, and many farmers faced financial ruin because their vineyards suddenly began deteriorating at an early age.

Poor affinity also causes a dramatic drop in yield after a few years. Since the 1920s, and particularly during the past 30 years, tremendous progress has been made in identifying ways to improve the compatibility and affinity of South African rootstocks to scions.

The ability or inability of scion and rootstock components to combine with one another either anatomically or physiologically after being grafted is called compatibility. Poor compatibility can be detected in the vine nursery where vines do not bud and produce only short shoots with yellow-tinted leaves. Other vines grow vigorously but break after they are dug up. The graft union is only partially joined when the graft union fails what is termed the 'twist-and-bend' test.

# Vine nurseries

There are many excellent vine nurseries in the Western Cape and one of the most progressive in the world is Ernita near Wellington. The staff there conducts comprehensive propagation, grafting and plant improvement programmes. The plant improvement programme in particular requires advanced technology that includes a selection of the best-performing clones, followed by heat therapy to rid vines of dangerous viruses. The first stage of the plant improvement programme involves clonal selection in existing vineyards. Promising plants are monitored and observed for at least three years. During this period they are assessed in terms of vigour, size, shape, compactness of bunches, colour intensity, bearing capacity, resistance to rot disease, climatic damage and viruses.

In the second phase, a selection of the best material of a specific variety is gathered and grafted separately onto a single variety of rootstock. These combinations are planted next to each other in commercial vineyards and closely observed for their viticultural and oenological qualities.

At this stage, the most promising clones are cleaned to eliminate harmful viruses.

# Nietvoorbij

The Nietvoorbij Institute for Viticulture and Oenology in Stellenbosch is a unique one-stop research facility. The institute provides leading technology for the advancement of viticulture and oenology in South Africa.

From modest beginnings in 1955, Nietvoorbij has developed into a world-renowned research facility for the grape, wine and brandy industries in South Africa. With a proud track record over the years, the Institute has won coveted awards locally and abroad for its technological and research achievements.

The Nietvoorbij Institute is probably the only facility in the world where all research pertaining to grapes and wine is executed under one roof. The different disciplines are organised into five divisions: soil science; wine grapes; table and raisin grapes; plant protection; and oenology.

One of its most important objectives is to translate complex research results into practical recommendations in order to enhance the wellbeing and prosperity of all people in the grape and wine industries.

Led by director Dr Johan van Zyl and deputy director André de Klerk, the institute has experimental farms in Stellenbosch, Paarl, De Doorns, Robertson and Lutzville, and trial plots near Upington. There it conducts trials in collaboration with producers on their farms. These field trials provide researchers with the opportunity to test new technology under diverse conditions.

*(left)* Propagated young vine.

*(right)* In vitro *vine propagation at the KWW nursery.*

*(below) Nietvoorbij Institute for Viticulture and Oenology in Stellenbosch.*

# Grafting

Before grafting was developed as a method of propagation in Europe, new vines were generated by means of cuttings. Taken from a specific grape variety, the cuttings were planted into moist ground in a protected place during late winter. In time they would develop roots and begin to grow. In the following year, during dormancy, the new cuttings would be planted out.

Today nurseries graft good quality plant material onto selected rootstocks. This plant material is known as a scion, and forms the top half of the vine above a graft. The rootstock provides for the roots and should be resistant to pests and diseases. Healthy strong vines are monitored over a period of at least three years before cuttings are taken.

Nurseries select scions from a specific grape variety from producing vineyards. The plant material for grafting is collected during winter when the vines are pruned. Canes are cut into 250- to 300-millimetre lengths, bound together and stored in cold storage or a cool moist place until required. Rootstocks are selected from one-year-old canes taken from mother vines, and then cut into 300- to 400-millimetre lengths. The rootstocks are then stored with the scions.

In South Africa, grafting usually takes place during the winter months of July and August. In the past, grafting was done by hand. Today it is mostly done by machine. With either method, the principles are the same. The two elements, scion and rootstock, must have the same dimension so that they can fit together. Also, the cut must be designed to create the largest growing face between one part and the other.

## Bench grafting

Two traditional types of bench grafting have evolved. The first and oldest type is called the long-whip graft. This method is still used today. Both components are cut diagonally through the wood. Equal portions from both scion and rootstock are taken and then the two are fitted together. The scion usually has two buds, and all buds are removed from the rootstock to prevent any growth other than roots. The second type, known as the short-whip graft, is similar to the long-whip graft but the scion has only one bud instead of two. The short-whip graft has an advantage over the long-whip in that tying is not necessary because the graft needs only a coating of wax to bind it together. Nevertheless, a grafter needs several years of experience to perform this type of graft.

## Machine grafting

The names given to machine grafts are derived from the shape of the various cuts that finally form the bond between scion and rootstock.

The most popular cut is known as omega. Omega-shaped cuts in the rootstock and scion are punched in by a machine. The two parts form a very neat join much like two parts of a jigsaw puzzle. About 10 000 to 15 000 omega grafts can be handled by one person in a day.

Other, less widely used, machine grafts include the Jupiter or zigzag graft and the Heitz or wedge graft.

Once the two parts of the graft have been fitted together, the union is usually dipped in warm wax to seal it and to prevent moisture loss. The grafted vines are then placed in callus boxes and stored in ideal temperatures between 24 and 28°C with a relative humidity of 70 per cent. Storage at this temperature and humidity ensures that scars created by the cuts grow together by forming a new protective tissue. At this stage, roots also develop. A callus box measures about

*Aerial graft*

*Amphi graft*

*Long-whip graft*

*Short-whip graft*

*Omega graft*

2.5 cubic metres and can contain about 1000 grafted vines. The callus box is filled with porous material, such as sawdust or sand, to keep the grafts moist.

After root formation has taken place, the cuttings are moved from the hothouse to a shade tunnel or similar structure where they acclimatise to more natural conditions. The process is gradual so the young plants are protected from strong winds and too much sunlight. The new vines are then planted fairly close together in rows in the vineyard nursery. They remain there for a year before being sold to farmers.

## Field grafting

Field grafting is done in South Africa's summer months of November and December. There are two basic methods. The first is known as chip budding or aerial grafting. This is when a small bud is grafted onto a rootstock that has been planted out during the previous winter. An incision is made on the rootstock about 30 millimetres above the soil, and a bud is inserted into the cut and secured with plastic tape. All other buds are then removed.

The second method, amphi graft (also known as the 'winter bud on a green shoot' method), was developed at the Stellenbosch University in the early 1950s by Professor C. Orffer. This graft is done in late spring on a green shoot about 450 millimetres long by making a cut between the nodes on the shoot. A dormant bud is inserted into the cut, secured with plastic tape, and sealed with grafting wax. The bud of the scion must be completely dormant. In other words, no growth is taking place, and leaves should not be removed from the shoot as they help sap flow. Once the bud has developed sufficiently, the shoot is cut away at the node above the graft. All other shoots and buds are then removed so the vine can develop its new scion. The amphi graft is time-consuming, and a good grafter can only graft about 300 vines a day.

## Soil grafting

During spring in the Cape, from September to the middle of October, soil grafting takes place in the vineyard and the nursery. A scion with two buds is cleft or whip-grafted onto the rootstock. Careful placing of an incision at a 90° angle to the prevailing wind is necessary to prevent the loss of contact between the scion and the rootstock in the graft union. The union is then secured with plastic tape and covered with fine soil. Care must also be taken in the packing of the soil, which must be light, warm and well aerated for the best results.

Favourable weather conditions play a role in the success of a soil graft, as does the attention paid to tending the vine following completion of the graft. After rain the soil must be repacked around the graft and young shoots should be staked to avoid wind damage.

*(right) Omega graft.*

(left) Tinta Barocca compound bud.

New growth

Flowering

Pinot Noir berry

# PHENOLOGY

Phenology is the study of the different times at which changes take place in vines. The following important phenological stages occur:

- Bleeding     approx. August
- Budding     approx. September
- Flowering     October to November
- *Véraison*     December to January
- Maturing     February to March
- Leaf drop     approx. May

Several factors influence the phenology of the vine. The first is undoubtedly genetic, as a variety's phenological stages are genetically inherent. Under comparable climatic and cultural conditions, these stages always occur at the same time each year. Differences from clone to clone do, however, occur.

The second factor is climate. Temperature and hours of sunshine have the most important influence on phenology, but it is not always possible to define the influence of these factors separately. Seasonal fluctuations can also not yet be explained, even though the 'earliest' and 'latest' season can differ by as much as four weeks.

Climate can be divided into three categories as follows:

- Macro-climate: the climate of an area within a district.

- Meso-climate: the climate of a specific vineyard block, influenced by slope, altitude, water masses and protection by hills, ridges or avenues of trees.

- Micro-climate: the prevailing climate within the vine canopy, influenced by row direction, trellising systems and the nature of the soil surface.

Several oenological practices can be used to create a warmer environment in order to advance or shorten the phenological stages. These practices include irrigation, fertilisation, snapping of the peduncle, topping, time of pruning, crop loading and bud stimulation, to name but a few. Both the rootstock and the phytosanitary (or virus-free) status of the plant material also influence the phenology of the scion variety. The difficulty remains in determining a definite phenology for each specific variety as there are so many variables.

Very good indications have, however, been obtained for the most important phenological times that are of interest to the producer. The times of budburst, flowering and maturing for several wine grape varieties at the experimental farms in Stellenbosch and Robertson are given in tables 2.1 and 2.2 respectively. In this experiment, conducted in 1987, maturity was reached when the white and red grape varieties had a sugar content of about 20 to 22° Balling respectively.

*TABLE 2.1 - Budding, flowering and maturing dates of several wine grape varieties at Nietvoorbij in Stellenbosch*

| Variety: | Budding Earliest | Latest | Flowering Earliest | Latest | Harvesting Earliest | Latest | Maturing time | Budding to flowering days | Budding to harvesting days |
|---|---|---|---|---|---|---|---|---|---|
| Chenin Blanc | 2/9 | 13/9 | 30/10 | 14/11 | 21/2 | 6/3 | Early midseason | 50 - 65 | 170 - 184 |
| Cinsaut | 11/9 | 23/9 | 4/11 | 17/11 | 13/3 | 26/3 | Late midseason | 49 - 54 | 171 - 191 |
| Colombar | 30/8 | 12/9 | 24/10 | 9/11 | 20/3 | 8/4 | Late midseason | 48 - 69 | 200 - 217 |

Rootstock: Richter 99     Trellising system: Perold     Soil type: Glenrosa or Clovelly

# Grape ripening

The development of a grape berry can be divided into four distinct stages. The first, or green stage, begins after flowering with the set of the berries and ends as they begin to ripen. During this stage, the berries change in size. The acid content is already high, and malic and tartaric acids reach their highest levels during this phase.

The second or ripening stage begins as the berries soften owing to dramatic metabolic change. The green colour fades, turning to white or yellow on white grapes, and shades of blue-red or black on red grapes. This period is called *véraison* and denotes the time when the berry changes from an organ that accumulates acid to one that accumulates sugar. As ripening progresses, the rate of the change in colour increases and the texture of the berries continues to soften.

The third stage commences once the berries are ripe and reach optimum maturity. This is not an absolute condition, nor does it represent a complete stop in the process of change.

During the fourth and last stage the grapes become overripe. Continuing changes subtract from, rather than add to, the berries' quality. Sugar no longer increases and acidity continues to decrease.

Colour is determined by the berry itself and not by the vine. The eventual intensity and brightness of the colour is affected by environmental factors, such as the duration and intensity of light, temperature, soil moisture and nutrition, coupled with physiological factors such as leaf area and crop levels.

Optimal maturity is really determined by the desired type of wine or style of wine making. When determining maturity, berries should have reached a stage of development where the relationship of the different components of sugar, acid, pH and tannin ripeness is optimal. The fruit must also be in a sound condition.

For the maturing times of most of the grape varieties grown in the Cape, see fig. 2.3.

| Variety | White/ Red | Maturing Time |
|---|---|---|
| Barbera | R | L |
| Bukettraube | W | EM |
| Cabernet Franc | R | L |
| Cabernet Sauvignon | R | L |
| Cape Riesling (Crouchen) | W | M |
| Carignan | R | M |
| Chardonnay | W | EM |
| Chenel | W | M |
| Chenin Blanc | W | M |
| Cinsaut | R | LM |
| Clairette Blanche | W | L |
| Colombar | W | LM |
| Fernão Pires | W | E |
| Furmint | W | LM |
| Gewürztraminer | W | M |
| Grenache Blanc | W | M |
| Grenache Noir | R | M |
| Hárslevelü | W | M |
| Kerner | W | E |
| Malbec | R | LM |
| Merlot | R | M |
| Muscat d'Alexandrie | W | LM |
| Palomino | W | M |
| Pinotage | R | EM |
| Pinot Blanc | W | E |
| Pinot Gris | W | E |
| Pinot Noir | R | EM |
| Pontac | R | M |
| Raisin Blanc | W | L |
| Ruby Cabernet | R | L |
| Sauvignon Blanc | W | EM |
| Sémillon | W | EM |
| Shiraz | R | LM |
| Souzão | R | LM |
| Sylvaner | W | E |
| Tinta Barocca | R | M |
| Trebbiano | W | L |
| Weisser Riesling | W | M |
| Zinfandel | R | M |

Fig 2.3.

### ☛ MATURING TIME KEY

E  = EARLY
EM = EARLY MIDSEASON
M  = MIDSEASON
LM = LATE MIDSEASON
L  = LATE

*(above) Berry.*

*(right) Grenache grapes at* véraison.

## TABLE 2.2 - Budding, flowering and maturing dates of several wine grape varieties in Roberstson

| Variety: | Budding Earliest | Latest | Flowering Earliest | Latest | Harvesting Earliest | Latest | Maturing time | Budding to flowering days | Budding to harvesting days |
|---|---|---|---|---|---|---|---|---|---|
| Chenin Blanc | 29/8 | 10/9 | 25/10 | 1/11 | 14/2 | 2/3 | Early midseason | 52 - 60 | 167 - 185 |
| Cinsaut | 15/9 | 27/9 | 31/10 | 8/11 | 1/3 | 12/3 | Late midseason | 41 - 53 | 166 - 176 |
| Colombar | 1/9 | 14/9 | 20/10 | 4/11 | 3/3 | 20/3 | Late midseason | 49 - 54 | 188 - 195 |

Rootstock: Richter 99    Trellising system: Perold or factory roof trellis    Soil type: Hutton or Sterkspruit

# VINEYARD PRACTICES

There are certain vineyard practices that influence the growth of a vineyard and the resultant wines. Along with their New World colleagues, South African wine grape growers have been able to adapt the lessons learnt by European farmers to local conditions. The result: optimum performance of the vines.

Developing a vineyard is a costly exercise, and no short cuts can be taken when preparing, planting and caring for the vines. First the farmer has to deep-plough the vineyard site and add the necessary lime and phosphates. In autumn a cereal crop such as rye or oats is planted. During late winter or early spring of the same year, the rooted young vines are planted and may be covered with a plastic mulch. The farmer then establishes trellising and irrigation systems if required. The current cost of establishing a vineyard is approximately R70 000 per hectare over the first three years.

Dry land viticulture is still practised in certain areas of South Africa. Under these conditions, new plantings require a plastic mulch to conserve moisture in the topsoil since the young vines still have shallow root systems. The plastic mulch also stops competition from weeds. Interestingly, trials conducted in new vineyards in the Cape indicated that during the first growth season, the growth rate of mulched vines was about 10 times the rate of unmulched vines. Towards the end of the season, the shoots of mulched vines were about four times longer, and their root systems were also three times greater than those of unmulched vines.

*Micro-jet irrigation*

*Mulched vine*

Weeds compete with the vine for both nutrients and water during the growing and ripening period, making eradication imperative, particularly in the vine row. Another way of controlling weeds is by using herbicides, which are usually applied at the end of winter prior to budburst. The chemicals eradicate the weeds either by scorching or by acting systemically within the plant. Herbicides are used in compliance with the Integrated Production Programme of the Wine and Spirits Board to ensure an eco-friendly environment.

Soil potential and climatic conditions often determine the type of trellising in the vineyard. In arid and hot regions where soils have little depth, some vineyards are not trellised at all in order to contain growth. Where trellising systems are established with moveable foliage wires, the most widely used are hedge systems varying from three to five strands of wire.

Mechanical cultivation is becoming less common in South Africa due to the fact that traffic through the vineyards results in soil compaction. Excessive cultivation can also be detrimental to the topsoil's texture and structure.

*(below) Spraying near Robertson.*

*(below right) Spraying near Malmesbury.*

*(far right) Pruned vines at Uiterwyk vineyards.*

# Canopy management

### Density

This is the most important factor in determining the micro-climate of the vine as well as the grape and eventual wine quality. The perfect canopy density, and by inference the ideal micro-climate, is created by correct canopy management. This involves suckering, tipping, shoot positioning, leaf removal and crop removal. The following is a brief description of each practice and includes timing when necessary.

Suckering is the removal of undesirable young shoots that hinder aeration and sunlight penetration, with the exception of those shoots positioned on the spurs. Suckering should be completed shortly after budburst when shoots are 5 to 10 centimetres long and again when the strongest shoots are 25 to 30 centimetres long. The frequency differs from variety to variety. For example, Sauvignon Blanc vineyards may be suckered three to four times during a season while Pinotage usually only once.

The advantages of suckering are:
❖ Improves sunlight penetration on producing leaves
❖ Decreases diseases and pests through better spray penetration and ventilation
❖ Facilitates easier pruning and harvesting
❖ Exposes more leaf area to sunlight
❖ Increases bud fertility through better bud differentiation
❖ Improves flowering, berry set and grape colour.

Tipping involves the removal of the growing tip from an actively growing shoot during the growing season. A shoot should naturally stop growing at the commencement of *véraison*, but if this does not occur, the shoot must be tipped. Tipping also takes place when the trellis system cannot support the vines' vigour. Varieties prone to poor berry set should be tipped during flowering to produce more compact bunches for certain varieties.

Shoot positioning is done by placing shoots in an upright position to create the ideal canopy. This allows the maximum amount of sunlight to fall on producing leaves.

Leaf removal is practised in cool viticultural areas to ensure better sunlight penetration onto the bunch zone. Leaf removal also leads to better colour in red grapes and better aeration, especially on rot-sensitive varieties. Yellow leaves, caused by a lack of sunlight exposure, must be removed from all vines since these leaves have a detrimental effect on pH and colour.

Crop removal should be practised to ensure that the grape crop is in balance with the vines' foliage. Over-cropping is detrimental to wine quality and young vines should not have too many bunches during the first three to four years.

## Mechanical harvesters

In 1987 the first mechanical grape harvester arrived in South Africa. Almost half of the Cape vineyard area has the potential to be harvested mechanically.

The machine straddles trellised vines as it passes along the rows. It has two series of flexible rods, one on each side, which shake the grape-bearing branches. The vibration of the rods releases the ripe grape berries from their stems and they fall into a series of containers. These containers run on a conveyor system circulating on the harvester, and are deposited into a tank. A powerful fan blows away any leaves from the grapes. The vine is left undamaged.

A magnetic device is employed to attract loose pieces of metal that may have fallen from the trellis wires. This avoids damage to the harvester, the wine-making equipment and, most importantly, it prevents the grapes, juice or wine from contamination. In addition, the many hydraulic motors, shafts and junction points on the harvesters are effectively sealed and covered with protective sleeves to prevent even the slightest contamination of the grapes.

The crop can be harvested quickly when the fruit is at its peak, a vitally important factor when striving for excellence in white wine making. Approximately eight to 10 tons can be harvested per hour.

*(above right) Three-wire vertical trellis.*

*(below) Mechanical harvesting near Stellenbosch.*

# TRELLISING

Grapevines are naturally climbing plants, but in modern viticulture they are trained on trellises for economic reasons. The only difference between trellised and untrellised vines is that the trellised plant has an elongated trunk with horizontally trained arms.

Vines are trellised to keep grape bunches off the ground, to keep the shoots in a more or less vertical position, thus facilitating the control of fungal diseases, and to stimulate growth by making use of polarity. The vertical position of the shoots will also facilitate cultivation, harvesting and pruning.

## Establishing a trellis

First, the end posts of the trellising system must be well fixed. They should be anchored with thick galvanised wire to either a concrete block or large metal plate buried underground. The wire is then attached to an end post. The depth of the hole in the ground, the weight of the concrete block or position of the large metal plate, and the distance between it and the end post, are largely dependent on the height of the trellis.

Row widths typically vary from 2.4 metres to 3 metres, depending on slope and soil type. In the row, spacing typically varies from 1 metre to 1.8 metres, depending on the vigour of the cultivar or variety. Properly trellised vines must be supported by a pole every five to seven metres within the row. Thus 740 poles are required per hectare if a pole is placed after every fifth vine. If the vineyard has 50 rows, 100 end posts must be added.

These end posts should be considerably thicker in diameter and planted at least 30 centimetres deeper into the soil than the wire-supporting poles along the rows.

## Trellising systems

To support a vine's shoots and leaves, trellis sizes must always be adapted to the vine's differing capacities. In shallow soil types, a two-wire vertical trellis with wires 20 to 25 centimetres apart is sufficient. Vines grown in deep soil should produce longer shoots and a larger canopy. As a result they would need a higher vertical trellis to prevent shading.

Trellising systems such as the lyre trellis are seldom used, but they are found on high potential soils where vigorous growth proves to be a problem. On the lyre trellis, the cordon is divided or split in two to slow down growth. Trellising systems such as the lyre trellis require extensive canopy management as the dense foliage on the canopy has a tendency to overshadow the lower shoots. If the basal eyes are not exposed to sunshine, they are always less fertile, and in very dense foliage the grapes do not ripen properly. Above all, the trellising system must be able to provide the correct balance between the vine's fruiting capacity and vegetative growth. As this is largely dependent upon the soil and climate in the vineyard, the correct choice of trellis becomes integral to the making of fine wines.

*Lyre trellis*

*Scott-Henry trellis*

*(right) Vertically trellised vines at Vergelegen in Somerset West.*

# PRUNING

Developing a trellis brings important advantages.

*First growth season*
Allow vines to grow undisturbed without topping.

*First winter pruning*
Retain best shoot. Prune back to two buds.

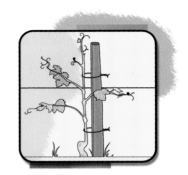

*Second growth season*
A green shoot is trained to grow towards the trellis as a stem and topped above the cordon wire. Two laterals below the cordon wire are trained from the stem onto the cordon wire. When the laterals on the cordon wire have grown about 60 centimetres past the halfway point between two adjoining vines, the laterals are then topped. The future bearers will grow from the lateral development on the cordon arms.

*Second winter pruning*
Cut secondary laterals to one-bud spurs and space the bearers according to the viticulturist's instructions.

*Third growth season*
Virtually every bud on the arms can develop into a shoot with grapes. Strict crop control is required, together with suckering where needed.

*Third winter pruning*
Cut back spurs to two eyes and if necessary lengthen the arms by pruning the leader shoot according to its vigour and that of the vine. Arms are lengthened further by means of the leader shoot.

(right) Pruning sequence.

*Fourth growth season*
Strict crop control is required and unnecessary growth must be removed from the bearer spurs through judicious suckering. Three shoots are now left on a bearer spur.

*Fourth winter pruning*
Cut away the 'old' bearer on bearer spurs. Cut back 'new' bearer to two eyes.

*Fifth growth season*
Development is now mostly completed. Control the crop by suckering to two or three shoots per bearer.

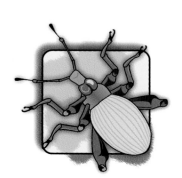

## Definitions

To understand pruning, it is important to know the meaning of the following terms:

*Arms:* laterals older than one year.

*Canes:* mature shoots carrying between 8 and 15 buds. Produce fruit and are pruned yearly.

*Spurs:* when a vine is pruned in winter, spurs are left to produce the shoots that will bear the next crop.

*Suckers:* water shoots which develop on the trunk and between the spurs. They can be used to replace old growth but will not bear during the first year. If the suckers are not needed, then they must be completely removed.

*Trunk:* the undivided main stem of the vine.

# Pests and diseases

The following are the most important pests and diseases that affect Cape vines:

South Africa's vineyards have not been immune to the deadly *Phylloxera vastatrix*, which caused economic ruin for hundreds of Cape farmers in the mid-1880s. The presence of this soil-borne louse can first be detected when several batches of vines start deteriorating. Not visible to the naked eye, phylloxera feeds on the roots, especially the root tips, causing galls. The galls decay as a result of infection by secondary organisms present in the soil. This results in a reduction of the root system and a subsequent decline in the vine's growth.

Phylloxera spends its entire life on vine roots. The adult female louse remains almost stationary on the root and her eggs pile up around her. As soon as the young hatch, they begin to feed. Some travel by crawling through cracks in the surface of the soil during the dry season. They move a short distance, crawl down another crack, and then start a new colony on another vine. The only practical control measure in South Africa, as in Europe, has been to graft onto phylloxera-resistant American rootstock.

Another economic scourge of the Cape's vineyards are microscopic roundworms called nematodes. Of these, the root knot nematode, *Meloidogyne*, and the dagger nematode, *Xiphenema index*, are considered the major pests. Some nematodes feed on the root system, while others transmit viral diseases. A decrease in growth occurs, as well as a subsequent yield loss of vines grafted to rootstocks susceptible to these nematodes.

It is the snail, however, that takes first place as the most common and damaging pest today. Snails are particularly attracted to young vines in spring and early summer. The damage to buds and shoots caused by snails can retard the growth of the vine and virtually destroy small developing bunches.

Snout beetles are also very active in the growing season. The first signs of their presence are holes in the leaves and possibly 'bite' marks on the edges of the leaves. Later in the season, these beetles also attack the rachis of the young bunches and berries, causing them to dry out and even drop off.

The presence of vine mealy bug and associated ants can be detected on the vine when the secreted honeydew turns into a black mould. Badly affected bunches are not suitable for wine making.

Bud mites are minute, but the damage they cause can be huge. This mite damages the buds, which can diminish the yield or crop. The bud mite can also deform shoots, bunches and leaves. This can lead to the development of secondary shoots. Mites can only be identified microscopically by experts in the winter months.

Powdery mildew, *Oidium*, is a fungal disease that can develop on any green part of the vine, including the grape bunch. The first sign is a small yellow spot on the leaf surface, which can be seen when held up to the light. In time it spreads over the entire leaf, leaving a powdery film as its name indicates.

*(right) Mealy bug.*

*(top right) Life cycle of* Phylloxera vastatrix.

*(above) Snail on vine leaf.*

*(above right) Snout beetles.*

Downy mildew is a pale yellow spot that can be noticed on the upper surface of the leaf and has an oily appearance. Eventually these spots turn brown. During humid conditions a fluffy fungal growth develops on the underside of the leaf. If a very young bunch of grapes is infected, it will die. Infected berries also turn brown, shrivel and fall off.

*Eutypa* dieback, or dying arm disease, occurs when small, yellow leaves develop early in the growing season. Although bunches still develop on these shoots, they dry out after flowering and fall off. If they are able to develop further, an uneven growth of both small and large berries will be evident. A cross-section of an affected arm that is brown instead of a creamy colour will show that it is dying.

When dark brown scars or lesions appear early in the season on the bottom two or three internodes of shoots, dead arm disease may be the cause. As the scars enlarge, the tissue cracks and dries out. Dead arm sometimes also affects the leaves, which will be wrinkled in appearance.

*Phytophora* is a soil-borne fungus that is first noticed when the vine leaves are a paler green than would normally be expected on a healthy vine. The leaves gradually change to yellow and then brown as the vine dies, and the roots turn a brown-black colour. *Phytophora* causes a disruption in the primary tissues of susceptible varieties and therefore young roots are more likely to be attacked.

The first sign of a grape bunch being infected by the fungus *Botrytis cinerea,* or Botrytis bunch rot, can be detected when the skin of the berry becomes brownish. In time the whole berry becomes infected. If conditions are too humid, spores develop on the surface of the infected berries. The condition is then known as grey rot. Whole grape crops can be lost as the fungus spreads.

If, however, the weather turns dry, the infected berries shrivel. Chemical changes in the berries can result in what is known as noble rot. Some of the most highly regarded, complex, sweet wines in the world are made from these grapes.

Viral diseases can also occur in vineyards and their prevention depends upon the virus status of the plant material. Chemical control is not possible in the vineyard, but virus-free material can be obtained by means of heat therapy prior to propagation.

The most common viruses found in Cape vineyards are leaf roll, corky bark, fanleaf, yellow mosaic, yellow speckle and asteroid mosaic.

| | BEFORE BUDBURST | SHOOTS 1-2 CM LONG | SHOOTS 10 CM LONG | SHOOTS 25 CM LONG | 14 DAYS LATER | FULL BLOOM | 80% CALYPTRA FALL | 14 DAYS LATER | PEA-SIZE BERRIES | RIPENING BEGINS | POST-HARVEST |
|---|---|---|---|---|---|---|---|---|---|---|---|
| SNAILS & ANTS | ● | ● | ● | ● | ● | ● | ● | ● | ● | | |
| ANTHRACNOSE & DEAD ARM | ● | ● | ● | | | | | | | | |
| ERINOSE MITE | | ● | ● | ● | | | | | | | |
| VINE BUD MITE | | ● | ● | ● | | | | | | | |
| MEALY BUG | ● | | | | | ● | ● | ● | ● | | |
| POWDERY MILDEW | | ● | ● | ● | ● | ● | ● | ● | ● | ● | ● |
| DOWNY MILDEW | | ● | ● | ● | ● | ● | ● | ● | ● | ● | |
| BOTRYTIS | | | | | | ● | ● | ● | ● | ● | |
| SNOUT BEETLE | | | | ● | ● | | | | | | |

**STAGES OF DISEASES AND PEST CONTROL**

● INDICATES: WHEN TREATMENT SHOULD BE APPLIED

# SEASONS OF THE VINE

For optimum development, the vine and its grapes are dependent on a balance of climatic conditions during its annual cycle of growth and dormancy.

During winter in June, July and August, the vine is dormant and must be allowed to rest. This period should provide adequate rainfall and the temperature must be cold.

September, October and November, the spring months in Cape vineyards, are a particularly sensitive time in the vines' annual cycle. Severe spring frosts may injure young shoots, while strong winds can prevent good pollination at flowering time. Cold snaps during blossoming or flowering time can lead to poor berry set, an effect referred to as 'millerandage'. This becomes evident quite early after berry set, when bunches are loose and then ripen unevenly.

In summer, during December, January and February, the vine has a steady supply of warmth essential for the growing season. This warmth is expressed in terms of both temperature and the amount of sunshine. Heat and sunlight are needed to create the necessary photosynthesis that produces sugar in the grapes. The 'not too much, not too little' principle is crucial for the making of fine wines. Without adequate sunshine, the sugar content is low, resulting in a light wine, high in acid and low in alcohol.

At the opposite extreme, problems can arise in a climate with too much sunshine. Generally, in a very hot climate the aromatic qualities of grapes, with the exception of Muscat flavours, are not as delicate or rich as those which develop in more temperate conditions. The high rate of photosynthesis results in a high sugar content in comparison to fruit acid production, and this yields an unbalanced wine. The effect of wind is also important. Many areas in the Cape winelands are within reach of cooling breezes from the sea that naturally compensate for the effects of summer heat. When protected by a mountain, the natural conditions necessary for the making of fine wine with a high fruit acid content and well-balanced sugar can prevail.

An adequate supply of moisture is also essential throughout the summer growing season. In the coastal region, the ideal water supply to the vine is approximately 300 to 350 millimetres. Too much water can be harmful, however, resulting in soft cell structures in the plants and fruit that can then become susceptible to rot. Excessive moisture can also lead to the growth of denser foliage, causing variations of the same problem. Heavy rainfall after grapes have reached their optimum ripeness can be disastrous, causing berries to split and rot. The sugar content of the berries will also decline considerably, owing to dilution of the berry juice.

The autumn months of March, April and May herald great activity in the vineyards and cellars. By mid-April, late-ripening varieties are finally brought to the crusher. Vineyards build up reserves for the next season, and if rain is delayed, supplementary irrigation is added. By early May cover crops are planted. If the leaves have fallen, pruning begins in June with the removal of all unwanted growth. Canes are selected and left for the final pruning at the end of winter.

*(far left) Vine leaf infected with* Erinose *mite.*

*(left) New growth in spring.*

*(right) Autumn vineyards at Buitenverwachting and Klein Constantia.*

# 3 Varieties

The old adage that great wine begins in the vineyard does not tell the full story about the many grape varieties that have developed in so many regions of the world. The modern market is sadly replacing some of the older, less well-known varieties as economies of scale and fashion dictate new planting.

This phenomenon, however, has actually been reversed in South Africa as viticulturalists have been able to obtain new planting material. Cape vineyards have long been dominated by white varieties but now premium reds are gaining ground. In particular, Rhône-style varieties are becoming popular and great Italian, Spanish and Portuguese clones are being viewed as possible candidates for the Cape's terroir with increasing enthusiasm.

The classic varieties are necessarily covered in detail, but the list is neither comprehensive nor exhaustive. Certain varieties that are planted on a very small scale in the Cape winelands have been intentionally omitted. These include Fernão Pires, Furmint, Gamay, Hárslevelü, Pinot Blanc, Schönberger, Servin Blanc, Sylvaner, Therona, Touriga Francesca, Touriga Naçional and Trebbiano.

## Chenin Blanc

# BARBERA

*Origin: Italy*

Barbera is the second most planted grape variety in Italy. Predominantly planted in Piedmont, this grape accounts for more than half of the region's red wine production. Wines developed from Barbera are made in many styles and the better wines can be aged for years. When overcropped, which is a tendency in southern Italy, the grapes develop a natural high acidity. The wine then can be thin and acidic. In certain areas of Alba and Asti, however, artisan winemakers have begun to limit yields and age their wines in barriques. This practice has certainly enhanced the reputation of wines made from these grapes.

*Distribution*

Barbera is planted in South America, particularly in Argentina. In the United States, it is grown mostly in California's hot San Joaquin Valley. The wine made from Barbera is largely used for blending to supplement the acids lacking in other varieties.

*South Africa*

Barbera is planted primarily in the Paarl District and Durbanville Ward.

*The wines*

To date, only Altydgedacht bottles Barbera.

# BUKETTRAUBE

*Origin: Germany.*

Bukettraube was developed from unknown vines in Germany. It is now grown on a small scale in the Alsace region.

*Distribution*

Bukettraube has not been a great traveller. The only country that has made something of this variety is South Africa.

*South Africa*

The variety reached the Cape winelands about 30 years ago. It has adapted to various climatic conditions, although it remains quite susceptible to wind damage. Bukettraube gives its best quality grapes in the cooler wine-producing areas of Paarl, Tulbagh and Stellenbosch.

*The wines*

The first experimental Bukettraube wine was made by Nietvoorbij in Stellenbosch and it has since proved popular as a blending partner. Bukettraube can produce commendable varietal wines which have a greenish tinge, a delicate Muscat aroma and honeysuckle, malva pudding and vanilla undertones. The wine tends to have a good sugar/acid balance.

There are about 10 wines bottled under the Bukettraube label. Most of them are off-dry to semi-sweet, in a style that promotes the Muscat aroma of this variety. None of the wines are wooded.

*(left) Bukettraube.*

# CAPE RIESLING

*Origin: France*

The correct name for this variety is Crouchen Blanc. It originated in the Pyrenees, where it is now virtually extinct owing to its susceptibility to both downy and powdery mildews.

*Distribution*

Cape Riesling has been more successful in Australia and South Africa, although Australia has only about half the amount of South African plantings. This variety was taken from the Cape winelands to Adelaide in South Australia as Riesling. After that it was grown in the Clare valley and Riverland areas as Clare Riesling, and later in the Barossa valley as Sémillon.

*South Africa*

There is no record of this variety's arrival at the Cape, but it is thought to be one of the earliest varieties planted here. When first planted in South Africa a century or two ago, it was thought to be Weisser or Rhine Riesling. It does not, however, resemble Weisser Riesling in any way. While Cape Riesling remains its official name in South Africa, it is sometimes also known as Paarl or South African Riesling.

Cape Riesling represents 2.7 per cent of the total plantings in South Africa. Most of the wine-producing districts grow this variety, with the largest concentration in Paarl, Worcester, the Swartland and Stellenbosch.

*The wines*

Cape Riesling remains a popular wine. It is usually made as a dry unwooded wine, and is undemanding in style with a light grassy or straw-like bouquet. The best wines are to be found in the cooler areas. When this variety is grown in very hot regions, the wines tend to be coarse and lack varietal character. About 20 wines are bottled under this label, of which the most notable are the Theuniskraal, Nederburg Paarl and Swartland Rieslings.

## *Physiology*

*Vigour: Very strong, but may suffer wind damage when shoots are young and brittle.*

*Phenology: Usually buds in mid-September. Flowers during the first half of November. Matures in the first two weeks of March. At full maturity, a favourable sugar/acid ratio is obtained with a total titratable acid concentration of 7 to 9 g/l and sugars of 18.5 to 20° Balling.*

*Diseases/pests: Extremely sensitive to fungal diseases such as downy and powdery mildews. In unfavourable conditions botrytis can develop into grey rot. Because of normal good leaf cover, there is usually no bird damage or sunburn.*

*Leaves: Medium-sized, five-lobed and dark green in colour. Underside has cobweb-like hairs on the veins.*

*Cluster/bunch: Compact, small to medium and conical. Sometimes shouldered. Peduncle has reddish tinge and is short and thick.*

*Berries: Small, oval and green, with a thin, soft skin.*

*Aromas and flavours: Sweet haystacks, canned peas, dried peaches and dried apricots.*

# CABERNET FRANC

### Origin: France

Cabernet Franc is the third most planted grape variety in Bordeaux, after Merlot and Cabernet Sauvignon. Generally, it shows its best wines in the Saint Emilion and Médoc districts of Bordeaux, where it is often used for blending. It is an important variety in the Loire valley, particularly in Anjou and Touraine. Cabernet Franc is also planted extensively in south-western France.

### Distribution

This variety is popular in Italy and produces its best wines in the north-east. Extensive plantings are also found in eastern Europe, and to a much lesser degree in Australia and California.

The variety is extremely adaptable. It is best suited to good soils, but can thrive better than Cabernet Sauvignon in wet clay soils. It is inclined to yield more and ripens earlier than Cabernet Sauvignon. During the wetter and cooler vintages in Europe, it is more likely to ripen fully.

### South Africa

Plantings have increased from an extremely small base in the 1980s, and Cabernet Franc is now found more often as a component of Bordeaux-style blends. Most of the Cape's Cabernet Franc plantings can be found in the Stellenbosch District.

### The wines

Fewer than 10 wines are bottled under the Cabernet Franc label. The wines are generally very aromatic and accessible early, but are not as structured and 'masculine' as Cabernet Sauvignon. This is one of the reasons why Cabernet Franc is popular in the Médoc area of France. There, when used in a blend, it softens the wine but allows it to retain its Cabernet character.

The most notable blended wine made from this variety is Cordoba's Crescendo which contains 70 per cent Cabernet Franc. Highly recommended varietal wines include Warwick, Bellingham and a new label, High Constantia.

## Physiology

*Vigour: Very strong. Yields are better than Cabernet Sauvignon under similar conditions.*
*Phenology: Matures before Cabernet Sauvignon, but still relatively late in the season. At full maturity the average sugar content is 23 to 24.5° Balling and total titratable acids are 6 to 7 g/l.*
*Diseases/pests: Susceptible to powdery mildew. Rot seldom occurs because of its thick skin.*
*Leaves: Lighter green than Cabernet Sauvignon.*
*Cluster/bunch: Cylindrical, conical, small, loose and sometimes winged.*
*Berries: Blue-black in colour. Round and slightly larger than Cabernet Sauvignon.*
*Aromas and flavours: Mint, blackberries, green olives, nutmeg, ripe plums and violets.*

# CABERNET SAUVIGNON

# CABERNET SAUVIGNON

*Origin: France*

Bordeaux is the home of Cabernet Sauvignon, particularly the deep, well-drained soils of the Haut-Médoc and Graves where some superb wines are produced. Cabernet Sauvignon is normally blended with varying proportions of Cabernet Franc or Merlot, and sometimes with a small percentage of Petit Verdot or Malbec. These are the only five varieties allowed in Bordeaux red wines. There is no doubt that Cabernet Sauvignon has produced some of the very finest wines in the world. In Bordeaux and many other parts of the world, it is considered the king of red varieties, even though Burgundians, who are passionate about their own grape varieties, would disagree. Nevertheless, this is the consensus of the wine-drinking world.

*Distribution*

Cabernet Sauvignon is found in most wine-producing countries. When properly managed in the vineyard, it retains its identity and nobility wherever it travels. As a late-ripening variety, it particularly prefers warmer climates and if planted in very cool areas the desired sugars cannot be obtained. It requires good, well-drained soils and has a medium production potential. Since budbreak is very late, it is not usually affected by spring frosts when planted in Europe.

*South Africa*

There is no record of Cabernet Sauvignon's first arrival in South Africa, but it is possible that this variety has been present in the Cape vineyards for the last two centuries. Cabernet Sauvignon makes up about seven per cent of total plantings and currently is the most planted red grape variety in the Cape. The most extensive Cabernet Sauvignon vineyards can be found in the Stellenbosch and Paarl districts.

*The wines*

Well over 200 good Cabernet Sauvignon wines are bottled under the varietal label. Cabernet Sauvignon is also used in the Cape's Bordeaux-style blends. In the past, Cabernet Sauvignon was blended with Cinsaut or Shiraz in order to soften the tannins. Today, Cabernet Sauvignon is still blended with Shiraz, which is considered to be a typical South African combination, but many winemakers are now more in favour of the traditional Bordeaux-style blend of Cabernet Sauvignon, Merlot, Cabernet Franc and sometimes Petit Verdot.

## *Physiology*

*Vigour: Exceptionally vigorous growth. Produces hard wood.*

*Phenology: Fertility may be a problem. The last grapes ripen late in the season. At full maturity the average sugar content is 24 to 25° Balling with a total titratable acid of 6 to 7 g/l.*

*Diseases/pests: Rather susceptible to downy and powdery mildews. It has a strong resistance to botrytis because of its thick skin.*

*Leaves: Medium-sized, shiny and dark green. Five-lobed with lobes overlapping. Perforated, giving the impression of five holes in the leaf.*

*Cluster/bunch: Medium-sized, cylindrical, conical and winged. Often shouldered and quite loose.*

*Berries: Small, round and very black, giving wonderful colour to the wine. Lots of bloom. Skin tough and thick. Pips quite large, which contributes to the tannin extracted during fermentation.*

*Aromas and flavours: Should be complex and rich with layered aromas of cassis, ripe fruits such as prune plums, berries, green walnuts, slight pepper, cigar box, pencil shavings, depending on clones. Some have mintiness or nuances of eucalyptus or mineral overtones. These characteristics should follow through to the flavour or palate.*

# CHARDONNAY

### Origin: France

Burgundy has made Chardonnay famous; the region's Montrachets and Meursaults are the benchmark for winemakers all over the world. Chablis also produces excellent Chardonnay wines from its calcareous soils. Chardonnay is one of the traditional varieties used for the production of Champagne, and the Champagne region, totalling 20 000 hectares, accounts for nearly a third of the total French plantings of this variety.

### Distribution

Chardonnay is very adaptable and is found in most wine-producing countries, wherever the climate and soils are suitable. The variety appeals to viticulturists and winemakers alike, because it is not temperamental in the vineyard and presents a variety of options in the cellar. In the late 1980s Chardonnay became Australia's most planted white grape variety.

### South Africa

Sydney Back of Backsberg is credited for pioneering Chardonnay in South Africa in the early 1980s. Chardonnay now accounts for approximately six per cent of the total white grape plantings. It is planted mainly in the Coastal and the Breede River valley regions.

### The wines

Fine Chardonnays are now being made in the Cape with a range of styles. If unwooded, these wines do not have the racy acidity and almost steely dryness of most Chablis wines. Nevertheless, this style is popular locally and in some export markets.

Some partly wooded Chardonnays are used in most of the Cap Classique sparkling wines, and are also popular as a blending partner with Sauvignon Blanc. The fully wooded wines are now starting to rival the best that the world has to offer. Approximately 180 wooded Chardonnay wines are being bottled in the Cape.

Noteworthy wooded Chardonnays with excellent ageing potential include Avontuur, Backsberg's Chardonnay Reserve, Buitenverwachting, DeWetshof Bateleur, Glen Carlou Reserve, Hamilton Russell, Meerlust, Overgaauw, Rustenberg Five Soldiers, Saxenburg Private Collection and Vergelegen Reserve.

## Physiology

*Vigour: Medium. Not affected by very cold weather, which explains its suitability to the Champagne region of France.*
*Phenology: Buds from late August to early September. Flowers at the end of September. Matures between the end of February and early March. At full maturity, musts with a total titratable acid content of 5 to 7 g/l and sugars of 23 to 24° Balling are easily obtained.*
*Diseases/pests: Sensitive to downy mildew. Moderately sensitive to powdery mildew and botrytis. Vulnerable to damage from birds and baboons.*
*Leaves: Medium-sized, very slightly lobed, thick, convex edges.*
*Cluster/bunch: Small, cylindrical to conical and winged. Well-filled to compact. Short thin peduncle.*
*Berries: Round, small, pale green to yellow. Thin, tough, transparent skin.*
*Aromas and flavours: Citrus fruits, especially lemon peel, peaches and cream, buttered toast and marmalade, honey, roasted almonds and cloves.*

# CARIGNAN

*Origin: Spain*
Carignan originates from the town Cariñena. Today it is the third most planted variety in Spain.

This variety was planted extensively in the Midi in southern France during the 1960s. It became the most abundantly planted red grape variety, and the main component in the *vin ordinaire* wines from the Languedoc-Roussillon area. Carignan Blanc and Carignan Gris are mutations. If well managed, Carignan may produce a commendable wine. It also makes a good blending partner because of its good colour, acid and tannins. Carignan has lovely redcurrant aromas with whiffs of strawberries and fennel.

*Distribution*
Carignan is widely planted in Algeria and Italy and to a lesser extent in the Americas, particularly in California, Mexico and the wine-producing countries of South America.

*South Africa*
Plantings are minimal in South Africa, but they are increasing.

*The wines*
Fairview and Welgegund have bottled wines from this variety. More are expected.

# CHENEL

*Origin: South Africa*

Released in 1974, Chenel was the first South African cross to be perfected after Pinotage, and the first white grape. Chenel is a combination of Chenin Blanc and Trebbiano and was produced by Professor Chris Orffer at the Elsenburg College of Agriculture. The name is derived from 'Chenin' and 'Elsenburg'.

*Distribution*

Chenel performs well under irrigation and high trellising, and can produce yields of over 30 tons per hectare. It is planted mainly in Worcester, Paarl and Malmesbury.

*The wines*

Because the wines from this variety are inclined to be neutral, they are mainly used for flavoured wines, which can be either red or white. They are easy-drinking, semi-sweet wines that have been flavoured with a natural fruit flavouring agent. Monis Esprit is the most popular local example of this style of wine.

# CHENIN BLANC

*Origin: France*

For hundreds of years the production of Chenin Blanc was concentrated in the Loire River valley, specifically in the Anjou-Touraine area. It was known as Chènere during the 13th and 14th centuries and was possibly named Chenin Blanc after Mont Chenin in the Touraine area.

Chenin Blanc has travelled successfully, but unlike Chardonnay and many other varieties, it undergoes a definite change in character away from home.

In France it produces notable wines with very good acidity. The styles range from dry to sweet. For memorable Chenin Blanc wines, the grapes are picked late to allow as much sugar as possible to develop. Depending on the weather, the vines are sometimes infected with *Botrytis cinerea*. This leads to noble rot, adding another dimension to the wine. The wines from the Coteaux du Layon, specifically from Bonnezeaux and the Quarts de Chaume, are made exclusively from botrytised Chenin Blanc grapes. These grapes produce a greeny-gold nectar that can be aged for decades. In Saumur and Vouvray, a very good sparkling wine is produced from Chenin Blanc by the traditional French method. One of the disadvantages of these northerly situated vineyards is that Chenin Blanc ripens late, usually in November, and rain often causes low sugars and grey rot.

*Distribution*

In France Chenin Blanc is grown mainly in calcareous soils. In the newer wine-producing countries, including South Africa, it is planted in various soils with differing climatic conditions. Extensive plantings are to be found in the United States, mainly in California. Chenin Blanc is also planted in Canada, Chile, Argentina and New Zealand.

*South Africa*

Chenin Blanc was probably introduced to the Cape by Jan van Riebeeck. It currently covers 23 per cent of South Africa's vineyards and is by far the most planted grape variety. Chenin Blanc was called Steen until the mid-1960s and considered a mutation of Chenin Blanc that was unique to the Cape. In 1965 experts finally established beyond all doubt that Steen was, in fact, Chenin Blanc. Since then, the wine may be called Steen or Chenin Blanc, as the producer wishes. Some very good Chenin Blanc is produced in a distinctive South African style that is very fruity and accessible.

Walter Finlayson of Glen Carlou was one of the first to start taking Chenin Blanc more seriously by wooding his 1994 Chenin Blanc. He released the wine as Glen Carlou Devereux in memory of Peter Devereux, South Africa's well-loved food and wine *aficionado*. Moreover, in 1995, a number of British Wine Masters visited the Cape and could not understand why so many good Chenin Blanc wines were losing their identity in various blends. These comments encouraged the Cape Wine Masters to organise a stimulating Chenin Blanc symposium the following year. The 1996 symposium generated a great deal of interest among growers and winemakers who were motivated to use their best vineyards to produce memorable wines. These would be older, well-established vines that deliver low yields and thus more concentrated musts.

A few winemakers immediately started with the 1996 vintage, and the wines have been well received by wine lovers. The prime example of this style was Jean Daneel's Morgenhof Chenin Blanc, which won *Wine* magazine's 'Chenin Blanc Wine Challenge Champion Wine'. This Chenin Blanc was made from a vineyard that is 27 years old, and the wine was not only matured in second-fill barrels for five months, but also underwent malolactic fermentation in the barrel.

### The wines

Chenin Blanc is extremely versatile. In South Africa this variety is used in the making of natural dry to natural sweet white table wine, sparkling wine and small quantities of white port, sherry and brandy. In 2000 Chenin Blanc accounted for 60 dry unwooded wines, 50 oaked wines and more than 40 off-dry to semi-sweet wines. Of these 10 were new labels.

Cooler areas in the Cape produce lighter, fruitier wines, while the hotter areas produce more robust wines with higher alcohol.

The yield of Chenin Blanc vines varies tremendously, depending on soil, trellising, pruning, and whether the vines are grown under dry land conditions or not. Under irrigation, tonnage can exceed 40 tons per hectare. The resultant wine is normally used for distillation.

The greatest wines ever made from Chenin Blanc in the Cape are Noble Late Harvests, which are made from grapes affected by *Botrytis cinerea* (noble rot). They are fragrant, honeyed and can be aged for many years. Nederberg Edelkeur is an excellent example of this style of wine.

### Physiology

*Vigour: Medium to medium high, depending on soil. Moderately resistant to wind.*

*Phenology: Buds in early September. Flowers in the first half of November. Matures in the second half of February, which is mid-season.*

*Diseases/pests: Sensitive to powdery mildew. Mildly affected by downy mildew. Very susceptible to botrytis.*

*Leaves: Dark green, medium round, no lobes to three lobes.*

*Cluster/bunch: Medium-sized, conical, very compact, winged bunches prominent. Short, tough peduncle.*

*Berries: Oval, small, greenish yellow, thinnish skin. Very juicy.*

*Aromas and flavours: Varied, depending on vineyard practices. Fruit salad consisting of peaches, sweet melon, pineapple, orange and so forth. Wooded examples are not as forthcoming.*

# Cinsaut

### Origin: France

For centuries Cinsaut has been associated with the Languedoc region of southern France. Today it is grown from Provence to the Midi. Since the 1970s, however, this variety has lost a certain amount of popularity among French winemakers. It is used mainly as a blending partner, and remains one of the varieties that are permitted for the Châteauneuf-du-Pape wines of the Rhône.

### Distribution

Cinsaut is found in Morocco, Tunisia and the Middle East. It has also found a home in Italy, some areas of eastern Europe, and Australia.

### South Africa

Cinsaut was first planted during the mid-19th century. In 1980 almost 13 per cent of the Cape's vineyards were planted to Cinsaut, making it the most planted red variety. By 1999 this figure had dropped to 3.6 per cent.

### The wines

Twelve wines are bottled under the Cinsaut label. The best serious wine made from Cinsaut is from Landskroon Estate, but Tassenberg is the largest selling red wine in South Africa.

If grown as a bush vine with correspondingly low yields, Cinsaut can produce a worthwhile wine. The berry is considerably larger than other red grape varieties. The ratio of juice to skin can cause a problem with colour extraction. Cinsaut is also popular for the production of rosé wines and as a blending partner.

## Physiology

Vigour: Moderate to low.
Phenology: Ripens late mid-season. Achieves sugars of 22 to 24° Balling and a total titratable acid of 5 to 7 g/l at optimum maturity.
Diseases/pests: Susceptible to dying arm. High humidity causes berries to crack. Sensitive to sunburn.
Leaves: Medium-sized, five-lobed. Light to medium green.
Cluster/bunch: Large, cylindrical, conical and quite compact.
Berries: Large, oval, with conspicuous bloom. Dark blue. Colour even darker under less fertile conditions.
Aromas and flavours: Soft, ripe berry fruits with nuances of strawberry jam, stewed plums and when young wet wool or wet dog. These wet wool or wet dog aromas soon disappear when aerated.

# CLAIRETTE BLANCHE

*Origin: France*

Although this variety has lost popularity in France over the past two decades, Clairette Blanche is still one of the grape varieties found in the wines of Côtes-du-Rhône Villages, Châteauneuf-du-Pape and other wines of southern France. Clairette Blanche produces the popular Clairette de Die sparkling wines.

*Distribution*

Clairette Blanche can be found in Sardinia, Algeria, Israel and Australia's Hunter valley.

*South Africa*

Until about 25 years ago Clairette Blanche was popular in this country for blended and sparkling wines. Today it is used primarily for wines at the lower end of the market and for distillation, although Fairview have begun using this variety in its popular Goats do Roam blends. Clairette Blanche is planted mainly in the districts of Stellenbosch and Worcester.

*The wines*

Only two wines are bottled under the varietal label and they are from the hotter inland district of Worcester. These wines can be almost colourless and if the vines have been over-cropped, the wines are quite bland. Cold fermentation is essential as Clairette Blanche oxidises easily.

# COLOMBAR(D)

*Origin: France*

Colombar was once important in the production of Cognac, but has since lost favour; nearly half of its plantings were uprooted during the 1970s. Colombar is currently grown to the north and west of Bordeaux, and makes up part of the blend of generic Bordeaux Blanc wines in south-western France.

*Distribution*

California and the Cape share an almost equal enthusiasm for Colombar. Both countries use it successfully for brandy distillation and natural table wines. Much smaller plantings are found in Australia.

*South Africa*

Twenty-five years ago Cape winemakers discovered that Colombar could produce extremely pleasant drinking wines. Previously the variety had been planted for distillation purposes. Colombar thrives on a variety of soils, particularly high-potential calcareous soils in warmer areas. Oxidation can be a problem during production, but this problem has largely been eradicated through the use of cold fermentation.

*The wines*

Twenty dry white wines are bottled under the Colombar label, while a number are off-dry or semi-sweet. Colombar is popular as a blending partner in medium-priced wines and for carbonated sparkling wines. Nuy Wine Cellar, Goed Verwacht Estate and Rooiberg wines are good examples.

## *Physiology*

*Vigour: A vigorous vine with dense growth.*
*Phenology: Ripens late mid-season with an average sugar content of 20 to 21° Balling and total titratable acid of 8 to 10 g/l.*
*Diseases/pests: Resistant to botrytis. Reasonably resistant to downy and powdery mildews.*
*Leaves: Medium-sized, round, almost kidney-shaped, lobes often absent. Petioles rose-coloured.*
*Cluster/bunch: Cylindrical, usually winged, medium loose.*
*Berries: Pale gold-green and medium-sized. Skin thin and tough.*
*Aromas and flavours: Fruity, luscious ripe peaches, apricots with an unmistakable aroma of guavas, jasmine, cantaloupes and pineapples.*

# GEWÜRZTRAMINER

### Origin: Undecided

The Traminer grape was grown in the Tyrol near the village of Tramin about a thousand years ago. Some ampelographers consider Traminer to be a descendant of a Greek variety brought to Europe by the Romans.

Since the Middle Ages, Traminer has been planted in Alsace, where some of the best Gewürztraminers are made. 'Gewürz' is the German noun for 'spice', and the wine remains one of the most aromatic and easily recognisable grape varieties. Gewürztraminer makes a definite statement of its identity even before the glass of wine reaches your nose, and perhaps its glorious aroma is synonymous with its most attractive pinkish copper-coloured grape.

### Distribution

Gewürztraminer is grown in Austria, eastern Europe and Russia. The variety is heavily dependent on *terroir* and does not grow well in warmer climates. Gewürztraminer does well in the cooler areas of the United States of America and New Zealand.

### South Africa

Relatively new to South African vineyards, this variety was first planted here 20 years ago.

### The wines

When the vines are planted in the cooler areas of the Cape, the resultant varietal wines are easily recognisable as Gewürztraminers. Some interesting and assorted styles of wines are being made and vary greatly from dry to sweet. Twenty wines are currently bottled under the varietal name.

Altydgedacht Estate is one of the very few dry wines made from this variety. Neethlingshof shows some sweetness. Bon Courage Estate's Special Late Harvest won a Diner's Club Award in 1999. Other comendable wines are Villiera, Neethlingshof and Vlottenburg.

### *Physiology*

*Vigour: Low to moderate yields. Heavy soils with some clay produce the most aromatic wines.*
*Phenology: Ripens mid-season. Develops good sugars if planted in favourable conditions.*
*Diseases/pests: Very susceptible to powdery mildew. Develops botrytis, depending on whether or not the thicker-skinned clones have been used.*
*Leaves: Petiolar sinuses with overlapping edges, teeth convex and wide.*
*Cluster/bunch: Small, conical and fairly loose.*
*Berries: Oval, pinkish copper, good fruity flavour.*
*Aromas and flavours: A sweet-smelling nose of roses in full bloom, orange blossoms with a touch of orange rind, and litchis.*

# Grenache Noir

### Origin: Spain

Grenache Noir is Spain's most planted red variety. It originated in Aragon in north-eastern Spain and was eventually cultivated in Rioja and Navarre. Grenache Noir forms part of the blend known as Vega Sicilia, one of Spain's most respected wines. It is the world's second most planted red wine variety.

### Distribution

Grenache Noir was first planted in Roussillon in southern France. It was then grown in the Languedoc, the Midi and the southern Rhône regions. During the past two decades, however, Grenache Noir's popularity has decreased in south-western France. Although there are still 87 000 hectares planted, many vineyards were replaced with more classical varieties.

Grenache Noir produces great wines under hot, windy, dry conditions. The vines are not trellised, ensuring a low yield which results in concentrated wines. The popular Tavel and Lirac rosés are made from Grenache Noir, but more often this variety is used as a blending partner with Shiraz.

In Australia Grenache Noir was the most planted red grape variety until the late 1970s, when it was superseded by Shiraz and later Cabernet Sauvignon. Producers in the Barossa valley now use Grenache Noir as a blend with Shiraz.

### South Africa

Grenache Noir plantings are increasing, especially in the Swartland as winemakers find the correct *terroir*.

### The wines

Grenache Noir is paler than most reds, especially if the yield is large and the wine tends to oxidise early. If the yields are restricted, the wine can produce dense reds that age for decades.

## Physiology

*Vigour: A productive variety with vigorous upright shoots.*
*Phenology: Budbreak is early and maturity is late.*
*Diseases/pests: Sensitive to downy mildew and botrytis.*
*Leaves: Cuneiform, superior sinuses are very pointed and narrow. Smooth, clear green, very shiny. Yellow veins, teeth are narrow and pointed.*
*Cluster/bunch: Large, conical, winged.*
*Berries: Black, slightly oval, fairly thick skin.*
*Aromas and flavours: Usually chosen for blending rather than varietal character. Skins do not have deep pigmentation, thus colour can be a problem. A great deal depends on soils and vineyard practices. Under ideal conditions, can produce big, voluptuous wines rich in mixed berry fruit nuances and flavours.*

# MALBEC

*Origin: France*

Malbec is one of the five grape varieties permitted in a red Bordeaux blend. Known as 'Côt' in Bordeaux, it has lost favour, however, because it is susceptible to disease, frost and poor berry set. Over the years Malbec has been grown in many parts of France, but plantings are now concentrated in Cahors in south-western France.

*Distribution*

Malbec is grown extensively in Argentina, where some very good varietal wines are made. It is also planted on a smaller scale in Chile and Australia.

*South Africa*

Plantings are limited in the Cape, but they have done extremely well.

*The wines*

Malbec is a fruity wine with flavours of cassis, mulberries, plums, hints of eucalyptus, and occasionally prunes. Ashanti, Backsberg, Bellevue Estate and Fairview bottle this variety. The remaining wine tends to be used in blends.

# MERLOT

### Origin: France

Merlot is the most popular variety in the Bordeaux region, and is France's third most planted grape variety. It produces magnificent wines in Saint Emilion and Pomerol, where it has been grown for over 200 years. Pomerol's Château Pétrus commands some of the highest prices in the world. Merlot ripens earlier than Cabernet Sauvignon and is also more productive. Unfortunately, it is affected by severe frost in early spring, but this is not a problem in Cape vineyards.

### Distribution

Merlot is found in Italy, Switzerland and, to a lesser extent, in Hungary and Spain. In the past decade Merlot has become a fashionable wine in the United States, where plantings have increased dramatically in California. Merlot is very popular in Chile, but Argentina has relatively small plantings. Australia has few vineyards planted with Merlot, but plantings are increasing due to international demand.

### South Africa

There has been a dramatic increase in the planting of Merlot in the districts of Stellenbosch and Paarl. New vineyards are also being developed along the west coast, where irrigation has to be carefully controlled in order to produce quality rather than quantity. Currently Merlot accounts for nearly four per cent of the total area planted to vines.

### The wines

About 150 wines are currently bottled under the Merlot label. The very best Merlots can definitely hold their own internationally. While most varietal wines are wooded, there are some unwooded Merlots, particularly from co-operatives, and these wines are produced for early and easy drinking. Styles vary a great deal from different areas. Highly recommended wines include Buitenverwachting (the first since 1991), Hartenberg Estate, Jean Daneel, Jordan Vineyards, Rust en Vrede, Saxenburg Private Collection and Veenwouden.

## Physiology

*Vigour: Medium to good. Very susceptible to drought during the ripening period.*
*Phenology: Ripens mid-season. At optimum maturity produces sugars of 23 to 24° Balling and total titratable acidity of 6 to 7 g/l.*
*Diseases/pests: Susceptible to downy mildew and botrytis if planted in very fertile soils.*
*Leaves: Medium-sized. Lateral sinuses, deep club-shaped, often with a tooth at the base. Smooth, dark green.*
*Cluster/bunch: Not too compact. Cylindrical, quite large. Peduncle medium-long and thick.*
*Berries: Medium-sized, black, round, thin-skinned.*
*Aromas and flavours: Should have really rich fruitcake/plum pudding aromas and flavours, with good spiciness. Smell and taste of the best dark chocolate, with hints of good roasted coffee and almonds. Styles vary with a more gamy, maraschino cherries aroma from Italian clones.*

# MOURVEDRE

*Origin: Spain*

Mourvèdre is often referred to as Mataro, particularly in the New World. After Grenache, it is Spain's second most planted black grape variety. Mourvèdre is also popular in southern France, where it has possibly been grown since the sixteenth century. Mourvèdre is far easier to grow in sunny Spain where it buds and ripens extremely late. It also adapts well to a wide range of soils in warm climates.

In France, Mourvèdre is considered an important blending partner, adding structure to wines from Côtes de Provence and Côtes-du-Rhône. It is particularly used as a blending partner with Syrah, Grenache and Cinsaut in Châteauneuf-du-Pape.

*Distribution*

In Australia, Mourvèdre is found mainly in the Barossa valley, where it is often combined with Shiraz. In California, plantings are concentrated in the southern coastal districts where the quality is inferior to those found in Spain and France. This is possibly the result of poor plant material.

*South Africa*

Mourvèdre is mainly planted in the Swartland, Paarl, Robertson and Overberg districts by approximately 10 growers. Most of the vineyards are no more than three years old.

*The wines*

Beaumont, situated in the Overberg district at Bot River, is the only producer bottling this variety. The remaining wine is currently being used as a blending partner.

## Physiology

*Vigour: Good, depending on soil and site.*
*Phenology: Buds late, making it a good choice for sites subject to frost. Ripens late, limiting it to areas with long growing seasons.*
*Diseases/pests: Resistant to botrytis, but quite sensitive to powdery and downy mildews.*
*Leaves: Cuneiform, truncated, lyre-shaped, average 'saw tooth'.*
*Cluster/bunch: Medium, compact, narrow and conical, winged.*
*Berries: Small, round and black, with a heavy bloom.*
*Aromas and flavours: Extremely intense blackberry and mulberry flavours. The variety tends to have high acids and can be astringent due to tannins extracted from thick black skin/husks.*

# Muscat d'Alexandrie

### Origin: North Africa

Muscat is possibly the largest and oldest 'grape family', with well over 200 different types or derivatives of its kind. Muscat d'Alexandrie is thought to have originated in Egypt, and was possibly taken to Greece by Phoenician traders. Later it was grown in the rest of Europe. Wherever it is grown, Muscat d'Alexandrie is best known for the sweet wine it produces. It is also an excellent table grape and produces delicious raisins when dried.

### Distribution

Spain has the largest area planted to this variety. It is found mostly on the Mediterranean coast, where fortified sweet wines called Muscatel are made from this variety. Also found in Portugal, France, Italy, California, Chile and Australia, it thrives in hot climates. In some countries the wine is distilled, as in Chile, where it is used for the production of Pisco.

### South Africa

One of the first grape varieties to reach our shores, Muscat d'Alexandrie is thought to be the 'Spaanse druyfen' to which Jan van Riebeeck referred in his diary. Today it is the fourth most planted grape variety in the Cape, accounting for 5.9 per cent of total vineyard plantings. Most wines made from these grapes are not famous. However, any book on important grape varieties grown in the Cape winelands would not be complete without the mention of Muscat. Muscat d'Alexandrie is also known as Hanepoot in South Africa and the grapes are considered a great delicacy by the local population.

### The wines

Fortified wines made from Muscat d'Alexandrie are usually labelled Hanepoot, which is popular with the local market as a good 'winter warmer'.

### Other Muscat wines

A Muscat de Frontignan wine is produced by Thelema Mountain Vineyards. Wines from Muscat Ottonel are usually much lighter than wines from other Muscats and have a subtle bouquet of honeysuckle and jasmine.

## Physiology

Vigour: Not a vigorous grower.
Phenology: Ripens late mid-season. Cool weather during flowering can result in poor berry set.
Diseases/pests: Susceptible to all diseases, pests and sunburn.
Leaves: Medium-sized. Petiole red. Petiole sinus lyre-shaped. Teeth pointed, narrow and in two series.
Cluster/bunch: Cylindrical to conical, winged and loose.
Berries: Large, attractive yellowish white, almost pale gold if exposed to the sun. Delicious to eat.
Aromas and flavours: Distinctive, very concentrated, honeyed, sweet nose. Typical of grapes at their ripest.

# Nebbiolo

### Origin: Italy

A variety that produces some of the most memorable and long-lasting wines, Nebbiolo is one of Italy's best-kept secrets. Only in the past decade has it been planted outside its home in the Piedmont area of north-west Italy. Nebbiolo was the first candidate to be considered for the Denominazione di Origine Controllata e Garantita (D.O.C.G). The designation was introduced in Italy in 1963 and denotes a legal category for the country's finest wines.

Even in Piedmont, Nebbiolo is restricted to a few specially selected areas. The variety represents merely three per cent of Piedmont's production because it is difficult to grow and does not produce large yields.

### Distribution

Nebbiolo is sparsely planted in North and South America. In Argentina, growers are inclined to over-crop. This detracts from the quality of the wine.

### South Africa

Nebbiolo is planted in small quantities in the Constantia Ward, and in the Stellenbosch and Paarl districts.

### The wines

Steenberg released the first Nebbiolo wine. L'Ormarins has some promising and eagerly awaited wine still in cask.

# PETIT VERDOT

*Origin: France*
Today, Petit Verdot is one of the five classic varieties that are grown for blending in Bordeaux. It was once considered a more important grape in the Médoc than Cabernet Sauvignon, but lost its overall popularity because of problems with late ripening. It remains popular in southern Médoc, however, where the soils are lighter.

When used in a Bordeaux blend, Petit Verdot provides concentrated flavours and depth of colour. Wines from Châteaux Lascombes and Léoville-Las-Cases are some excellent examples of this variety.

*Distribution*
Limited plantings of Petit Verdot are found in Chile and California's Napa Valley.

*South Africa*
In 1979, Billy Hofmeyer of Welgemeend Estate was the first Cape winemaker to use Petit Verdot in a Bordeaux-style blend. More Petit Verdot has been planted in South Africa during the past five years. The grapes are found mainly in the Stellenbosch, Paarl and Robertson districts.

*The wines*
As the vines are still young, Petit Verdot is used for blending.

## *Physiology*

*Vigour: Moderate to good.*
*Phenology: Ripens late. Planted in the wrong soils or on the wrong rootstock, Petit Verdot can be an irregular cropper.*
*Diseases/pests: Does not have any specific problems and, like Cabernet Sauvignon, is particularly resistant to rot.*
*Leaves: Medium-sized, rich, shiny dark green. Five-lobed, usually overlapping.*
*Cluster/bunch: Bunches are branched.*
*Berries: Medium-sized and very dark in colour.*
*Aromas and flavours: Spicy, peppery and fragrant. Quite similar to Syrah in character. Rarely bottled as a varietal wine. Provides wonderful colour to a blend because of its thick black skin.*

# PINOT GRIS

*Origin: France*

Pinot Gris is a mutation of Pinot Noir and has never decided whether it is a dark or a light grape. The husk or skin of the grape can be a greyish blue to a pinky brown colour.

Sometimes it resembles a black grape and sometimes a white grape. Nevertheless, it is used for the production of white wine.

Originally from Burgundy, Pinot Gris has a chequered history. In the Middle Ages it reached Switzerland. In the late fourteenth century it arrived in Hungary, where it is called Szürkebarat, and then circa 1570 it took root in Alsace, where it is known as Tokay. The grape has also travelled as far afield as Russia.

In 1711, a wine merchant named Johann Ruland found a semi-wild, uncultivated vine growing in the Palatinate, Germany's second most important wine region at the time. Ruland propagated the vine and named it Rülander. Each region produces wines that are distinctively related to their *terroir*.

### Distribution

In France, where Pinot Gris is also called Pinot Beurot, there are some well-reputed vineyards in the Côte d'Or. Small plantings are also found in certain areas of the Loire valley.

In Burgundy, Pinot Gris is often intermingled with other varieties. It is also sometimes planted in Germany and northern Italy, where it is called Pinot Grigio.

The wineries in Alsace produce rich, dry wines. There are limited plantings on South Island in New Zealand. In Europe, Pinot Gris produces a soft, delicately perfumed wine with more flavour and colour than most other white wines. If the climate is too hot, the wines become rather dull. Pinot Gris is at its best when grown in cooler climates.

### South Africa

Pinot Gris is grown in the Paarl and Robertson districts.

### The wines

Pinot Gris is a useful blending partner. Only two wines are bottled under the varietal label, by L'Ormarins and Van Loveren.

## *Physiology*

*Vigour: Could be identical twin to Pinot Noir, with moderate vigour.*
*Phenology: Ripens early, before Chenin Blanc.*
*Diseases/pests: Fairly resistant, except for downy mildew. Susceptible to birds.*
*Leaves: Large, orbicular, dark green and thick.*
*Cluster/bunch: Small and cylindrical.*
*Berries: Slightly oval; although light red/black in colour, is used only for white wine.*

# PINOT NOIR

### Origin: France

One of the oldest wine grape varieties, Pinot Noir originated in Burgundy where it is recorded to have existed since the 4th century. About 20 mutations of this variety exist. The most cultivated are the colour mutations Pinot Gris and Pinot Blanc and the red grape Pinot Meunier. The French ampelographer Pierre Galet has discovered 46 Pinot Noir clones, whereas Cabernet Sauvignon has only 34 clones.

### Distribution

Pinot Noir is difficult to grow outside Burgundy. Although planted in most wine-producing countries, winemakers are still tilting at windmills in an effort to achieve the ultimate quality that is found in the best Burgundy. Preferring cooler areas where the soils are rich in lime, this temperamental variety presents a challenge to any winemaker.

Apart from Burgundy, Pinot Noir is planted extensively in Champagne for sparkling wines, and there are more Pinot Noir vines planted in the Champagne region than there are in Burgundy. The variety has also been planted in Germany for some time with no notable success, although Pinot Noir is one of the red wine varieties that stands a chance of ripening in its cool wine-growing areas.

As in Champagne, Pinot Noir is used for the production of sparkling wine in many countries. Some good Pinot Noir wines have been made in New Zealand and areas of the United States such as in Oregon and the cooler areas of California. Australians have planted Pinot Noir since the early 1990s, but only time will tell whether their winemakers will be able to succeed where others have failed.

### South Africa

Professor Abraham Perold of Stellenbosch University originally imported Pinot Noir to South Africa on the Swiss BK5 clone. These vines are prone to leaf roll, but this problem has largely been overcome since the introduction of new clones.

### The wines

Currently about 30 wines are bottled under the Pinot Noir label. Early success with this variety came from winemaker Peter Finlayson, formerly of Hamilton Russell, who pioneered this variety in the cool Overberg District. Subsequently he established Bouchard Finlayson, which is unique in that it is not only planted to the new 113 Dijon clone, but also pruned to the French double guyot method.

Bouchard Finlayson, Cabrière Estate, Glen Carlou, Hamilton Russell, Meerlust and more recently Paul Cluver and Whalehaven are successful Pinot Noir producers.

## Physiology

Vigour: Moderate.
Phenology: Buds early. At full maturity reaches 23 to 24° Balling and total titratable acids of 6 to 7 g/l.
Diseases/pests: Fairly resistant to disease, except downy mildew. Susceptible to birds.
Leaves: Large, round, entirely or poorly three-lobed, dark green and thick. Rosy petiole.
Cluster/bunch: Fairly compact, small and cylindrical.
Berries: Slightly oval and small, dark violet-blue/purple/black when fully ripe. Skin thick and tough.
Aromas and flavours: Lovely ripe, summer berries mingled with wet leaves, compost of a forest floor, mushrooms and earthy farmyard smells.

# PINOTAGE

*Origin: South Africa*

Pinotage is the result of cross-pollination between Pinot Noir and Cinsaut (Hermitage), developed by Professor Abraham Perold of Stellenbosch University during the 1920s. His work with Pinotage was continued by Professor C. J. Theron, who headed the Department of Viticulture and Viniculture at Stellenbosch University in the 1940s and 1950s. Using Perold's four original seedlings, he evaluated specific vines from which he continued to propagate, and eventually established experimental vineyards of the new variety. During the 1950s only three farmers in the Stellenbosch District planted Pinotage vines. In 1959, the prize for the best wine on the Cape Young Wine Show was awarded to this unknown variety. The same wine was released in 1961 by Stellenbosch Farmers' Winery under the Lanzerac label.

Some 40 years later, it has become tradition for the opening and closing lots of the Nederburg Auction to be a case of a 1960s vintage Lanzerac Pinotage. Since the lifting of sanctions in 1994, a choice wine in the international marketplace is definitely Pinotage.

In 1996, the Pinotage Society, comprising some 80 members, was formed under the chairmanship of winemaker Beyers Truter of Kanonkop. The aim of the society is to promote Pinotage internationally, to assist Pinotage growers with technical information and to ensure quality among winemakers.

*Distribution*

Pinotage is found in small quantities in Zimbabwe and New Zealand. There are also isolated plantings in the United States.

*South Africa*

Pinotage accounts for 5.5 per cent of the total vineyard plantings. Although yields can be controlled on trellised vines, winemakers still believe that the best quality grapes are grown on bush vines with a total yield of no more than seven tons per hectare.

*The wines*

In the past decade, there has been a general awakening to the quality of Pinotage. Winemakers now understand that this quality can only be attained if the grapes are picked at optimal ripeness with very low yields.

About 60 wines are bottled under the Pinotage label. Most are good quality wines, but the style varies tremendously. There are three main categories: unwooded; wooded in large and often well-used wood; and the more serious wines that are wooded in barriques.

There is no doubt that Pinotage has inherited the best qualities of both parents, with each having a charm of its own.

Top Pinotage producers include L'Avenir, Bouwland, Clos Malverne, Jacobsdal, Kanonkop, Kaapzicht, Middelvlei, Stellenzicht, Uiterwyk and Vriesenhof. These wines have proven consistency and staying power. There are another 20 producers not far behind them. New labels include Spice Route, Neil Ellis and Bellevue Estate where the famous first 1959 Pinotage was made and bottled under the Lanzerac label. Bellevue has recently released its 1999 vintage – a huge complex wine.

## Physiology

*Vigour: Moderate to good. Fairly erect growth habit.*
*Phenology: Buds early September. The older clones are usually the last of this variety to ripen. Pinotage at full maturity produces average sugars of 22 to 24° Balling and total titratable acids of 7 to 8 g/l.*
*Diseases/pests: Susceptible to powdery mildew and botrytis. Very susceptible to downy mildew.*
*Leaves: Medium, oblong and five-lobed. Dark green. Teeth often occur in sinuses.*
*Cluster/bunch: Small, conical, compact, with a short peduncle.*
*Berries: Small and oval. Medium strong skin is blue-black in colour.*
*Aromas and flavours: Ripe bananas, plums, cherries and candyfloss. Sweetness from rich, ripe fruits with a hint of spice. Other nuances depend on the type of wood used.*

# ROOBERNET

*Origin: South Africa*
This variety was developed by Professor Chris Orffer of Stellenbosch University's Department of Viticulture. Roobernet is the 'offspring' of the parent varieties, Cabernet Sauvignon and Pontac. It became commercially available in the early 1990s and although very new, it appears to be extremely promising. Roobernet is a more prolific grower and a better bearer than either of its parents. It has no affinity problems and is highly resistant to *Botrytis cinerea* and bunch rot. Since it ripens before Cabernet Sauvignon, it can be planted in cool as well as hot regions.

*Distribution*
Roobernet has been planted at Uiterwyk and De Trafford Wines in Stellenbosch and at KWV's Laborie Estate in Paarl.

*The wines*
The juice of Roobernet grapes is as red as Pontac, and the wines have a deep colour without needing long skin contact. The wines are not too tannic and therefore easily accessible. Roobernet wines also have a distinctive Cabernet Sauvignon character.

## Physiology

*Vigour: Moderate.*
*Phenology: Buds 10 to 15 days before Cabernet Sauvignon. Sometimes flowers and ripens later than Cabernet Sauvignon.*
*Diseases/pests: Very resistant to rot. Resistant to downy and powdery mildews.*
*Leaves: Large, dark green and wedge-shaped. Lateral sinus moderately deep. Petiole sinuses U-shaped, closed with edges folded over each other. Teeth large, bulged and even.*
*Cluster/bunch: Moderately large and well-filled. Peduncle moderately long and brown.*
*Berries: Small, oval to round, and black. Skin thin and moderately strong. Bloom moderate. Pulp red, with good grassy flavour.*
*Aromas and flavours: On first impression, quite similar to a young Cabernet Sauvignon, but more simplistic without the complex nose or flavour.*

# RUBY CABERNET

*Origin: California*
A crossing of Cabernet Sauvignon and Carignan was perfected by Dr Olmo of the University of California at Davis in the late 1940s. Although it was developed specifically for hot regions, Ruby Cabernet has also proved successful in cooler areas. It was very popular in California in the 1960s, and as many as 3 000 hectares of Ruby Cabernet can still be found in this region.

*Distribution*
A few plantings exist in Australia.

*South Africa*
Ruby Cabernet has done very well at the Cape since it was first planted in 1982. This variety produces up to four times more per hectare than Cabernet Sauvignon. It is planted mainly in the Worcester District and other irrigated areas.

*The wines*
More than 20 wines are bottled under the Ruby Cabernet label. The rest of the wine is used for less expensive blends. Some interesting examples are Long Mountain, McGregor, Merwida and Robertson Wineries.

## Physiology

*Vigour: Strong.*
*Phenology: Buds in the second half of September and ripens late, shortly after Cabernet Sauvignon.*
*Diseases/pests: Not sensitive to disease. Resistant to wind.*
*Leaves: Large, dark green and five-lobed. Lateral sinuses deep, wide, pointed and folded. Teeth broad, blunt, with edges turned down.*
*Cluster/bunch: Compact, medium, conical, long, well-filled and shouldered. Peduncle moderately short and tough. Fairly difficult to harvest.*
*Berries: Small and oval. Skin dark. Texture watery. Slightly grassy flavour.*

# SANGIOVESE

*Origin: Italy*

Sangiovese is Italy's most planted red grape variety. It is indigenous to Tuscany, and plantings are documented as far back as the sixteenth century. Sangiovese produces some of Tuscany's most famous wines. It is the only grape permitted in the production of Brunello Di Montalcino and is the dominant grape for Chianti. Clonal selection is important because if not done, the resultant grapes can produce ordinary wines.

*Distribution*

Due to quality fluctuations in the grapes, plantings are limited outside Italy. Some Sangiovese is planted in Argentina and in California, particularly in the Napa valley. The original producers of Sangiovese in the Napa valley are linked to Italy's famous maverick Piero Antinori, and they are now making some interesting wines in their own Californian style.

*South Africa*

Sangiovese has recently been planted by Plaisir de Merle, Boplaas, L'Ormarins and Morgenster.

*The wines*

Sangiovese is a wine of typical Italian flair. It is spicy with hints of cinnamon, black pepper, stewed plums, maraschino cherries and fresh rich earthiness. In younger wines there can be a slight underlying floral aroma.

To date only Plaisir de Merle, Boplaas and L'Ormarins have bottled Sangiovese under the varietal label.

# SAUVIGNON BLANC

# SAUVIGNON BLANC

*Origin: France*

When blended with Sémillon, Sauvignon Blanc produces some of the exceptionally fine dry white wines of Bordeaux. It is an important component in the blending of the famous sweet wines of Sauternes.

In the Loire valley, Sauvignon Blanc produces the fine, racy, unique and identifiable wines of Sancerre and Pouilly-sur-Loire. These areas are known for their famous Sancerres and Pouilly-Fumés, which are unblended, varietal wines.

### Distribution

Sauvignon Blanc can be found in parts of Italy, Austria and eastern Europe, as well as in Australia and areas of North and South America. The variety has made an excellent name for itself in New Zealand, where it was first planted less than two decades ago. Wherever it is planted, Sauvignon Blanc is certainly identifiable, but it does have variances in character.

### South Africa

Extensively planted in the Cape from the beginning of the 20th century, Sauvignon Blanc vines were uprooted in the 1940s because of poor plant material. Replanting started in the late 1970s. By 1980, just 0.2 per cent of Cape vineyards were planted with this variety. Today Sauvignon Blanc accounts for five per cent of total plantings and the demand for quality grapes is increasing. Most of the Sauvignon Blanc vineyards can be found in the Coastal and Breede River valley regions.

### The wines

The Cape produces some extremely good examples of this variety. The best Sauvignon Blanc wines come from the coolest areas of specific districts, where canopy management is particularly important. About 180 unwooded Sauvignon Blanc wines are bottled, and less than 30 are oaked. The variety is also a popular blending partner with Chardonnay. Some of the best Sauvignon Blancs include Klein Constantia, Neil Ellis, Plaisir de Merle, Steenberg, Vergelegen and Villiera Bush Vine. Buitenverwachting has a more flinty style.

## Physiology

*Vigour: Performs well on medium-potential soils in cool climates.*
*Phenology: Ripens early mid-season. At optimum maturity average sugars are 21 to 24° Balling with a total titratable acidity of 6 to 7 g/l.*
*Diseases/pests: Susceptible to botrytis if grown on fertile soils, as the bunches are then very compact. Not very susceptible to downy or powdery mildew.*
*Leaves: Medium to small, usually five-lobed. Petioles pale rose-coloured.*
*Cluster/bunch: Medium to small, conical, slightly shouldered, almost cylindrical and very compact.*
*Berries: Short, oval and medium to small, with thin skin that has a distinctive grassy or herbaceous aroma. Very juicy.*
*Aromas and flavours: Some variance in character from French examples. The best from the Cape are excellent wines with more character and mouth-feel than many French wines. The Cape offers two styles: a wine with a more forthcoming nose of ripe fruits, especially fig and gooseberry, with a little grass and green pepper nuances; and a wine that is more French in style, being flinty, steely or chalky, with more defined grass and fig-leaf flavours.*

# SEMILLON

### Origin: France

Sémillon is one of France's premier varieties. It is also an important white grape variety in Bordeaux and is responsible for the luscious sweet wines of Sauternes and Barsac. Château d'Yquem, which is the best known producer of great Sauternes wines, has planted about 80 per cent of its vineyards with Sémillon, the balance being Sauvignon Blanc. When produced as a dry wine, Sémillon is usually blended with Sauvignon Blanc. The best of this style comes from Graves in Bordeaux.

### Distribution

Sémillon is planted in most of the wine-producing countries of the world, particularly in Chile and Argentina. Australia also has substantial plantings of Sémillon, and some excellent wines, especially those from the Hunter valley, have been produced from this variety. Sémillon responds best if planted in cooler regions and when not over-cropped, otherwise the wines can be bland. When new growth develops it is very susceptible to strong wind, but otherwise Sémillon is a relatively easy vine to cultivate.

### South Africa

Sémillon is considered to be one of the first grape varieties brought from Europe to the Cape, where it used to be known as 'Green Grape' or 'Groendruif'. For most of the 19th century it was the most planted grape variety, representing more than 90 per cent of the total plantings. By 1995, however, Sémillon made up just under one per cent of total plantings. It now seems to be gradually regaining popularity.

### The wines

About 24 wooded and 12 unwooded wines are currently bottled under the Sémillon label, with Stellenzicht Reserve and Boschendal Jean Le Long being the most noteworthy. New wines with high expectations include Constantia Uitsig, Landau du Val, Steenberg and Vergelegen's Show Reserve White.

## Physiology

*Vigour: Grows well in medium- to high-potential soils.*
*Phenology: Ripens early mid-season and at optimum maturity has good sugars and satisfactory acidity.*
*Diseases/pests: Resistant to anthracnose and slightly resistant to powdery and downy mildews. Berries susceptible to botrytis.*
*Leaves: Medium-sized. Very light and bright in colour. Remain distinctive even when mature, at which stage they are a very dark green.*
*Cluster/bunch: Conical, medium-sized and compact, with a tough peduncle.*
*Berries: Round, tending to slight oval, medium-sized. Berries very juicy and at full maturity have a slight grassy flavour.*
*Aromas and flavours: Very soft. Not readily definable fruit. Waxy pleasant nose, some lemon and herbs in the best examples.*

# Shiraz

### Origin: Possibly Persia

It is claimed that Syrah, or Shiraz as it is called in South Africa and Australia, originated in the Persian town of Shiraz in present-day Iran. It is also sometimes argued that it came from Syracuse in Sicily. For the last few hundred years the grapes have been grown in the northern Rhône valley of France. The most notable French Syrah wines are those from Hermitage and Côte-Rôtie. Since the 1970s, Syrah's popularity in France has grown steadily. It is now being planted with great success in the southern Rhône valley and the Languedoc.

### Distribution

The most important producer of Shiraz outside France is Australia, where its wines have achieved great success. Shiraz enjoys a really warm climate to ripen fully. California, Chile and Argentina have some plantings of this variety.

### South Africa

Shiraz has a history of producing good quality wine. Its popularity, however, was limited in the past because it was not a prolific bearer and producers were not rewarded for quality as is the case today. The Shiraz plant material was also virus-infected in the early days, but this has now been corrected. Most of the Cape's Shiraz vineyards can be found in the districts of Stellenbosch, Paarl and the Swartland. This variety accounts for 3.5 per cent of total plantings and continues to grow in popularity.

### The wines

Wherever it is grown, Shiraz is known for producing big, bold wines with good fruit and tannins and a very good maturation potential. The style of wine depends on viticultural practices, and especially on the yields of the vine. Approximately 105 wines are bottled under the Shiraz label. The most notable are Allesverloren, La Motte, Saxenburg, Stellenzicht, Lievland and Rust en Vrede. Successful labels new to the scene include Cordoba, Graham Beck, Hartenberg, J.P. Bredell, Slaley, Spice Route and Villiera.

## Physiology

*Vigour: Very good. Performs well on medium- and light-potential soils. Adapts well to various climatic conditions. Susceptible to wind.*
*Phenology: Ripens mid-season, with an average sugar content of 24 to 25° Balling and total titratable acidity of 6 to 7 g/l at optimum maturity.*
*Diseases/pests: Reasonably resistant to disease.*
*Leaves: Fairly large, elongated, orbicular, five-lobed, quite dull green.*
*Cluster/bunch: Fairly loose, cylindrical and medium-sized. Long, brittle peduncle, breaks easily.*
*Berries: Medium to small, conspicuously oval, blue-black in colour. Skin thin. Heavy bloom. Very juicy.*
*Aromas and flavours: Gamy or meaty, leather, wild herbs, subtle spices, black pepper, maraschino cherries and raspberries, black chocolate. The type of oak used will also influence the aroma and flavour.*

# SOUZAO

*Origin: Portugal*
This variety originated in the Douro valley in Portugal. It is generally regarded as one of the better varieties for port, with its high fruit acid content and highly pigmented skin.

*Distribution*
Souzão is planted and used for the making of port in Australia and California.

*South Africa*
There are small plantings of Souzão, mainly in Paarl, Stellenbosch and the Swartland. The wines from this variety are so deep in colour that they appear almost black. Souzão produces a complex, mouth-filling wine with excellent maturation potential. If not used for port production, it is blended into red natural table wines.

*The wines*
No varietal wines are bottled under the Souzão label.

# TINTA BAROCCA

*Origin: Portugal*
Tinta Barocca was first planted in the Douro valley in northern Portugal about a century ago. It is used mostly for the production of port.

*Distribution*
Tinta Barocca has not gained in popularity in the wine-producing world.

*South Africa*
Although Tinta Barocca was originally planted for port production, some varietal wines have been bottled over the years.

*The wines*
Six wineries bottle a natural table wine under the varietal label, including Allesverloren, Die Krans and Rust en Vrede.

# VIOGNIER

*Origin: France*

This white variety has been planted for centuries in the northern Rhône region, but it almost became extinct because of its low yield. In the late 1960s only 15 hectares were still planted. Ten years ago, Viognier plantings increased dramatically and it is now also found in the Languedoc-Roussillon region. A hardy vine, Viognier does well in hot and dry areas. The best wines from this variety are intense, rich and certainly memorable.

*Distribution*

Viognier is planted in California and Australia.

*South Africa*

Viognier has taken a long time to reach South Africa, but there are now plantings in the districts of Paarl and Stellenbosch, with at least eight producers planning to cultivate Viognier as soon as material is available.

*The wines*

Those who know the wines of Condrieu, which are considered the best from this variety, eagerly await the release of more Viognier wines. Fairview is now making a particularly good example, followed by sister cellar Spice Route and Uiterwyk. The wine is rich and golden in colour, with hints of ripe pears, dried apricots and peach pips. The bouquet is interesting but elusive.

# ZINFANDEL

*Origin: Uncertain*

Possibly of European origin, Zinfandel today is synonymous with California where it has been planted since the mid-1880s. It was very important to the Californian wine industry until a few decades ago, when it was superseded by more fashionable varieties. Zinfandel has proved to be extremely versatile, producing both red and white wines in various styles.

*Distribution*

Zinfandel is found in Australia and South Africa. Since the late 1970s, small plantings of Zinfandel are found in the Stellenbosch District.

*The wines*

There are four red wines bottled under the Zinfandel label, of which Blaauwklippen's is the oldest, best known and most consistently well rated, even in California. Ashanti is a notable rising competitor, as is Hartenberg.

# WEISSER RIESLING

*Origin: Germany*

In South Africa, there is sometimes confusion between the locally named Weisser or Rhine Riesling (just called Riesling in Germany) and Cape Riesling, which is a completely different variety better known as Crouchen Blanc in Europe.

Experts claim that Riesling is the greatest and most noble of all white grape varieties because of the longevity of its wines. In Germany, Riesling wines are made in many styles, from dry to sweet, and the best have excellent acids and extract.

Possibly the most famous of these wines is Trockenbeerenauslese, considered the finest sweet wine of the Rhine, and particularly the Rheingau and Mosel areas. Riesling is Germany's second most planted variety after Müller-Thurgau, which has the advantage of ripening earlier than Riesling.

*Distribution*

Alsace is the only region in France where Riesling is found and the plantings produce fine wines. Riesling is also grown in Austria, throughout eastern Europe and extensively in Russia. Large plantings are found in Australia, where it is called Rhine Riesling, and in South and North America, where it is known as Johannisberg or White Riesling.

*South Africa*

On the recommendation of Dr Hans Ambrosi, a German consultant who worked at the Nietvoorbij Institute in the 1960s, a number of Riesling clones were imported from Germany during that decade and evaluated under South African conditions. The results proved promising, allowing the variety's release for planting in 1974. Weisser Riesling now accounts for less than one per cent of total vineyard plantings and can be found mainly in the Coastal Region.

*The wines*

Just over 30 wines are bottled locally under the varietal label of Weisser or Rhine Riesling, and there are some very good examples that range in style from dry to sweet. The most outstanding wines made from this variety are those affected by *Botrytis cinerea*. Called Noble Late Harvest wines, they have a distinctive floral, spicy, peppery aroma, and when aged tend to have a waxy character. A particularly good wine made in this style is the Neethlingshof Estate Weisser Riesling Noble Late Harvest.

## Physiology

*Vigour: Moderate, with a fairly erect growth habit.*
*Phenology: Buds early season. At full maturity, has a sugar concentration of 20 to 22° Balling and a total titratable acid level of 7 to 9 g/l.*
*Diseases/pests: Not particularly susceptible to disease, except botrytis, owing to its compact bunches. Fairly resistant to wind. Susceptible to sunburn.*
*Leaves: Medium to large. Round and five-lobed. Shallow lateral sinus, teeth medium, convex.*
*Cluster/bunch: Cylindrical, small, short and compact, tending to conical. Peduncle reddish, very short and lightly held.*
*Berries: Round and medium to small. Skin medium to thick and soft. Very juicy, with aromatic fragrance.*
*Aromas and flavours: Spicy, peppery, flowery, fruity. When older, very honeyed with overtones of kerosene. Distinctly oily smell on the nose.*

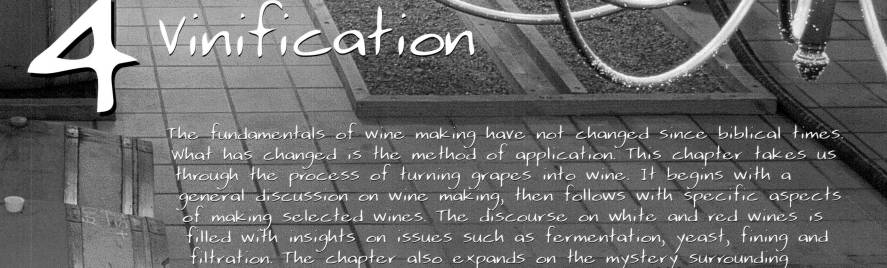

# 4 Vinification

The fundamentals of wine making have not changed since biblical times. What has changed is the method of application. This chapter takes us through the process of turning grapes into wine. It begins with a general discussion on wine making, then follows with specific aspects of making selected wines. The discourse on white and red wines is filled with insights on issues such as fermentation, yeast, fining and filtration. The chapter also expands on the mystery surrounding tannins and how contact with the lees will improve certain wines. It continues with a discussion on sparkling wine, sweet wine, sherries and ports, and finally closes with oak-ageing and bottling.

Waterford maturation cellar

# Wine Making

In the early 1960s, during the Natural Wine Revolution in South Africa, the MacKenzie press and drainers were revolutionary. South Africa, however, did not maintain its leading role in the world of wine production. Europe took over in the so-called 'hi-tech' wine-making arena. The basic wine press had hardly changed for centuries, but suddenly the traditional basket press gave way to all manner of variations. Early attempts at mechanisation were impressive in saving labour, but the then modern press was so rough in its handling that a coarseness of wine was associated with these innovations.

The pneumatic press was then introduced. This worked with an inflatable rubber bladder that squashed the pulp more gently, but it could not be easily cleaned. A 'tank' press with its single membrane was easier to clean, however, and could, seemingly, be built to almost any size.

Slowly but surely the development in technology ironically took us back to where things began. In the 1990s we returned to a press design that resembled the old-fashioned basket press yet added the convenience of modern technology and computerisation. This transformation has not been the only back-to-the-future-type movement. Backed by a better understanding of chemical changes that occur during the wine-making process, most stages are now left as close to the natural process as possible.

There are those who think electricity should be kept out of the winery. There is a strong belief that using open fermenters for red wine that has its 'caps' punched through is better, by far, than pumping over. Many won't agree. It is difficult to argue, however, with the quality of wine that is currently being made with the guidance of the winemaker rather than the interference of same. Electricity is essential for refrigeration and this plays a major role in all aspects of modern wine making.

There is no doubt that technology has done wonders for the improvement of our standard everyday drinking wine. The massive new wineries that have developed all over the New World and the re-developing areas of the Old World make use of ultra-modern technology and their wines are very drinkable and win all kinds of awards. There is a very definite place for these wine production units. They make huge volumes of wine available for the everyday drinker. The top wines will still be made from the best fruit on a smaller scale with much more hands-on involvement. Small can be in thousands of cases while large is in hundreds of thousands of cases.

The 'rule' should be not to try and improve on nature. Rather the winemaker should use technology to reproduce the best possible natural conditions. Usually, the less manipulation used, the healthier the wine. The more natural the wine making, the more expressive the wines.

Mechanical harvesting is considerably less expensive than picking by hand, possibly by as much as 25 to 33 per cent. Harvesting during the cool of the night also contributes to quality and reduces cooling costs, especially when making white wines. It also greatly reduces the oxidation factor, as the containers in which the grapes are transferred to the winery can be closed to the atmosphere and are more easily protected by ascorbic acid.

Initially machine harvesters collected material other than grapes (called MOG in the industry), such as leaves, canes, snails, insects and even the occasional bird's nest or snake. These problems have now been largely overcome with

technical advances and better vineyard management with pruning and trellising. The machine is, however, still unable to distinguish between fully ripe and not-so-ripe bunches, but even this is less of a problem with improved vineyard practices.

Most modern wineries use similar basic equipment such as crushers, presses, filters, tanks, pipes and pumps to transform grapes into wine. No matter how sophisticated the machinery may be, the quality of the fruit and the winemaker's skill are essential for the making of fine wines.

Most big wineries start with loads of grapes arriving in tractor-drawn trailers or on the backs of trucks fitted with a tipping apparatus to unload 'mechanically'. The vehicles are weighed before and after dumping the grapes to determine the tonnage of grapes that has been received. Although the winemaker analyses the grapes for sugar, acid content and the pH before determining when to harvest, he has the juice analysed again once the grapes have been crushed. He must know the analysis to determine exactly how he will handle the wine.

*(above and left) Mechanical harvesting.*

*(below left) Tipping grapes at Kanonkop.*

*(below) Chardonnay harvest arrives at the Rustenberg cellar.*

The crusher splits the berries to liberate the juice and can be combined with revolving beaters that remove the grapes from their stems. The winemaker can select to crush without destemming or destem just a proportion of the grapes. This allows him or her to have just the right amount of stem needed for either causing drainage furrows through the mass of skins and pulp or to provide the amount of tannin required. When making certain white wines, or even some reds, the destemming may be omitted completely and the whole bunch goes to the press for 'whole-bunch pressing'. This is a much slower process and can yield finer, cleaner juice. It allows much more skin character to be imparted to the wine. If done with red grapes, the mechanical action liberates some of the colour from the skin, which flows out with the juice, giving it a pale pink tint before any fermentation takes place. This is how blanc de noir is made.

Whole-bunch pressing is also used in carbonic maceration for the production of nouveau-type wines in South Africa, along the lines of the famous Beaujolais of France. This method may be partially used in making some of the younger-drinking, fresh, fruity red wines. Despite some opinions, cooling is a fundamental process of modern wine making in warm climates. The process starts with the cooling of the must, followed by cooling during fermentation, mainly for white wines, and finally storage of the finished wine under cool conditions in tanks to retain its freshness. Very cool conditions can encourage the deposition of tartrates. Of course, most barrel maturation cellars are also cooled.

The first cooling takes place immediately after crushing, through a series of pipes arranged in such a way as to get the longest length of piping possible into a relatively small space. The pipes have narrower piping on the inside and it is through these pipes that the mash is pumped. In the outer pipe a cold solution of below-freezing brine or other refrigerant such as glycol is passed in the opposite direction. This reduces the temperature of the must. The must is then transported to the fermentation tank, where once again cooling is employed. Sometimes the juice is pressed from the skins at this stage. There are many different types of modern presses to express the juice and hold back the skins, but the principal remains the same. Old wooden slatted basket presses are still in use, and those that are not can still be found

decorating the entrances to wineries. In the early part of the 20th century, a major change took place when the French company, Vaslin, helped pioneer a horizontal, wooden slatted press. This innovation became an important development in gentle pressing.

The modern pneumatic airbag press could well have been inspired by the horizontal press. The pressing plates have been replaced by inflatable bags that press against a cage through which the juice is expressed. The airbag press enables a greater surface area to be pressed, and the operation can be done far more gently than the old-style presses could ever do. This ensures that the pips are not broken and that the subsequent introduction of harsh tannin character to the wine does not occur. These presses are batch operated and have to be emptied and refilled after each pressing.

Continuous presses are associated with large wineries and for making everyday drinking wines, rather than high quality wines. The resulting pomace, which is the residue from the pressings, can be used either for making compost or for the distillation of grappa or marc, since it still contains some sugar if pressed before fermentation.

Centuries ago all fermentation took place in wooden casks. Slowly these were replaced by concrete and eventually mild steel tanks, which were lined to prevent the wine from coming into contact with the steel or the concrete. These linings were once made of wax for concrete or glass, enamel or even ceramic for steel tanks, but these were later replaced by epoxy plastics.

Since the late 1950s and early 1960s, stainless steel has become the preferred product for the manufacture of not only tanks, but also almost every other container or process equipment in the cellar. The exception, of course, occurs when wine is fermented or aged in oak. Some open concrete tanks can still be found in operation, and indeed, some of the world's great red and fortified wines are still fermented in open-topped tanks.

In the old-fashioned open-topped fermenters, whether wood or concrete, rising skins, known as 'the cap', were regularly punched down. As pumps became more practical, the wine was pumped from the bottom of the tank onto the top of the 'cap' to submerge the skins into the fermenting wine for colour and character extraction and to release the build-up of heat in the 'cap'. In modern closed tanks the cap still occurs, but within a sealed vessel the only outlets are valves that release the generated carbon dioxide. Rotating paddles or other agitating devices can also be found inside these tanks. In some cases the entire tank is able to rotate. Pumping over can still also be done in a closed tank.

When fermentation is finished, the wine is allowed to settle. It is then decanted or racked off its sediment or 'lees', which are made up of dried yeast cells, skins, and any other solid matter that might have been present in the wine. Racking is usually done two or three times. This will help to clarify the wine. The longer the settling process, and the more gently it is carried out, usually the better the wine. If, however, the wine is needed for early sale, the sediment can be removed by centrifuging, fining or filtration or a combination of those three. Fining is a term used when an agent is added to the wine to remove the coarsest particles and even some flavours, while filtration takes place when the wine is passed through a filtering medium.

*(left) Bucher press in Rustenberg's new cellar.*

*(from top) Wooden slatted basket wine press (circa 1880), early wine press (circa 1715), oak wine press (circa 1790), all housed at the Stellenryk Wine Museum in Stellenbosch.*

# WHITE WINE

South Africa makes far more white wine than red. More than 80 per cent of all wine produced in the Cape is white. Whole-bunch pressing is traditionally associated with champagne production, but is increasingly being used for the production of still wines with more complexity. Gently done, it yields the clearest juice with the lowest phenolics, resulting in finely flavoured, well-structured wines.

In the cellar the grapes are crushed and the stalks removed. Sometimes the stalks are left on until after pressing, since they allow the juice to drain more easily. Because of the tannin content in the stalks, great care must be taken, although some tannin does add complexity. The stalks, skins and seeds are high in phenolics and these are undesirable in most white wines. When stalks are removed from the juice, it is done as quickly as possible. At this stage sulphur dioxide is added as protection against oxidation and microbiological spoilage. Along with cooling, this also results in better colour and increased primary grape flavours.

There are winemakers who believe in allowing the juice to oxidise deliberately for more complex flavours at the expense of the primary fruit flavours. When fermentation is in progress, however, oxidation is avoided at all costs.

Better wine is made from free-run juice, and this is cooled to 12 to 13°C using a must chiller. It is then left to settle for about 24 hours. Cooling inhibits the activity of micro-organisms and allows the fermentation of clean juice containing only the flavours of the fruit. Cooling also allows the settling of solid matter, such as skins, seeds, vineyard dust and any other impurities that have a detrimental effect on the taste and give adverse odours to the wine. Cleaning the juice also clears the way for better control of the fermentation to follow. The same effect can also be achieved through centrifuging, but this is not the preferred method for high-quality wines. A period of skin contact might be required at this stage, depending on the style of wine. The more extended the skin contact, the more full-bodied the wine. Lengthy skin contact is risky though, as the chances of oxidation and microbiological infection increase. Careful monitoring is essential to avoid bitter flavours in the wine.

## Fermentation

Under normal conditions, sugars in the must consist of equal proportions of fructose and glucose. These simple sugars are monosaccharides that are converted directly into ethyl alcohol and carbon dioxide by yeast enzymes. When the sugars are exhausted, the wine is dry and no further fermentation can take place. If the alcohol reaches a level which the enzymes cannot tolerate, the fermentation will cease, leaving a wine with natural sweetness.

Should the winemaker wish to stop fermentation before the wine is completely dry he may raise or lower the temperature of the fermenting wine. If the temperature of the wine is raised to about 80°C for one minute, the micro-organisms in the wine will be destroyed. This is called pasteurisation and is only applied to wines destined for early consumption. On the other hand, if the wine is chilled to less than 10°C, the yeast becomes dormant, ceases to work and will only reactivate when the temperature is raised again. The yeast can be removed by centrifuge or made inactive by the addition of sufficient sulphur dioxide, although this is avoided when making top-quality wines. Extremely fine filtration is another way to remove yeast.

One of the most common methods to ensure no further fermentation takes place is to add extra alcohol, which overpowers the yeast. This will completely change the character of the wine, however, and is the basis for port, sherries, muscadels and other fortified wines.

After alcoholic fermentation has taken place, some wines undergo a secondary or malolactic fermentation. During this process, the malic acid present in the recently fermented wine is converted into lactic acid and carbon dioxide. For malolactic fermentation to occur the temperature must be above 15°C. It can happen spontaneously, or can be induced by the inoculation of bacteria, primarily *Bacterium leuconostoc*. Malic acid is produced naturally in the grape and is responsible for the sharper, fresher character of the wine. During malolactic fermentation, the strong malic acid is converted into the weaker lactic acid and in this way the high acidity of certain wines is reduced and the acid character 'softened'.

*Yeast*

In the past, Cape winemakers almost automatically added acid because local juice was considered lacking in fruit acid. This was done by using crystallised tartaric or malic acid. Today this practice is no longer necessary in the production of better wines and seldom used for less expensive big-volume wines because better-quality fruit is being grown in the vineyards.

The clean juice is introduced to a fermentation tank along with an inoculation of selected yeast cultures. The selected yeasts will overpower any wild yeast already present in the juice.

Fermentation follows, with the generated heat being reduced to around 14°C. Different winemakers use different temperatures at different stages. Too high a temperature during tumultuous fermentation causes a loss of many of the aromatic fermentation and flavour compounds into the atmosphere. During cooling, the reaction is slowed and aromas are retained.

If fermentation is uncontrolled, heat will kill the yeast and terminate fermentation before all the sugar has fermented to dryness. This might sound acceptable for a wine requiring some sweetness, but heat imparts unacceptable flavours and leaves the wine vulnerable to bacterial spoilage. When the alcoholic fermentation is complete, a few days are allowed for the motion to subside and for the suspended matter, mainly

## Lees Contact

In barrel ageing, white wines are left on their lees during the time they spend in the barrel. The wine is left in the barrel to gain extra complexity and continuous agitation of the lees, to keep them suspended in the wine, adds a richness of flavour and texture. The lees also act as an anti-oxidant, keeping the wine pale-coloured and fresh. To a degree, the suspended lees protect the wine from oak tannins and from picking up any wood colour.

dead yeast cells, to settle at the bottom of the tank. The wine is then removed from the lees by what is termed racking. This simply means pumping the wine off the lees. If this is not done at an early stage, the wine picks up unwanted odours from the yeast as it undergoes cell autolysis. These smells are very beefy (similar to Marmite) and totally unacceptable in white wine. Some contact with the lees, however, can add flavour to the wine, as well as freshness, which is retained by early bottling.

During the first racking it is common practice to add a small amount of sulphur dioxide. This keeps the free content at about 30 mg/l in order to prevent oxidation. From that point on the wine is protected from contact with the air to prevent even the slightest oxidation. Depending on the style of wine, it may now be transferred to casks for oak ageing, kept in stainless steel for future blending, or sent for early blending and bottling. If it stays in the tank, another racking will take place within two to three weeks, to remove the wine from the sediment. For wines that will be bottled early and sold at a relatively low price, the winemaker will use a centrifuge to remove the solids, although this will also remove some of the flavours and aromas. Wines for early bottling undergo cold stabilisation, which chills the wine to –4°C, thereby causing tartrates in the wine to form crystals. These tartrates settle naturally in time, but if they are not removed from the young wine they will appear as crystals in the bottle. The wine also requires some clarification to remove any remaining solids either by fining, filtration or centrifuging, or a combination of all three processes. Young wines will certainly be filtered before bottling and fining may remove some unwanted flavours that might have developed.

Usually some form of blending occurs in order to give the wine balance or consistency. Even single varietal wines are usually blends from different tanks or perhaps from wines of different origins.

While some white wines are fermented in a tank and later introduced to wooden barrels, others are fermented in barrels and may be left on their lees for a period of months. This is often referred to as *sur lie*, a French term meaning 'on the lees', and refers to the way a wine develops special characteristics from the lees, including a creamy complexity.

The lees are also powerful anti-oxidants, but they must remain sweet, otherwise foul flavours develop. By stirring up the lees, a practice called *bâttonage*, the effects can be accentuated.

Wood ageing adds greater complexity to the wine, but can be very costly and time-consuming since careful, constant monitoring by the winemaker is required. Wood ageing is reserved for selected, higher priced wines. Today many inexpensive wines have attractive oak characteristics, and this is achieved by submerging selected oak chips or staves in the wine for a period. This has the benefit of adding the oak flavours to the wine without the cost of buying a cask or the time required for ageing.

Some white wines undergo malolactic fermentation to soften excessive acidity before ageing. This can take place in wood, without wood, or using a combination of both. It can also continue in the bottle, but this would be considered a fault. Ageing times in wood are at the winemaker's discretion, and can last from a few weeks to a year or two, depending on what he or she wants to achieve. Combinations of new and used wood also add to the complexity of character.

White wines can be finished bone dry, off-dry, semi-sweet or in the styles of Late Harvest, Special Late Harvest, Noble Late Harvest or Sweet Natural, or as sparkling wines of various kinds.

*(above) Filter at Rustenberg.*

*(background) Refrigerated stainless steel tanks at Vergelegen.*

# RED WINE

There is no set path for making red wines. The winemaker has a myriad of options to choose from, and the choice depends on whether he is making a classic wine in small quantities or large volumes of early-drinking red.

Red wine is made only from red grapes, and as most of these grapes have their colour in their skins, it is imperative to include the skins in the wine-making process.

The grapes arrive at the cellar after being picked either by hand or machine. There they are broken to release the juice and to encourage fermentation. Some winemakers destem while crushing, while others retain some of the stems to help with juice drainage. In most cases the stems are removed to avoid a high tannin content in the wine. With some varieties, such as Pinot Noir, the winemaker may choose to do whole-bunch fermentation, followed by pressing with the stems intact. This allows a gentle pressing to be employed, with the stems forming what can be described as draining channels for the wine to flow more easily.

The winemaker then either adds selected yeast or allows spontaneous fermentation to occur from the yeast on the skins. The skins are mixed on a regular basis through the wine during fermentation. This encourages the extraction of colour and flavour compounds in the skins. These are mainly of a phenolic nature and are extracted by the alcohol produced during fermentation. The extraction is also assisted by heat generated from fermentation. Too high a temperature will lead to a loss of fruit character. Therefore careful control and a stable temperature between 20 and 25°C is necessary to extract colour while keeping the fruit character.

During open tank fermentation, the winemaker frequently plunges the cap down into the must, using a device that looks like a broom without bristles. The cap is brought to the surface by rising carbon dioxide, and plunging ensures that the skins are thoroughly mixed in the fermenting juice to promote good extraction. Plunging also has a cooling effect. Sometimes fermenting juice is drawn up from the bottom of the vessel and then pumped onto the cap at the surface. This alternative method also mixes and cools the juice.

In modern stainless steel tanks the cap can be held below the surface using a perforated plate. Pumping over can be employed or, as in the case with roto tanks, the entire tank can be revolved in order to mix the skins and juice. The length of time allowed for skin contact is critical. In the past, the juice would be drained from the skins when the amount of colour and tannin extracted was considered sufficient. Fermentation would then be completed without the skins. Today it is common practice to ferment to dryness on the skins and then to allow even further contact. This practice is sometimes called post-fermentation maceration. It not only allows more colour and tannin extraction, but also has the effect of 'softening' the existing tannins.

After fermentation the juice is drained away from the skins and the skins are pressed. The winemaker has the option of either returning the pressed wine to the original juice or using it to bolster another wine needing a component fuller in tannin and colour.

Today it is common for red wines to undergo malolactic fermentation, a process that stabilises the wine and adds complexity to its character. It is often done while the wine is still in bulk so that the entire volume undergoes the same process. The wine is usually inoculated, but if it is introduced

## Malolactic Fermentation

Malolactic fermentation has nothing to do with alcohol production, but instead modifies the acidity of a young wine. Grape musts usually contain two predominant organic acids in very differing quantities. Tartaric acid is the acid particularly associated with the grape whereas malic acid, which is widely distributed in the fruit world, is particularly associated with apples. Tartaric acid does not change that much as the grape ripens, but the level of malic acid is high in green grapes and low in ripe grapes. There are strains of bacteria that are often present at the start of the alcoholic fermentation and develop and build in population as the alcoholic fermentation ends. At a certain point the population is such that secondary fermentation, known as malolactic fermentation, will begin. If the amount of bacteria is not sufficient and malolactic fermentation is desired, then it can be inoculated.

The cells attack the malic acid, not the tartaric acid, and convert it to the more feeble lactic acid which is not present in the original juice and is associated with milk. During the reaction, carbon dioxide is given off and this needs to be able to escape. If malolactic fermentation takes place in the bottle, an unsightly deposit is formed and the gas produces an unpalatable prickly sensation. If it is going to happen, it must take place before bottling.

The replacement of malic acid with lactic acid causes a decided reduction in the wine's acidity. Sometimes this is highly desirable in many red wines. In addition to reducing acidity, the reaction can add aromatics that were not previously in the wine and it certainly contributes to the texture and roundness of the wine. It would seem that spontaneous malolactic fermentation gives greater character but can also add unwanted dairy-like smells. Cultured strains leave little in the way of aromatics.

*(from top) Jacques Borman and assistant pump over red wine in open tank fermenters at La Motte, punching the cap at Kanonkop, assistant winemaker Jann Buchwalter clearing the lees at Rupert and Rothschild.*

*(right) Cellar at Rustenberg with suspended tanks for ease of operation.*

to old barrels prior to malolactic fermentation, it might be left for this type of fermentation to begin spontaneously. This occurs because old barrels often contain bacteria residue from previous periods of malolactic fermentation.

Maturation in oak is a popular practice. The oak contributes vanilla and oak tannins to the wine, adding even more complexity. A winemaker needs to make crucial decisions with regard to the type of barrel, whether new or used, the choice of wood, and the length of maturation, with costs always in mind.

Whether or not it is to be aged in wood, the wine needs regular racking off its lees. From tank to tank racking is a relatively

## Yeast

Although man has used micro-organisms for fermentation since the dawn of time, fermentation was never fully understood until Louis Pasteur (1822 to 1895) opened our eyes to the true nature of micro-organisms, including yeast.

Yeast is the agent that makes the reaction happen, converting sugar in the juice into equal proportions of ethyl alcohol and carbon dioxide. While the gas is released into the atmosphere during fermentation, the alcohol remains in the juice. Fermentation gives special characteristics to the juice and they combine with those of the grape variety, resulting in flavours and aromas that make wine so attractive.

In wine making both cultured and natural yeasts are used. Although cultured yeasts are also considered natural, they have been cultivated and specially selected in the laboratory for reliability during fermentation. Winemakers select the type of yeast that best suits their requirements. Some yeasts react better under certain conditions, such as warmer temperatures, while others give higher alcoholic concentrations.

Prior to a fuller understanding of yeast and its role in fermentation, all fermentation was considered to be 'spontaneous'. In other words, it occurred without a catalyst. Some yeasts are naturally present on the skin of the grape while others are airborne. The skin of the grape is covered with a waxy substance, called *pruine* in French or 'bloom' in English, which contains millions of yeast cells. Only one per cent of these cells are the preferred 'wine' yeasts, as opposed to 'wild' yeasts, which can be blamed for unwanted flavours, objectionable odours and a cloudy appearance in the wine. Although there is a diverse range of yeast types, the most desirable species of 'wine' yeast is *Saccharomyces cerevisiae*. Those that are present in the greatest quantity will eventually determine the fermentation characteristics.

A grape has everything required for fermentation, not only sugar for conversion to alcohol, but also nutrients, such as amino acids, vitamins and minerals, which are required for stimulating yeast growth. For yeast to grow, it needs carbohydrates, which in the grape take the form of sugar. The sugar varies in each grape variety and its ripeness. Higher sugars can be obtained by allowing the grape to dry out slightly, taking on a slight raisin-like appearance.

Under favourable conditions, a single yeast cell can split 10 000 sugar molecules a second in the course of fermentation. On one grape, as many as one billion sugar molecules can be split every second. After fermentation begins, the appearance is that of a boisterous bubbling mass.

simple process, but from barrel to barrel it is considerably more tedious, and the intensive use of labour adds to the cost. Two to three rackings are usually required. Some winemakers do rackings before transferring the wine to wood.

When the wine is removed from the wood it undergoes a fining and this is sometimes followed by a light filtration before bottling. Some red wines are labelled 'neither fined nor filtered', and these wines will certainly throw heavy sediments with time and need to be decanted before serving. Some winemakers believe that these wines will have a far more satisfying character of flavours and aromas than wines that have been fined and filtered. Other winemakers, however, opt for a light egg-white fining and the softest filtration just before bottling to ensure that no solid matter is introduced to the bottle.

Ageing in wood, whether for six months or for more than a year, naturally stabilises the wine, but it remains vulnerable to oxidation and needs to be bottled to avoid this and to continue its ageing process. Some unwooded red wines which are bottled in their youth need to be tartrate stabilised after blending and before bottling.

Some red wines are kept in stainless steel tanks and blended with wines that have been aged in wood, and although the wood-aged component may have deposited some of its tartrates, the blend might also require stabilising before bottling.

## Fining and filtration

Fining and filtration are processes used to clarify wine. During fining a material is passed through the wine, causing suspended matter to sink to the bottom of the tank or barrel as sediment. The clear wine can then be racked from the sediment. During filtration wine is passed through the filtering medium, leaving the suspended matter behind on the filter. Sound wines usually settle naturally with clarity. This can take time, but if the winemaker needs to bottle the wine before this stage is reached, usually for economic reasons, the sedimentation process can be speeded up. This is done by fining. Fining can, however, be used for reasons other than clarification, including stabilisation. Fining is a complex reaction, the simple explanation being that of electrostatic attraction.

A fining agent carrying a particular electrical charge reacts with wine constituents carrying the opposite charge, and the neutralised combination precipitates. The type of fining agent used depends on the type of colloid or particle to be removed from the wine. The main fining agents include gelatin, isinglass, casein, albumin, bentonite and silica. Fining materials may absorb flavouring components and bentonite can even reduce the flavour of the wine. For this reason, fining and filtration are being used less often in the making of hand-crafted wines in an attempt to keep as much character in the wine as possible. This can lead to sediment in the bottle and the wine should be decanted before serving.

Winemakers also use filtration as a method of speeding up the production process. This can be done either through depth filtration or surface filtration. Used at an early stage of the wine-making process, the former is a rougher form of filtration, where the wine is passed through a porous type of silica. At a later stage, the wine is passed through a thin film of plastic material perforated with tiny holes. This surface filtration ensures that the wine is sterile and rid of potentially harmful organisms just prior to bottling.

## Tannins

Tannins belong to a group of chemical compounds found in grapes and are known as polyphenols. They include anthocyanins that give colour to red wines. In the grape they are mainly in the skin and the pips.

As much as tannins are important in red wines, they are very difficult to isolate and measure, and they continually change their chemical nature which reflects on their taste expression. A good deal of what winemakers know about tannins in their particular set up is discovered by experience. Get a group together and you will soon see, or hear, that scientifically, tannins remain pretty much a mystery. Hard tannins, ripe tannins and sweet tannins can be tasted, but apparently not easily measured.

Polyphenols increase in quantity as the grape ripens. The tannins become more acceptable the riper they become and so the makers of quality wine wait to pick their grapes when they are phenolically ripe. Not only do they taste the grape, but they also check the development of the pips and will only pick when the pips have all turned brown. It is pretty well accepted now that the later a red grape is picked, the softer the tannins become in texture. They also become easier to extract and certainly more pleasing to the taste. Almost without exception, harvesting at this time is way beyond the old accepted optimum of sugar/acid ratio of ripeness. Like everything in nature, if the development is allowed to go too far, the wines end up unbalanced and too low in acids, making them 'jammy' or overripe.

Wines that are made with 'development through ageing' in the mind of the winemaker might have tannins that are initially not that pleasant to most people's palates. As the tannin molecules grow larger with time, they 'polymerise' and their ability to combine with proteins change. Early on this is more apparent and as the tannins react with the proteins in our saliva the wine appears to be hard. As the tannin molecules enlarge, their activity seems to become less astringent. Some become too large to remain soluble and settle out of the wine and form part of the sediment. This has a great softening effect on the wine.

# Rosé and blanc de noir

In Europe, rosé wines were traditionally made from grapes without much colour, but as the demand for these wines grew, grapes with better colour were used. Once the desired colour is achieved, the fermenting juice is drained away. In the Cape some rosé wines are made in this manner, but most of the inexpensive brands of semi-sweet rosé are made by blending some deep red wine into white wine until the desired colour is achieved.

Some Cape rosé is made dry, such as the Felicite made by Newton Johnson. There are others made from Pinotage, such as the one released by Delheim early each year. It is almost like a Nouveau, but it has some ability to age. Other red varieties such as Shiraz and Merlot are also used in the production of rosé at the Cape. Good rosé is making a minor return to popularity, with some innovative products such as the dry Chardonnay/Cabernet Sauvignon rosé from Steenberg.

The blanc de noir style first achieved commercial success in South Africa during the early 1980s. Blanc de noir was first introduced by Boschendal and it is still very popular after its 22nd vintage. The difference in taste between a blanc de noir and a rosé can be attributed to different wine-making methods. Rosé obtains its colour from fermenting on the skin, and the alcohol produced during fermentation extracts the pigment from the skin. In the making of blanc de noir, red grapes are crushed and the juice is slowly drained away, and whatever colour is leached out as the fresh juice moves through the mass of skins is retained as the only colour of the final wine. Because there is no reaction in the skin during fermentation, the colour and character of the wine are distinctly different.

In South Africa, blanc de noir has to be certified that it has been made in the approved manner. In contrast, a rosé is certified for origin, vintage and variety, but not for the method in which it was made. Wines that are not certified as blanc de noir are sometimes called 'Blush' in order to avoid the more difficult method of making a true blanc de noir.

*(previous page) Plaisir de Merle maturation cellar.*
*(below) Massed stainless steel tanks and Bucher press at Rustenberg.*
*(right) Vaulted Cap Classique cellar at Twee Jonge Gezellen.*

# SPARKLING WINE

The great tradition of Champagne immediately comes to mind when sparkling wine is mentioned, but the world produces many other excellent sparkling wines, made in the same manner as Champagne but not labelled as such.

There are two very broad categories of sparkling wines: some with many bubbles, which most people think of as 'champagne', and others with fewer bubbles, which in South Africa we generally call perlé.

The first category has as its most illustrious role model the sparkling wines from the Champagne area, and to be able to use that name, the wine must originate from that part of France. It is a wine that gets its bubble by means of secondary alcoholic fermentation which takes place in the bottle. It is also one of the most modern styles of wine, having its origin in France in the mid-17th century.

There are other sparkling wines that are packaged in the same manner as the famous wine from Champagne in the familiar bottle with a cork and wire muzzle. Nevertheless, they have not been made by the *méthode champenoise*, which is both labour intensive and time-consuming. Price can be a very accurate indicator as to how the wine was made. In the medium price range are the better non-bottle fermented sparkling wines, made by the Charmat method. During this process, the wines undergo secondary fermentation in a tank rather than in a bottle. There are also those sparkling wines that are even less expensive, and these have been carbonated either in a tank or in a bottle.

Excellent wines made by the *méthode champenoise* can be made in all parts of the wine-producing world, and each has its own character. None, however, is identical to those produced in Champagne. The Champenoise are understandably very proud of their name, and no wine made anywhere other than in Champagne can be sold using that name or anything alluding to that name. Hence other names have developed, such as Cava in Spain and Cap Classique in South Africa. In Australia and the United States the marketers of bottle-fermented sparkling wines have so far relied on their brand names rather than any generic term to sell the product.

Interestingly, the major Champagne houses have set up production facilities for their style of wine in different parts of the world, particularly in the United States, but also in Australia and Argentina. In South Africa, only Mumm has as yet become involved with a local producer.

Comparisons of wines made by the *méthode champenoise* are difficult, and even house styles within Champagne differ greatly. The tremendous variation in vintage conditions plays a role in the distinct differences in the character of the vintaged wines of Champagne. Wines made in the same manner in the New World, including South Africa, do not have such dramatic differences caused by the vintage. Non-vintage Champagne of the *grandes marques* is, however, remarkable in its consistency. There is no doubt that in Champagne the skills of making, managing and marketing a particular style of wine have reached a peak not matched anywhere else in the world of wine.

# *Cap Classique*

In the Cape, sparkling wines called Cap Classique are made using the *méthode champenoise*. In recent history Frans Malan of Simonsig was the first to market a bottle-fermented sparkling wine, Kaapse Vonkel. Made in 1971, the first wine was produced from Chenin Blanc, but since 1988 only the classic combination of Pinot Noir and Chardonnay is used for the base wine.

Other producers have experimented with their blends. Jeff Grier of Villiera has used Pinotage in his successful Tradition Carte Rouge, and Jean Daneel, previously at Morgenhof, used a combination of Chardonnay and Pinotage. All agree, however, that the composition of the blend and the use of a proportion of aged wine are essential for the best wines.

Top quality is achieved only by using the very best fruit, and as whole-bunch pressing is *de rigueur* in the making of Cap Classiques, hand picking is necessary. Most Cape winemakers use the pneumatic bladder press with its sensitive controls to express the juice very gently. Usually only the free-run juice, or that from the most gentle pressing, is collected for the production of Cap Classique.

The fresh must is usually chilled and settled. The clean juice is then racked to a fermenter and fermented dry with selected yeast under controlled conditions. A few winemakers ferment a portion of their production in wood for extra complexity, while others encourage malolactic fermentation. The wine is racked again and may undergo a light fining for clarification prior to cold tartrate stabilisation. Further fining and filtration follow.

The winemaker then blends the wine according to the house style. For a non-vintage wine he uses the current wine and small quantities of base wine from previous vintages. Alternatively, he may choose to highlight the very best of a particular vintage.

After blending, a final stabilising procedure follows before the addition of enough sugar to generate the second alcoholic fermentation. The sugar is added in the form of a syrup, along with the selected yeast.

The wine is then bottled and closed with a temporary metal crown cap that will eventually be replaced with the traditional cork we all know. The second fermentation takes place in the closed bottle, under the pressure generated by the carbon dioxide that cannot escape. The length of time the wine is kept in contact with the yeast inside the bottle further enhances the character and flavour of the wine. Most of these wines are kept under these conditions for at least a year, while the best wines might remain like this for as long as five years. It is this second fermentation that gives the wine its bubbles. The temperature is kept low so that fermentation proceeds slowly, and this eventually generates the desirable fine bubble.

The bottled wine is then stacked on its side, almost always in bins so that it can be handled by a fork-lift truck, although previously stacking on wooden slats was the norm. If bins are used, the bottles are normally stacked neck down so that during mechanised riddling on *gyropalettes* the bottles do not need to be handled again. Those winemakers who do not use *gyropalettes* move the stacked bottles to A-frame wooden racks for riddling or *remuage*, which is the painstaking process of shifting each individual bottle from the angle it was placed onto the rack to a vertical neck-down position. Each time the bottle is moved, the slight bump as it is set down helps to move the fine yeast deposit down towards the inside of the closure. This operation can take months by hand, while mechanised *gyropalettes* do the same job in as little as a week.

The use of the latter is a much more efficient process, and essential in the modern world where every attempt is made to reduce cost and improve quality.

There have been various developments in the removal of the yeast from the bottle, including the capturing of the yeast in 'beads' of calcium alginate, which gather in the neck of the upside-down bottle in a few seconds. Eventually new developments could do away with the traditional need for *remuage* and the human riddlers or *remueurs*.

It is important to remove the sediment. When the cork is released, the bubbles rise to the neck of the bottle, and if the yeast sediment has not been removed, the gas will bring the solids to the surface, leaving the wine cloudy and unattractive. In the early days, before Madame Clicquot perfected the *remuage* process, champagne glasses were opaque in order to disguise the murky wine. When the yeast has gathered in the neck of the inverted bottle, disgorgement follows. This process involves freezing a small amount of wine in the neck of the bottle, where the yeast has collected in a little plastic cup on the inside of the metal cap. When the cap is removed, the pressure of the gas ejects the frozen plug of wine and yeast, leaving clean wine. During this process the wine is exposed to oxygen, and the operation must be carried out as quickly as possible.

During disgorgement, the wine's sweetness or dryness is determined and some sweetening or *dosage* is usually added.

This style of wine is naturally high in acid, and carbon dioxide, which gives the bubble, is also acidic and needs to be smoothed.

Traditionally a sugar syrup with brandy, called *liqueur d'expédition* in France, was added to the wine, but today sugar and wine form the *dosage*.

After the *dosage* has been added, a regular sparkling wine cork is forced into the bottle neck, and wired down with a metal muzzle to prevent the pressure from discharging the cork. The bottle is then immediately shaken to mix the *dosage*.

The recently corked bottle is stored for a while to allow the cork to lose some of its elasticity and to facilitate eventual easy removal. The pressure in a bottle of Cap Classique is between five and six atmospheres, which is about the same pressure as that of a tyre of a haulage truck. It is therefore understandable why the glass of the Cap Classique bottle is thick and strong and why great care must be taken when removing the cork.

The date of disgorgement is becoming an important part of the information on the labels of Cap Classique wines. The longer they are kept before disgorgement, the more character they develop. Wines from the same vintage could well have different disgorgement dates; the later disgorged wines always have better character.

# Other sparkling wines

Cap Classique represents only a fraction of all the sparkling wine produced in the Cape. Some sparkling wine producers use the carbonation method to give the wine its bubble. The carbonation is applied slowly over time while the wine is held under pressure in a tank, and this ensures even, pin-point bubbles when the cork is released.

There are a number of sparkling wines that are produced by tank fermentation or the Charmat method. The secondary fermentation is started in a pressure tank and not in a bottle. When the wine reaches the required pressure (about five atmospheres), the fermentation is halted by cooling. The wine is clarified and bottled under pressure.

Another method is known as the transfer method. Here the wine undergoes secondary fermentation in the bottle. It is then transferred from the bottle to a bulk pressure tank without riddling or disgorgement. There the sediment is removed by filtration and, after the *dosage* has been added, the wine is bottled once again.

Perlé wines enjoyed their heyday in the early 1970s, but some fine wines with gentle bubbles are still very popular in certain areas of the country. Most perlés are carbonated in line to bottling. To meet the definition, perlé wines must have a pressure below 1.5 atmospheres, otherwise the producer has to pay the much higher rate of duty levied on sparkling wines.

*(above left) Corking Cap Classique.*

*(left) Frozen sediment in inverted neck bottle.*

*(below left) Metal muzzle cork fastener.*

## Base wines and cuvées

By all accounts, the most important element in the making of a good sparkling wine is not necessarily the method by which the wine produces its bubbles, but rather the quality of the base wine from which it is made.

Destined for blending into what will eventually be the desired sparkling wine, the base wine is made as a still wine. The bunches of grapes are picked by hand and are then gently whole-bunch pressed. The juice is clarified, fermented, and sometimes undergoes malolactic fermentation, and the base wine is blended. This wine can be used as the base wine for that year's sparkling wine or can be kept as a base wine for following vintages of sparkling wines.

When the base wine is blended with the current year's wine, the final blend is called the *cuvée*. Sugar and yeast will be added to this wine and then it will be transferred to the bottle or into a tank for second fermentation, depending on the method used to produce the bubbles.

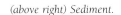

*(above right) Sediment.*

# SWEET WINES

Sweet wines are broadly classified. The wines may be 'Natural Sweet' wines or fortified with wine spirit. It should be remembered, however, that not all fortified wines are sweet.

## Natural Sweet wines

Natural Sweet wines make up a considerable proportion of the market. The modern industry developed from a natural semi-sweet wine called Lieberstein. Until the end of the Second World War, all natural wines made in South Africa were dry and sweet wines were fortified. With the arrival of European technology after the war, there was a tentative move in South Africa to make a natural wine that was not dry. One of the earliest commercial successes was Tasheimer Goldtröpfchen, a high-price category wine which was closed with a cork.

Today Late Harvest, Special Late Harvest, Noble Late Harvest and Natural Sweet wines are carefully defined. Late Harvest wines are usually blends of dry wine to which sweet must or even concentrated grape juice has been added in order to achieve the required sweetness.

Special Late Harvest and especially Noble Late Harvest wines derive their character from the effect of *Botrytis cinerea*. This micro-organism reduces the moisture of the grape and concentrates its sugars, and the fungus adds a specific character to the eventual wine. As it grows on the surface of the grape, the filaments of the fungus penetrate the skin. Moisture is removed and both the sugar and the acid content are degraded. The lack of moisture causes the grape to shrivel and as much as 40 per cent reduction in mass can take place. Various compounds develop, including glycol. All these effects combine to give the special 'botrytis' character to the eventual wine. Because of the concentration,

only very small amounts of rich wine are made from botrytis-infected grapes. The development of 'noble rot' by the fungus is a risky procedure, as once the fungus begins to grow, dry conditions are essential for full development. If it should rain or the skins are broken, 'grey' or 'sour rot' develops and the harvest is lost.

In its noble form the rot can be present in various proportions. Obviously, the greater the content of botrytis, the greater the amount of character the wine will show. This means that both higher or lower botrytised wines can be made. High sugar concentrations can also be achieved without any botrytis influence. For this reason the Natural Sweet category was introduced for Late Harvest wines that show no botrytis character but have the sugar concentration.

The making of a Special Late Harvest, or particularly a Noble Late Harvest, is a long, slow and laborious task and there is no set method. As a result these special wines are highly individual. Only bunches affected by botrytis are removed from the vine during harvesting. The shrivelled grapes are taken to the cellar, where they are inspected for grey or sour rot. These undesirable grapes are cut away.

The winemaker may choose to destalk the grapes or continue with a gentle press, using the stalks as a kind of stabiliser, as the mass of botrytis-infected grapes is very 'slippery'. This mass of stalks, pulp and skins may be broken up a number of times to release as much of the rich juice as possible. The juice is allowed to settle, or it might be clarified for a cleaner fermentation. Fermentation of this rich juice, with its highly concentrated sugar content, is not easy and it may take months to reduce to an acceptable alcohol level. The final composition depends, however, on the sugar concentration in the grapes at the time of picking.

Natural Sweet wines are made in much the same way, but without the effect of botrytis. The sugar content is developed in the grapes as they dry or 'raisin' on the vine. *Vins de paille* or 'straw' wines are now permitted in the Cape. To make this type of wine, the grapes are picked at a very ripe stage, and then dried on straw mats to concentrate the contents even further before fermentation begins.

# FORTIFIED WINES

Wherever wines are made, some kind of fortified wine is produced. The great fortified sherries, ports, Madeiras and Marsalas all have their origins closely associated with the United Kingdom. It is, therefore, no surprise that as a former British colony, the Cape of Good Hope excelled in the production of sherries, ports and muscadels. Most of the Cape's wines were of the fortified variety until the natural wine revolution of the late 1950s. Since then the volume has declined dramatically, but in recent years there has been a revival in the appreciation of good Cape port, and some interest is being shown in the best muscadels.

Fortified wines owe their existence to the fact that once the fortifying spirit has been added to the wine, it acts as a preservative and gives the wine a very long life.

## *Cape sherry*

Many people conveniently lump port and sherry together, probably because they are both fortified and originate on the Iberian Peninsula. That is where the similarities end.

Sherry is made from white grapes, fermented dry before being fortified, and then blended through a continuous process, year by year. Unlike port, sherry does not carry a vintage date, owing to the practice of blending different vintages.

Sherry is one of the best known fortified wines and often the name is given to wines that bear little resemblance to the original wines of Spain. Although similar wines are now universally produced, the label must state where the sherry was made, for example, in the Cape, Cyprus or Australia.

*Flor* sherry is the characteristic sherry of Spain and is the classic style on which the others are based. The name *flor* comes from the Spanish word for 'flower'. Sherry acquires its characteristic flavour and bouquet from the growth and action of a yeast that develops a film across the surface of the young wine. Under the microscope the yeast has the appearance of thousands of little flowers linked together, hence the name *flor*.

In Spain sherry is made mainly from the Palomino grape. Much of the best South African sherry is, however, made from Chenin Blanc.

Once crushed, the juice is fermented to dryness, racked a few times to remove its lees, and then slightly fortified to prevent the young wine from losing quality. The wine is not fortified too much, as this will then prevent the *flor* from forming. The young wine is placed into casks in what the Spanish call the *criadera* or nursery. The casks are only partially filled in order to leave a large surface area on which the *flor* can develop. The *flor* prevents the wine from coming into direct contact with the atmosphere. During the two or more years that the wine spends in the *criadera*, the unique sherry character develops. After the wine is removed from the *criadera*, it is fortified to full strength to preserve it. The wine then passes through the *solera*.

The *solera* is an ageing and maturing process that takes place through the continuous blending of one vintage with another, normally in three-tiered vertical rows of barrels that are never moved. At the start of a *solera* process, the first barrels are filled from the *criadera* of the first vintage. The next year another set is filled, and again in the third year.

*(right) Sherry solera at KWV.*
*(far left) Palomino grapes used in sherry production.*

Botrytis cinerea-*infected grapes.*

*Spier wine shop.*

When sherry is blended, a portion is drawn from the first or oldest layer of barrels; the space left is then filled from the next row and that space from the next. This last or youngest space is filled with new wine from the *criadera*. This is why a vintage sherry from a single year is not possible through the *solera*. It also means that if a wine has spent about two years in the *criadera*, and then at least three years to work through the *solera*, the minimum age for a good *flor* sherry is at least five years. The best sherry is more likely to exceed six or seven years as there will be more layers in the *solera*. The process produces uniformity and ensures that a well-known brand is always reliable. New branding is now being designed for Cape sherries, as legislation requires that the word 'sherry' may no longer be used in the export market.

## *Muscadel*

There are two very distinct types of muscadel produced in the Cape. There are those that are fortified before any fermentation takes place, and those that have undergone a slight amount of fermentation before the fortifying alcohol is added, giving the wine another dimension. This small amount of fermentation creates flavours and characteristics unobtainable other than through fermentation.

If Pinotage is South Africa's national red wine, then muscadel should surely be considered the national fortified wine. The really great muscadels from the Breede River and Klein Karoo regions can hold their own among the best of the world's fortified Muscat wines.

Hot climates encourage high sugar contents, as well as a certain amount of raisin development. This makes the removal of the berries from the stalks somewhat difficult. The concentration of character through simple dehydration without any botrytis effect shows very distinctly in the finished wine.

Very few Cape Muscats are wood aged, but those that are develop a particular magic, and these rich wines are magnificent.

# Cape port

South African winemakers are making considerable efforts to improve their ports with much success. The Cape has a long history of port production, but in the past most of what used to be labelled as port bore little resemblance to the port that originated from Portugal. Leading port producers have recently formed the South African Port Producers Association (SAPPA) to pool their knowledge, lay down guidelines as to the terminology for labelling and encourage the use of Portuguese port varieties. The best ports are made from blends that include Touriga Naçionale, Touriga Francesca, Tinta Barocca, Tinta Roriz, Cornifesto and Souzão.

Calitzdorp has become the unofficial capital of Cape port, and Boplaas and Die Krans have made great strides in the improvement of port in this area. Cape Wine Master, Tony Mossop, has also established a small port vineyard in the area. Calitzdorp now hosts a port festival each winter.

SAPPA recommends the use of traditional Portuguese varieties and has included sugar and alcohol levels in its guidelines, based on Portuguese regulations and adapted to suit local conditions. The name selected for use on export labels is 'Cape', and outside South Africa the wines are known as Cape Ruby, Cape Vintage and Cape Tawny. Port is fortified when enough fermentation has taken place to extract as much colour as possible and when enough grape sugar is left to give the wine the desired level of sweetness.

When making port, grapes are crushed by mechanical means. Fermentation takes place in either traditional open casks or in modern, closed, stainless steel fermenters. Winemakers may punch the cap or pump the wine over the cap to get colour extraction as soon as possible, so that the wine can be fortified when the correct sugar level has been achieved. The fermenting juice is pressed from the skins, and fortifying spirit is added to preserve the natural sugar. The wine is then aged in wood; the period of maturation depends on the type of port being produced.

## Port

SAPPA has set the following guidelines for different styles of port:

Ruby: lighter style, ruby-coloured, non-vintage port, aged in wood for at least six months.

Vintage: a port with a vintage date and bottled after about two years in wood.

Vintage Reserve: a port made from exceptionally good years, aged about two years in wood and vintage dated.

Late Bottled Vintage: a port with a vintage date and bottled after four to five years in wood.

Tawny: a port aged for many years in wood. It has developed a tawny colour. It need not necessarily carry an age indication.

(right) Cape port cellar at J.P. Bredell Wines.
(far right) A cooper assembling a barrel.
(following page) A cooper toasting a barrel.

# OAK AGEING

Originally wooden barrels were used as ordinary containers to hold wine, but it became apparent that if wine spent some time in barrels, a change occurred in its character and quality. As tanks with patent linings found their way into the industry, and eventually stainless steel, the use of wooden barrels declined, particularly in the New World, where small barrel maturation was not at all common.

This situation has changed, however, and the use of oak barrels has made an important comeback. Over the past 20 years New World winemakers have become important users of barrels, as well as leaders in the development and use of oak chips.

The most common oak barrel in use today is the 225-litre barrique, although the larger 300-litre hogshead and the 450- or 500-litre puncheon are also popular. Winemakers use different barrels for different purposes. In general, smaller barrels are used for quicker extraction of the oak character. The winemaker might also prefer to use 'new' barrels that have not been used before. He may rack wine from a new to an old barrel, or even back into a stainless steel container once the desired wood character has been achieved.

The origin of the oak is important, and names such as Limousin, Nevers, Allier, Tronçais and Vosges have set the standards by which other oak is judged. These names indicate the traditional forests in France from which the wood originated. Other forests in Europe, including those in Germany, Italy, Yugoslavia and Russia, are also used in the production of oak barrels. Across the Atlantic, American oak is gaining popularity for the maturation of the more powerful red wines such as Shiraz, Pinotage and Cabernet Sauvignon. There are many species of oak, but the most important in the making of barrels are two European species, *Quercus sessiliflora* and *Quercus robur*, and the American, *Quercus alba*.

Some of the wine industry's most colourful characters are coopers, and perhaps they still retain some of the Celtic myths and legends that are associated with the origins of this profession. They are highly skilled craftsmen who work in hot and tough conditions that demand a level of fitness few other jobs in the industry require. The wood is traditionally seasoned in the open air in stacks for up to two years. The ideal moisture content of an oak stave is about 17 or 18 per cent. Although oak can be dried in a kiln, which is a much quicker process than the natural method, kiln-dried wood is not preferred by top coopers.

An oak tree's grain is determined by soil and climate. Cooler climates result in slower growth and a tighter grain, which produces more of the desirable phenolics preferred by winemakers.

Another important influence on the wine is the amount of 'toasting' the oak undergoes during the construction of the barrel. An open fire is made inside the circle of staves in order to bend them, and the level of burning or browning of the wood is termed 'toast'. The fire increases the flavouring factor of all the compounds in the wood, and the slight 'caramelising' of the sugars in the oak has a distinct effect on the eventual aroma and flavour of the wine. Staves can also be bent by using steam, rather than over an open fire, but the oak obviously does not have the same toasted character. Winemakers re-use their barrels each year, filling them with different wines to achieve different results. This is cost-effective, and very important when one considers the expense of new barrels. Another cost-effective measure involves the shaving of the inside of the staves of used barrels. Although this does give the barrels a longer life, they are never quite as effective as new barrels.

# BOTTLING

Over the centuries wine has been available in many containers, but when cork was discovered as the best way to close a wine container, it revolutionised wine drinking. Until then, wine had to be consumed as soon as it was made, because of the lack of an effective stopper to keep air from entering the container and spoiling the wine. It was also discovered that as time passed certain wines underwent pleasing changes in the bottle. Modern bottling lines introduce wine to the bottle with the absolute minimum aeration. Inert nitrogen or carbon dioxide is also often used to eliminate any risk of the wine coming into contact with oxygen.

# 5 Virtuosi

Wine from South Africa tends to fall between the solid structures of 'Old World' wines and the upfront fruit and soft tannins of the 'New World'. Nevertheless, traditionalists have looked more to Bordeaux and Burgundy for inspiration. What has emerged over the past few years is an awareness that the Cape can produce new blends that are drawn from varieties from many regions. This awareness has matured into a serious debate over where Cape winemakers should be heading in the new millennium. The interviews in this chapter are focused on this debate in an attempt to place the Cape within the wider context of the world of wine.

Steel tanks at Vergelegen.

# RUSTENBERG

## Simon Barlow

Simon Barlow was elected as the youngest governor of the World Economic Food and Beverage Forum. He has a wealth of experience marketing wine abroad and has made some innovative changes. Rustenberg is among the leading cellars in the race to produce South Africa's icon red wine.

*Editor:* How would you characterise the South African wine industry in relation to the other major wine industries of the world?

**Simon:** *Fragmented. We lack cohesion. There is too much volatility by the big boys in the industry and no focused effort. This is confusing to the international market, which is not sure where we're at, or where we're going. As a country, we must be quality-focused and results-orientated. We need to work together to pool resources and know-how, as they do in Australia, where the big boys like Penfolds help lift the smaller players. We have to break free of the 'laager' mentality in which knowledge and resources are jealously guarded. Our competitors are not our neighbours, but the rest of the world. With the restructuring of Wines of South Africa (WOSA), hopefully we'll get it right.*

*Rustenberg gable*

Ed: What improvements have you seen since the change to a democratic government and how has this affected the wine-making scene in South Africa?

**Simon:** *Improvements are mainly window-dressing. We've lost our Mandela/new democracy advantage. It's time we started playing the bigger game more seriously in terms of a strategic marketing plan, service and delivery. There's still the feeling we're in the warm-up stage regarding exports when the real marathon has already started.*

Ed: South Africa does not have a wine with the recognition of Australia's Grange Hermitage. What does South Africa have to do to get international brand recognition for its wines, and is this process already under way?

*Vine-covered pathway*

**Simon:** *Bear in mind that Grange dates back to 1951. While I believe we should be hungry for success and aim for icon wines – the Granges and Le Pins of this world – we must not fall into the eternal trap of the 'Emperor's New Clothes'. Our top wines have yet to build up a track record of consistency. To do this, let's be more receptive to external criticism and use our energy positively to improve our wines. We're often too task-focused, instead of looking up to see what's happening in the rest of the wine-making world. Let's use world benchmarks, rather than local ones, as our quality standards.*

*Tranquil pond*

We've also got to improve our plant material. If we are to be competitive on international markets, cleaning up the vineyards must be a priority. It's no use building state-of-the-art cellars if the vineyards are not in a world-class condition. It's time we stopped looking at plant material as a competitive advantage. There should be a concerted industry drive to eradicate virus-infected vines and a focus on issuing wine farms with clean, healthy material.

The drive should be spearheaded by an independent and accountable third party, as it is in Australia, where the CSRIO is aware of the importance of healthy vineyards both locally and in terms of the broader international picture. Ideally, this initiative should be industry-funded.

Ed: Do you see a major change in the varietal mix of South Africa's wines? Where are we heading, and do you see any new varieties making a splash?

**Simon:** *There's a new enthusiasm to experiment among the young wine-making fraternity that augurs well for the future. Personally, in terms of icon wines, I'm very excited about the Rhône varieties as an addition to vines currently planted. The introduction of Spanish and Italian varieties is also welcomed.*

Ed: The UK is still South Africa's largest importer of wine, importing just on 50 per cent of the total volume. Is this trend going to continue, or do you see other markets rivalling the predominance of the UK as the major importer?

**Simon:** *I believe the United States will be a big player. In her opening speech at the 2001 Nederburg Auction, Zelma Long highlighted the opportunities presenting themselves in the US market, where wine is one of the fastest-growing consumer products. Her suggestion that we should position ourselves in the*

(above) Simon Barlow in his maturation cellar.

(opposite page above) Schoongezicht manor house at Rustenberg.

(opposite page below) Autumn on the farm below the Simonsberg.

super and ultra-premium wine categories is supported by encouraging statistics. Between 1990 and 1999, the US adult per capita spending on premium wine grew from $16 to $61, a compound annual growth rate of 18 per cent. Even more impressive is the fact that 50-year-olds drink more than younger consumers, and in the USA, 10 000 baby boomers will turn 50 every day until 2014. But on entering this market, we should be aware of the possibility of competition from Australia, which is reputedly re-inventing itself as regards wines.

*Ed:* To return to the United Kingdom. What are the current trends in this market and specifically do you see South African wines beating the high-end competition from Europe, the USA and Australia?

*Simon: The UK is definitely a consumer's market. British wine-drinkers are spoiled. They have access to the whole world's wines at amazing value for money. My advice to any local wine producer intent on beating the competition would be to aim high and then make it a pleasure for buyers to deal with your company. Regrettably, South African producers are not known for good service. It is easy to get a bottle off the shelf once, but without offering value for money, bottles will not move a second, third or fourth time. I keep trying to explain to local wineries that they have to make their wines accessible. At the correct price they can move a couple of tons off the shelf. The market also requires consistency. Wine buyers need to get used to their daily tipple…*

*Ed:* Before it's gone.

*Simon: Yes. Before it's gone. Also I think we are making a huge mistake in this country by exporting bulk wines for bottling overseas. I have never heard of most of the labels that are on offer. We must brand South African labels and I think by doing that we will be halfway there.*

*Ed:* How have you overcome this problem?

*Simon: Well, as of February 1st we have removed our wines from the large supermarkets. We have changed direction not only because our margins are being squeezed, but also because we want to brand ourselves in the old High Street bottle store. The specialised wine stores love this because they do not have to compete with the large multiples and they have something to market that is somewhat exclusive to the passing trade. The stores are given an enormous amount of information and in essence become an extension of the farm.*

*Ed:* How have you positioned Rustenberg in relation to the trends in the market? I know you have embarked on an extensive replanting programme.

*Simon: We've repositioned Rustenberg at the top end of the market – where else? We've set our sights high, but we're not there yet. I believe 80 per cent of wine is made in the vineyard. We're fanatical about eliminating virus-infected material. We've set up our own nursery and imported a cross-section of clones to improve the quality of our wine. In terms of land, we are one of the largest single-property players in the wine industry, and our diversity of altitudes, aspects and soils allows for site-specific clonal selection and planting.*

*Ed:* Do you think that clones really make a difference?

*Simon: Yes. Different clones on specific sites make huge differences. We have imported the newest generation of a specific clone. A clone might already be in South Africa, but it could be five generations older than the Bordeaux clone because it has undergone so many more selections.*

*New rootstock*

*Formal cellar garden*

*Steel tanks*

*Tasting room*

*(above) Top level of the gravity-fed winery under thatch.*

*(above) The historic cow byre restored to contain the new cellar.*
*(below) Schoongezicht manor house and surrounds below the Simonsberg.*

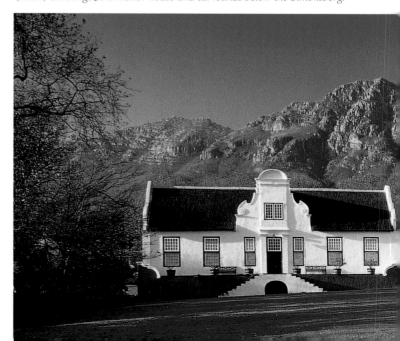

*Ed:* How does Rustenberg compare in terms of *terroir* to the great wine areas of the world? I am interested here in your views on soil and climate.

**Simon:** *The climatic conditions of the Stellenbosch District are near perfect. Our soils are far too good by comparison with those of the icon wines. I don't see this as a negative, it just requires good vineyard management. To control vigour we are using devigorating rootstock to get the vines in balance. We restrict yield and spend a lot of time on canopy management. To coin a phrase, we're into turning sunlight into wine.*

*Ed:* You talk about a devigorating rootstock. Are you planting on 101-14?

**Simon:** *Yes. We do plant on Richter rootstocks in certain areas where the soil is dry. We can get water up there, but since it drains so quickly, 101-14 is not the right rootstock. But in the main, we plant on 101-14.*

*Ed:* What is the composition of your soil?

**Simon:** *Mainly decomposed granite Hutton soils with effective depths of approximately two metres.*

*Ed:* I see that you are beginning to plant much higher on the slopes. What varieties can you ripen effectively at these elevations?

**Simon:** *We are now planting at 500 metres above sea level. At these levels we should be able to work with Merlot and Sauvignon Blanc. We are planting the slopes in bands of individual varieties at different levels on the mountain. We have also introduced Rhône varieties and the expectation is that we will have better blending opportunities as we draw from different blocks planted at different elevations.*

*Ed:* How are you giving expression to this *terroir* in your cellar?

**Simon:** *We're very much of the mindset that the vineyards and terroir determine the vintage. Our winery was designed to eliminate bottlenecks, allowing the vineyards, rather than the cellar, to dictate when the grapes should be harvested.*

*Ed:* But you say that you are making site-specific wines and grapes are picked separately. Certainly you have designed the cellar very differently from most cellars because you can work with small quantities.

**Simon:** *The cellar doesn't dictate anything to the viticulturist. We walk through vineyards; we taste grapes until we do not want to see another grape. But we find vineyards with different aspects and we pick them separately. Some of these parcels are quite small, perhaps only one ton and they will only fill three barrels. But when we blend, we have to go to these lengths if we are going to get ourselves up to a world-market standard. Our total crush is approximately 500 tons, but at the end of the day we have to do the hard work to get the quality.*

*Ed:* What does the future hold for the South African wine industry in general and Rustenberg in particular?

**Simon:** *I'm enormously optimistic about the future. The opportunities are huge if you take hold of them. We're definitely in the race for the SA icon wine. But for a true icon, it's going to take a long time. In this regard, it's worth remembering that the wine industry is not a business; it's a passion.*

# RUPERT AND ROTHSCHILD

## *Michel Rolland, Schalk Joubert*

Michel Rolland, world-renowned viticulturist from Pomerol, has teamed up with Schalk Joubert at Rupert and Rothschild to bring a touch of French flair to South African wine. In this interview, Michel discusses conditions in Bordeaux and how viticultural techniques applied in this famous region may be employed in the Cape. Schalk Joubert then follows with a brief analysis on how Michel's ideas are followed up in the cellar.

*Editor:* Michel, I want to open the interview by discussing *terroir* in Bordeaux. What do you believe are the core factors governing *terroir* in Bordeaux and how would you argue that this forms an expression of the wine from that region?

*Michel:* I think terroir is very important in France in general and in Bordeaux in particular. Certainly terroir has been the most controversial story over the years. But what exactly is terroir? There is terroir everywhere in the world and not only in France. In Bordeaux and Burgundy the vignerons understand their terroir very well since they have produced good wine, maybe great wine, for more than 100 years. They know where the gravel is, where the clay is, where the sand is, and what type of rootstock to plant, what cultivar to grow in any particular place.

Terroir, in the final analysis, really is an ability to match the right soil with the right rootstock and the right grapes to the right place. This is not easy because it takes time through experimentation. Only after years and years can we be convinced that Merlot will grow better in one vineyard than another. We had to decide whether Cabernet Sauvignon would grow better in certain areas and Pinot Noir in others. This is really what the arguments over terroir are really about. Outside France, or an old country like Italy or Spain, winemakers are still looking for this perfect match between terroir and grape varieties. This is essentially the question for everybody in the New World. They have to understand the perfect relationship between terroir and grapes. This is the challenge.

*Ed:* But specifically if I could discuss *terroir* in Bordeaux. What makes Bordeaux different? What are the soil types and what are those elements that make Bordeaux so great?

*Michel:* Terroir is not only soil. Terroir is definitely a combination of elements, a combination between climate, soil and grapes. We understood a long time ago that when we have a lot of clay in the soil, Merlot will grow better than Cabernet Sauvignon. Also we understand in gravel soil, Cabernet Sauvignon will grow better. In Bordeaux we have a lot of rain.

*Manor house*

*Manor house interior*

*View of the Simonsberg*

We have natural moisture, and that's very important. Clay retains moisture all year long, even when we have a dry season. The soil is never very dry or too hot. In gravel, the water table recedes slowly, allowing the vines to dry out during the maturing season. That is the essential difference in the optimal growing conditions for Merlot and Cabernet Sauvignon in Bordeaux and these soils lie only a few kilometres apart.

The soil makes a huge difference in terms of wine quality. Even though there is only a small difference in the climate, in the soils, in the ability of the soil to ripen a particular type of grape, it nonetheless makes a difference. Thus I have to return to my original remarks by saying again that we have to learn how to match any one type of soil to a particular variety. One mistake I see so often is that Chardonnay, Cabernet Sauvignon, Merlot, and even Pinot Noir, are planted on the same parcel of ground. I am convinced this is wrong. Maybe there is one good match, but there is also one bad match. It is impossible to grow all varieties in the same place. This is the big difference. In Bordeaux we understood our soils a long time ago because historically the old producers understood where the grapes would grow better.

*Ed:* Basically you are saying in order to understand wine we really have to understand the soil and the climate. That in turn will be expressed in the quality of the grapes.

*Michel:* Yes. We need a better understanding between grapes, soil and climate. These are the three factors which are important in the production of good or great wines. If we don't understand these factors, we have a chance to produce wine, but never great wine. This is the secret of an old region like Bordeaux where we have a

*(above) Michel Rolland (left) and Schalk Joubert.*

*(right) Manor house dining room.*

*background. Also, we don't grow a lot of grape varieties. We don't grow Shiraz for example. We are convinced that Shiraz will not do well in Bordeaux. We produce Merlot, Cabernet Franc, Cabernet Sauvignon and some Petit Verdot, and that is all. With whites, we have Sauvignon Blanc. Chardonnay could be good, but is not allowed in Bordeaux right now.*

*Ed:* If we move to South Africa, let's look at Stellenbosch and the Franschhoek valley. How would you describe the *terroir* here specifically? How would you differentiate between the *terroir* of Stellenbosch and that of Bordeaux? Let's take Bordeaux as a point of departure and start looking at the differences.

**Michel:** *Of course there is a huge difference between Bordeaux and South Africa. But if we look just at soil we are simply looking at geography. At Fredericksburg we have a completely different type of terroir. The farm is close to the mountains yet we find heavy soil, sandy soil and soils with granite decomposition. With these different types of soil the challenge is to identify soil type with variety. This is the great question.*

*Ed:* Well, then my next question has to be 'what goes with what?'

**Michel:** *Once we understand the soils, the next step is to choose the correct rootstocks. South Africa is problematic because vines tend to produce very high yields and there is often too much vigour in the vines. Most vines are grafted to Richter 99. This is a very vigorous rootstock. On good soils, Richter 99 produces a huge crop together with a large canopy. South Africans plant Richter 99 because it is very resistant to dryness. But we can use irrigation. I think it is much better to use a less vigorous rootstock and then manage the vigour with irrigation. In this way we can create the right canopy, control the vigour and develop the vineyard correctly. I am not sure that these practices are done properly right now in South Africa.*

*Ed:* Are there dwarfing rootstocks available in South Africa?

**Michel:** *I think they are available in South Africa. I think 101-14 or 3309 is available. Winemakers, however, do not use these rootstocks primarily because of a tradition of improving kilos or yield.*

*Ed:* So if we go on 101-14, would you argue that Cabernet Sauvignon is the right variety for Franschhoek in general and specifically at Fredericksburg?

**Michel:** *Yes, I think Cabernet will grow very well here. On the higher slopes where we have less heat, especially in the afternoon, Merlot should also do well. I think Cabernet and Merlot will grow very well and on good locations you can plant both with good success.*

*Ed:* And would there be any other varieties that you would recommend?

**Michel:** *I think Shiraz could be good in South Africa because there is a lot of sun. There is also a lot of light and light is very important, perhaps even more important than temperature. But I know there are problems. Shiraz is a very high producer. If we produce 15 or 20 tons per hectare there is no way we can make good wine with Shiraz.*

*Ed:* So would you recommend we drop down to say eight tons per hectare?

**Michel:** *I think eight is the limit, the absolute limit, to make really good wine. I think good wine could be made from between five to eight tons, but never more than eight tons.*

*Ed:* Just as a matter of interest, does making good wine depend on the age, or the maturity, of the vine?

**Michel:** *Of course. Of course the age of vines is crucial in making better wines. I think we can make good wines with young vines, but we have to be careful with production. The younger the vines, the lower the production because young vines are not built to ripen fruit. If the vines carry more than six or seven tons per hectare, they simply will not be able to ripen grapes in terms of tannin and aroma.*

Ed: If you had to compare South Africa with Bordeaux, what are the ripening characteristics in either area? Where do we go in terms of balling or tannin ripeness?

**Michel:** *I think there are a number of differences. In Bordeaux we certainly have cooler climates. We never have long periods with very high temperatures. We may have a week where temperatures exceed 30 degrees, but in the next week temperatures may drop to 22 degrees due to the influence of the ocean. Bordeaux also has a lot of rain and that is a problem because the berries grow too big and become diluted. In South Africa there is too much sun. It's very dry. As a consequence, the berries can be small but the sugar content rises too fast. When we assess ripeness, we assess it in two ways. The first is to evaluate ripeness in terms of sugar content, and the second is to evaluates ripeness in terms of tannin ripeness. Sugar rises and at the same time the tannins and the aromas rise. But normally tannins are always later than sugar. So if we have too much sun, sugar rises too fast and tannins are left behind. The goal is to reach balling ripeness and tannin ripeness simultaneously. This goal is possible with the right viticulture management. Not too much yield and the correct canopy. The vines must be open, not too closed, not too tight with a lot of vegetation. We have to give more light directly to the grapes because light helps with maturity. Bordeaux is different because Bordeaux does not have enough sun. Maybe in one year every twenty-five years sun is a problem. For Bordeaux the problem is water. We wait for maturity and 15 days before maturity we have 18 millimetres of rain and the grapes enlarge, become diluted, and we loose our quality in two days.*

Ed: If you had to plant a vineyard here, how would you advise South African farmers to plant in terms of planting distances, average trellising heights, this type of thing?

**Michel:** *I have a particular philosophy. If you asked the same question to my friend Richard Smart, who lives in Australia, he would certainly answer differently. But please… he is a good friend. My philosophy is to create a vineyard where we have a chance to get it right. We cannot change the weather. We have to take the weather as it comes – heat in South Africa, rain in Bordeaux. But we have a chance to get it right even in these differing conditions. The secret is to limit the crop to between one kilogram to 1.5 kilograms per plant. But if we want to maintain the production per hectare, we have to increase the number of plants per hectare. My feeling is that in South Africa we must plant no less than 5000 vines and I feel that 6000 would be even better.*

Ed: Per hectare!

**Michel:** *Per hectare. Distance between plantings is arbitrary, but my preference is a planting distance of one and a half metres between the rows by one metre in the row. That works out at 6600 plants per hectare. You can harvest six tons per hectare at one kilogram per vine and then you will have a chance to get it right in good conditions.*

Ed: How high will the canopy be then? Will it be a three-wire canopy?

*(above right) View of Fredricksburg manor house and surrounds across the vineyard.*

*(below right) Maturation cellar.*

*Michel:* Here I agree with Richard Smart. We both advocate that the canopy should reach about one metre above the cordon. A canopy one metre high by one metre wide should ripen one kilogram of grapes. So we don't need a huge two-metre canopy. It is not necessary.

*Ed:* What about clones? Are there any particular clones that you would advocate for South Africa? Let's say we can choose from 38 or 39 Cabernet clones. Is there anything special that you would recommend?

*Michel:* My thinking on clones is a bit controversial. Clone selection started, mainly in France, to avoid disease. But selection was driven more by production levels and berry size and this concerns me. I am also not sure that clones will travel. Clones change with climate and soil so we can't predict how clones will perform in different areas. I am more and more convinced that healthy plant material should be sourced from local plants as they react to climate rather like people. If you live in northern Europe, for example, you are more resistant to a cold rainy climate. Look at the English, they are very resistant to the rain. But if you are used to living in South Africa you prefer sun. You are more resistant to the heat and I think clones are exactly the same. They have to adapt to a particular soil, to a particular climate, to local conditions. I think we should select material from local plants that is disease resistant. The important point is to use clones that have had time to adapt to local conditions. Even clones with a good reputation produce too much. The numbers are very simple. We prune a vine to six buds. Six buds deliver six shoots. In good conditions, six shoots produce 12 clusters. Twelve clusters on 6000 vines equals 72 000 clusters. At 200 grams per cluster, we arrive at 14 tons per hectare.

*Ed:* So you have to reduce the crop by half in any event.

*Michel:* Exactly. There is no clone that produces the right yield. We have to green harvest any clone to improve quality. This is my definition of terroir and clone selection.

*Ed:* I'd like to take you back, if I may, to our discussion on planting density. When you talk about this density are you trying to plant the vineyards so there is a certain amount of stress on each individual vine?

*Michel:* Yes. It's a good point. There are two issues. First, if we want good quality, we must keep production down. I have advocated a planting density of 6000 vines per hectare to reach this quality. Second, if we plant to a density of three metres by three metres, for example, we see less competition and more vigour. Vigour is not very good for quality. A higher density leads to more competition and more competition leads to less vigour because the soil cannot feed 6000 vines as well as 3000 vines. So we see more stress and I think stress is much better for quality. So for both reasons we have to increase the density.

*Ed:* But if we can keep the vine in balance even though we plant at a density of say 3000 vines, because we need more room in the working row for tractors, could we make great wines?

*Michel:* Yes, it is possible. I have consulted in countries all over the world where there are low-density plantings. For example there are some very old vines planted in Chile and Argentina at very low densities. But both these countries are very dry and we can control vigour and stress the vines through irrigation. With stress we can control canopy development and see good results. In Argentina, they plant on a pergola system, three by three. Too much irrigation produces a lot of vegetation and too much shade, but when they control the water we see a small canopy with good light and the results are interesting.

*Ed:* Let's go back to ripeness. You made the comment that South African grapes ripen too quickly. Yet we know that if we increase the crop, we slow down the ripening process. Surely if we limit the crop to three clusters per arm, we hasten the ripening process?

*Michel:* Yes. You are right in terms of time. When we green harvest we hasten the ripening process. But this is exactly what I am looking for. Let's go back to Bordeaux. In Bordeaux we have between 100 and 108 days from flowering to maturation. In South Africa, the United States, Argentina or Chile we see that this period extends to 120 days, even 125 days, so we can add another 10 to 15 days to Bordeaux's ripening period. If we reduce the number of clusters, we shorten the cycle and this is what I am looking for. The key is to avoid picking over-ripe, because the shorter the cycle, the more chance there is to pick over-ripe. Our goal is to pick at the right moment and we have to be careful not to pick too green or too ripe. There are a lot of articles about me that say I prefer picking over-ripe. This is nonsense. But I prefer to take the risk on over-ripe grapes than to pick too green.

*Ed:* But when you talk about over-ripe, you are referring to tannin ripeness.

*Michel:* Yes, of course, of course, but it is effectively true. When the grapes are ripe, the next step is over-ripe and over-ripe grapes gives a port or raisin flavour.

*Ed:* I am a little confused. When you talk about 108 days in Bordeaux or 120 days in South Africa, is the problem of maturing quickly a South African problem or a problem in Bordeaux? I missed your point on this particular issue.

*Michel:* The issue is not to compare France with South Africa. The shorter the cycle, the better the wine.

*Ed:* In both countries?

*Michel:* Yes, in both countries. The shorter cycle right now is in Bordeaux versus South Africa, the United States or Chile, but I am looking to shorten the cycle in all environments. If we look at the great vintages we had in Bordeaux – 1961, 1955, 1947, 1945 or 1929 – they were all shorter cycles. Early budding and a very early harvest. Thus a very short cycle. So my conclusion is very simple and not very technical. My conclusion is, the shorter the cycle, the better the wine. So I try to shorten the cycle wherever I can.

*Ed:* You mentioned that Shiraz would be a good variety for South Africa. We know that Australia has done very well with it. Can South Africa make a wine that would compare with the best?

*Michel:* I think so. There is no reason not to. I think Shiraz is very adaptive to hot climates. Shiraz likes sun, it likes dryness and I don't understand why Shiraz is not planted more extensively in South Africa.

*Ed:* I have always felt that Shiraz has been grown more in the inland areas than at the coast. And perhaps South Africans feel that Shiraz is not suited to districts like Stellenbosch and Somerset West. Perhaps now ideas are starting to change and, as you say, we can plant it in Franschhoek as well.

*Michel:* Yes. But we have to take care of raw material of course, and secondly production, because Shiraz is a very high producer. With overproduction, Shiraz is not an interesting wine. It becomes very diluted and green. But with the right production, the right vineyard, I think Shiraz will go well here.

*Ed:* My last question. We all know you have a philosophy about wine. Just for the record, what is your personal philosophy about wine?

**Michel:** *About wine? I have a very simple philosophy. I was born in Pomerol. I love Pomerol. I love the wine from Pomerol and Saint Emilion, because my house is just on the border between Pomerol and Saint Emilion. I was born 300 metres from Livongene. I love these types of wine because I grew up there. My family owns vineyards there and I love the wine. Now my job is to consult, not everywhere, because I do not travel to Australia and New Zealand. My philosophy is very simple. Wherever I am, I try to improve the wine, to make the best wine possible. When I travel to Margese in Casteel, for example, where they produce approximately 10 million bottles of one type of wine, it is not the same as travelling to Allen Estate in the United States where they produce 2000 cases. It is completely different. But the goal is the same. To improve the wine, to make the best wine possible given economic and quality considerations. I try to find the right way to improve wine everywhere I may be.*

*Ed:* Schalk, you've heard what Michel has to say about vineyard management. How do you give expression to these methods in the cellar?

**Schalk:** *First, with high-density planting we need good, highly fertile Glenrosa-type soils. Second, we must have water. The reasoning behind this is that the vines must compete with each other, giving a slightly higher extract in the fruit. And then of course we have to control the canopy correctly. Our trellising tends to be quite low. We tend to place the cordon 650 millimetres above the ground, and we keep the vines as close as possible. We harvested 850 tons this year and less than 80 tons were inoculated with yeast. We ferment as naturally as possible, including malolactic fermentation. We do all the malolactic in wood and we tend to keep the wine on the skins for 32 days. I do not ferment warm. The average temperature during fermentation is about 22 degrees in the cap, not the juice, so fermentation is quite cold, giving a slow, long fermentation. My main aim is to preserve the fruit from the vineyard and not interfere too much. We keep the batches from each vineyard separate, and after malolactic I will start making a base blend with Michel's help. The sooner the different components are put together, the better they integrate. I use wood as a refining agent. I don't fine the wines after they go into the barrel and I will normally keep the wine in wood for 26 to 27 months. I like to use French oak and less than five per cent of total production is in American oak.*

*Ed:* Let's talk about the wines. Your top of the range is the Baron Edmond. What is the make-up of the blend?

*Manor house*

*Cellar*

*Cellar and fountain*

**Schalk:** *The Baron Edmond is made from five particular vineyards. Here terroir obviously does play a role. The 1998 is currently a blend of 60 per cent Merlot and 40 per cent Cabernet. We do have a Cabernet Franc vineyard as well, but it did not make the blend. The 1999 is blended with 75 per cent Cabernet and 25 per cent Merlot. The main thing about this wine is that it is made completely naturally; yield is minimised to about one kilogram per vine, and once again the wine is totally natural with no fining or filtration. I am really looking for elegance in the wine. Everything must be in balance and I am looking for harmony with nothing ostentatious jumping out of the glass. I want all the elements together with no particular flavour dominating another.*

*Ed:* Is there a large difference between the Baron Edmond and the Classique?

**Schalk:** *The Baron Edmond is a serious wine whereas the Classique is a wine with more upfront fruit and slightly less oak. I'd like to make it clear, however, that they are two completely different blends. The emphasis with Classique is on accessibility.*

*Ed:* In terms of your Chardonnay, are you looking more for a wine that's Chablis in style?

**Schalk:** *Chardonnay is the only white wine that we produce. Grapes for the Chardonnay come from Elgin, the West Coast and from one particular vineyard at Franschhoek. We do whole-cluster pressing and ferment very, very dirty. The juice, which is the colour of brown bread, goes into wood and ferments naturally. We keep it on the lees for 10 to 11 months but we do not battonage. We roll the barrels to minimise the levels of oxygen.*

*Ed:* Finally, are you planning any new blends for the future?

**Schalk:** *We are definitely not limiting ourselves to two or three noble cultivars. We have planted some Shiraz, but for the time being we are quite content with the three wines that we have and I think we are going to keep it as simple as possible. It allows me to really concentrate on these three wines. That might change in a couple of years' time.*

(below) Summer vineyards.

(far left) Cellar fountain.

# Meerlust

## *Giorgio Dalla Cia*

Giorgio Dalla Cia is a master of the Bordeaux blend. His signature wine, Meerlust Rubicon, has certainly stood the test of time, becoming a firm favourite both at home and abroad. He would be the first to say that terroir makes the wine, but the blender's art requires a special, elusive talent that separates great winemakers from lesser mortals. This interview concentrates on blending. We have attempted to tease out Giorgio's secrets in an effort to reveal the mind behind the man.

*Editor:* Giorgio, there is no doubt that you are considered the master blender in South Africa. Meerlust Rubicon has also been a benchmark for blenders for many, many years. I thought we should start by briefly discussing the philosophy behind blending wine and the secrets that make a blended wine something more than its parts.

*Giorgio: First of all, blending wine is a must if you want to make a wine with complexity. I remember when I was a young student in Italy. In those days we always thought of a blended wine as an inferior quality wine, because we thought a blended wine contained the left-over wine from the varietal wines. We thought blending was done more for practical reasons than to create a superior wine. Only after spending time in France where I went to improve my French as a student, was I able to buy good bottles of blended wine from Bordeaux, and I learnt the fundamental difference. On the one hand we see blends produced by the large wineries or wine merchants who try to mix wines from different regions in order to put together a generic, drinkable blended wine. On the other hand, we find blends where the winemaker is looking for finesse, complexity, elegance, and for a superb finish. That is the real pleasure of blending. So the two are completely different worlds. The word may have the same meaning, but the wines are worlds apart. The winemaker's art may be called a blend, but the other should be described more as a concoction.*

*Ed:* But essentially, how do you blend?

*Giorgio: First of all, when I begin a blend, I look for a particular wine that has a good chance of blending in with another wine, so one complements the other. One wine, for example, could be very mellow, very fruity, very elegant, like a Merlot. Yet this same wine may lack enough body or enough structure. Then I may have a Cabernet Sauvignon that has plenty of body and is well structured yet lacks fragrance.*

Manor house

Owner, Hannes Myburgh

*Therefore, I may use some of the Cabernet Sauvignon to give extra backbone to the Merlot. In another example, Bordeaux winemakers blend Merlot with Cabernet Sauvignon because Merlot, being an early variety, can be harvested before the rain. As such, the winemakers can leave the Merlot to hang for a longer period in the vineyard and thus raise the sugar. When the winemakers are forced to harvest Cabernet early because of weather conditions, they already know that they have harvested Merlot with 13 or 14 per cent alcohol to blend in with the Cabernet Sauvignon that may have only reached 11 or 11.5 per cent alcohol. This gives a more balanced wine. So one wine helps the other and vice versa. Generally this is what blending is all about.*

*Ed:* Could I just break in here? Why would winemakers in Bordeaux use wines such as Petit Verdot or Malbec?

*Giorgio: Petit Verdot is a wine that has very high tannins. It also has a very high colour concentration. So again in certain vintages when the grapes have not matured well enough, as in the case of Cabernet Sauvignon for instance, Petit Verdot adds a little bit of extra tannin or extra polyphenols to the wine. It supplies that portion that may be missing.*

*Ed:* Essentially Petit Verdot pumps up the blend or gives it more weight.

*Giorgio: Yes. Again to bring more complexity. Now if we look at Meerlust's Rubicon, we see that Rubicon is made up of 70 per cent Cabernet Sauvignon, 20 per cent Merlot and 10 per cent Cabernet Franc. Interestingly enough, when I arrived at Meerlust in 1978, my first blend was one third each of these three components. By*

(above) Giorgio Dalla Cia tasting wine.

(right) Meerlust manor house in its tranquil garden.

1980, I came to the conclusion that I should change the composition of the blend completely. Cabernet Sauvignon is quite raw. As you know, 'Sauvignon' means savage or wild in French, and the wine is difficult to work on its own. To get it right and mellow is problematic and depends on the vintage. In one vintage we may have a great Cabernet Sauvignon, in another we may have a less complex Cabernet Sauvignon, a third may develop into a truly elegant wine. Inevitably, the wines will be so structured that they will only become drinkable after 10 to 15 years. So what we do, and I must point out that French winemakers have been doing this for years, is add Merlot. Merlot is more fragrant, more mellow, more round and more elegant on its own. By adding a certain amount of Merlot to the Cabernet, we add a touch of finesse. Cabernet on its own is very much like a raw diamond that has not been cut and polished. Simply put, Cabernet needs to be polished. By adding Merlot, we bring to the Cabernet that lovely touch of finesse.

Ed: What about Cabernet Franc?

Giorgio: When we add Merlot, we essentially dilute the concentration of the Cabernet Sauvignon aromas. So we are not drinking a true Cabernet Sauvignon but a diluted Cabernet Sauvignon. To counterbalance this dilution, we use Cabernet Franc as Cabernet Franc is very similar to Cabernet Sauvignon but has more concentrated aromas.

Ed: Are you referring to spicy aromas?

Giorgio: Yes. When we dilute the Cabernet by adding Merlot, we give it that touch of finesse, but at the same time we need to re-establish the concentration of the original aroma. So we add Cabernet Franc. Cabernet Franc is also less tannic and is therefore much easier to work. As such, we can make the blend easier to drink; it's more upfront and we may drink it sooner.

Ed: Do we not need Petit Verdot in South Africa, given that the climate is so much hotter?

Giorgio: A certain amount of Petit Verdot should do well in South Africa. Unfortunately, until recently we couldn't get good plant material in this country. Eventually we succeeded in planting some Petit Verdot at Meerlust and if all goes well we should be able to

*Manor house porch*

*Historic stable*

make use of some Petit Verdot in three to four years. I believe we would use possibly three, four or a maximum of five per cent Petit Verdot in the blend. The idea is not to use Petit Verdot just to bring in another wine. In fact, you shouldn't be able to pick up Petit Verdot in the blend, but it will allow us to make a more classic blend. We will have to re-adjust a little bit and I can't be narrow-minded. I shall have to adapt to the particular vintage. I can't take for granted that this component will be of a higher level. Of course, if the quality is not there, I would rather leave it out.

Ed: As a matter of interest, how would you describe a classic blend?

Giorgio: To my mind, the classic blends are the wines from Médoc, but you must have an idea of what to look for. If you want to learn how to blend in a broader sense, it is very much like studying a painter, learning how to mix his colours. If you want to paint like Tiziano, you have to study Tiziano so that you can mix the same colours Tiziano made. You will paint in a style with very strong intense red colours. If you want to paint like Botticelli, you will have a different style altogether. Each master had his own school where he trained his students to mix the colours. Each painter had his own formula for mixing minerals and herbs or whatever he was using. This was a well-kept secret and the secret was actually the blend of different colours that achieved that particular tonality. The same ideas apply when blending wine. You have to learn how to mix the different wines in order to achieve something else that is better. If you mix different wines and get something disappointing, you are blending the wrong varieties. To achieve success you have to understand the components of the blend. You have to understand each wine separately and you have to know if each wine has an affinity for the other. For instance, Merlot has a good affinity with Cabernet Sauvignon and Cabernet Franc because Merlot is a variety that originates from Cabernet Sauvignon. They are almost part of the same family. If we blend them, they can integrate easily with each other. I would never blend Cabernet Sauvignon with Shiraz for instance.

Ed: But isn't that what we call a Cape blend?

Giorgio: If we add Shiraz to Cabernet Sauvignon, in the end we have no Cabernet and no Shiraz. One actually destroys the other

instead of one helping the other, and to my mind there is no way to blend these varieties. I think it is very important that when you decide to blend, first of all you must know whether the wines are compatible with one another.

*Ed:* So that they complete each other…

**Giorgio:** *For instance, I can't see blending Sauvignon Blanc with Chardonnay. Although this does occur, it simply does not make sense to me. It's like mixing meat with fish. Perhaps you can mix meat with fish, but then you would have to call the dish 'Nouvelle Cuisine'. Basically the idea of blending is 'blend to improve'. Blend to bring out the complexity of the wine. Just as you add salt, pepper and spice to bring out the flavour of your meat or fish, so you do exactly the same thing to bring out the flavour of a Cabernet. I see Rubicon basically as a Cabernet with greater complexity and richness than a normal Cabernet because the components that are added are compatible and well integrated. One other point, just as*

Historic door

you would use Merlot to mellow down and give a touch of finesse to Cabernet, so you use Cabernet to give a little bit of extra structure to the Merlot. Of course, you must not blend too much Cabernet into the Merlot, otherwise the Merlot is overwhelmed. But if you use just a touch, you will add a final complexity and structure to the Merlot. This will allow the Merlot to age correctly in the barrels, not mature too fast, and it will last much longer.

*Ed:* Why would Château Pétrus use so much more Merlot in its blend rather than Cabernet? In other words what is the fundamental difference between the Médoc and Saint Emilion?

**Giorgio:** *Pétrus is grown in a completely different area. Look at the map of Bordeaux. Médoc is on the left of the river and Saint Emilion and Pomerol are on the far right. The different soils and micro-climates mean that Cabernet doesn't do terribly well in the Saint Emilion area. Cabernet does much better in the Médoc, while Merlot thrives in Saint Emilion. Winemakers use Merlot as a base in Saint Emilion and Pomerol and then use Cabernet as a blending partner to give extra strength and extra structure to Merlot. In the Médoc, just the opposite is true. In the end, it is pure expedience – pure necessity.*

*Ed:* So it is just based on *terroir* in other words.

**Giorgio:** *You have to adapt yourself. That is why, for instance, my blend here is 70, 10 and 20. That doesn't mean my formula is good for the whole of South Africa. In Stellenbosch you may blend at 80 and 20 or 50, 10 and 40. You have to see what you can get out of your soil, out of your vineyards and then blend accordingly.*

*Ed:* I wonder if we couldn't move across to Italy. Could you describe some of the famous Italian blends? What are the great wines that you can mention from Italy?

**Giorgio:** *Twenty-five years ago there were some open-minded people in Tuscany. People with vision like the Antinoris for instance. Piero Antinori is a great wine man. Together with his oenologist, Giacomo Tachis, he wanted to expand into the American and English markets. He soon realised that the only way to do so would be to improve the quality of Tuscan wine. In the old days, Chianti was a mix of different red varieties, but included between 25 and 30 per cent white grape varieties. This was done, and probably decided on about 100 years earlier, in order to make a wine that was easier to drink. Without the white grape varieties, the wine was too coarse and needed too many years in the barrels. Chianti was not even recognised on the local Italian markets as a great wine and consumption was basically limited to Tuscany. Chianti became popular with the tourists and of course they wanted to take the wine home. Once they opened the wine at home they realised that the wines were not really that special. Antinori thought it would be a good idea to remove the white varieties from the blend. But you know the*

(left) View of the manor house from the south side.

(opposite page above) Geese on parade.

(opposite page below) A quiet corner in the garden.

legislation in Italy is very strict and changes are not readily allowed. Antinori had the courage to produce a wine he could not name Chianti and he simply named it 'Vino comune da tavola' which means 'common table wine' in Italian. This put the wine at the bottom of the quality scale, technically speaking according to the law, but by doing so he made a wine that was far superior to the Chianti made by anyone else. Eventually he proved that by removing the white varieties and by adding a little bit of Cabernet Sauvignon and eventually some Merlot, he had made a better blend.

Ed: Is Sangiovese the foundation wine for Chianti?

**Giorgio:** Yes, Sangiovese is the backbone. Again, what is interesting is the way Antinori began selecting clones. There was a time in the 1950s when there was a rush to plant. In order to meet the huge demand, farmers looked for clones that could be cropped at high production levels because they wanted to produce as much as possible. In contrast, Antinori began to select clones from much older vineyards which produced more character and more complexity. He also introduced small French oak instead of using the traditional big vats made of Slovenian oak. By using small French barrels, the ratio between wine and wood is much higher. Therefore the wine can develop faster in the barrel. You know, if you use a huge vat, very little oxygen goes into the wine and the wine has to stay in barrel for up to 6 to 8 years before it mellows down. By putting the same wine into smaller barrels, the oxygen interaction with the polyphenols and tannins allows the wine to develop faster. Again the change in the quality of the wine was

dramatic. In Piedmont, Angelo Gaja went down the same route with his barrels to make his Barberesco. I remember in the first few years his colleagues hated him. They thought he was a traitor because he broke away from the old traditions. Nevertheless, he eventually proved he was right. Together with the Antinoris, he radically changed the history of great wine making in Italy.

117

# FAIRVIEW

## Anthony de Jager, Eben Sadie

The old adage that a man is as good as his team certainly applies to Charles Back at Fairview. Charles is rated by the cognoscenti as one of the most innovative winemakers in South Africa. He is constantly developing new blends and rich single varietals. In Anthony de Jager and Eben Sadie he has found two young winemakers with a passion for their craft that suits the mood of this enterprise. Both Anthony and Eben specialise in Rhône-style wines. As such, this interview concentrates on Rhône varieties, the terroir in the Côte du Rhône and the differences and similarities which apply to South Africa.

*Editor:* As a point of departure, I would like to talk about the Rhône valley and specifically Rhône-style wines. So may I begin by asking why the Rhône is so special?

*Eben: Well, I think the Rhône is an area with an extended family of varieties like Syrah, Grenache, Carignan and Mourvèdre that were introduced many years ago. As a result, the viticulturists have had sufficient time to sort out how to deal with these grapes. Secondly, the Rhône valley has a number of diverse regions. Hermitage and Côte Rôtie may fall within the northern borders of the Rhône valley, but there are immense differences. The way the farmers work the vines in Hermitage is totally different from Côte Rôtie, and this leads to differences in the wines themselves. Everybody thinks of the Rhône as an integrated area, but this is simply not true. When you think about the Rhône, you must think about the northern Rhône and the southern Rhône, which runs into the Languedoc-Roussillon area. The northern Rhône's poor, well-drained soils are definitely responsible for the great wines there. If you plant Syrah, Mourvèdre or Viognier on vigorous soils, as we do on some South African farms, you can have disastrous results.*

Ed: Would you consider Fairview to be more like the northern or the southern Rhône?

*Anthony: I think the upper reaches of Fairview copy the Rhône in a way, but down in the bottom section of the farm we find shallow sandy soils where we have had to adapt to suit the environment. Fairview is no longer an estate, and where we have hit limitations on this farm, we have bought in grapes from Paarl. There are beautiful sites in Paarl, or on the outskirts of Paarl, towards Perdeberg, that produce terrific grapes.*

Ed: How would you describe Spice Route's *terroir?*

*Eben: Spice Route is definitely not northern Rhône. It is more like the south, very much more like Languedoc. If you walk through Roussillon there are a lot of rough forms of slate still around. We do not have too much of that in South Africa, which is a pity. Our soils are well developed. The climate is similar, but much more Mediterranean. I cannot really understand how farmers can work with Bordeaux wines here. Even the cooler areas like Constantia or Elgin are more Mediterranean than temperate.*

*Anthony: I worked for Chapoutier in 1997. It was a warm year. We all talk about climatic similarities, but I picked on the slopes in Hermitage and we had to wear sweaters in the middle of the day. Eben referred to the similarities between Spice Route and the Languedoc, but I think Paarl is much hotter and more severe. At Spice Route the night-time temperatures are much cooler and this mitigates against the heat. In Paarl we stay warm at night. So even a warm year in Hermitage is cool when compared to South Africa.*

Ed: How do these climatic differences affect the wine?

*Eben: Well to begin with, they pick in autumn and we pick in mid-summer. When we start comparing climatic conditions, this alone is a huge difference. In the main, all southern hemisphere grapes are picked in mid-summer, which is in the middle of the growing season. I don't feel this is the best time to pick because the vine is still in a vegetative stage. In France the vines are picked when they have basically finished their growing cycle and are calming down. After picking in France, winter can set in within two weeks. The leaves are already yellow, phenolics are ripe. The grapes typically reach phenolic maturity at 12 per cent alcohol. To reach the same level of phenolic maturity here, we need to pick at 14 or 14.5 per cent alcohol. In many years we struggle to ripen our grapes, while the French struggle to reach optimum sugar levels.*

(above) Anthony de Jager, winemaker at Fairview (left), and Eben Sadie, winemaker at Spice Route.
(opposite above) Autumn colours.
(opposite below) Artifacts in the tasting room.

*Anthony:* I could also add there is a major difference when we speak about the age of the vines. In France, winemakers are working with vines which are often 50 years old and even 80 years old. They are part of the total harmony in the environment. In South Africa, we consider a vine old if it exceeds 15 years of age, and that's if we are lucky and a virus hasn't wiped it out.

*Ed:* Let's talk about the blending of Rhône wines and why winemakers blend certain varieties.

*Anthony:* I think the principle purpose behind blending is to fill in the gaps. For instance, when we first planted Mourvèdre, it was difficult to ripen the young vines. As a result, we didn't quite have the mid-palate in the wine and we blended in a huge Shiraz. The final blend ended up as our 1998 Shiraz and was a stunning wine. The wine was purpose-blended. But there are different reasons for blending. First, we must ensure that the consumer can buy the best possible wine. If this means that we have to make up a blend, that's fine. Second, we have to locate the wine for a blend. For instance, if the Mourvèdre is too young and can't stand on its own, it has to be blended. We are currently busy with a programme for Carignan. Carignan doesn't have a fantastic record of ageing well. We also have a problem with the mouth-feel. Over the past three years we have developed a programme of blending in 15 to 25 per cent of a nice high-powered Shiraz, and I think we have arrived at the best possible wine. The same goes for Grenache. There is some beautiful Grenache in France that can stand on its own and age well. But we still have to work on Grenache a bit. We have to reduce the crop more, and in the meantime we still need a nice Shiraz to fill out the palate.

*Ed:* When you work up a Rhône blend that includes Grenache, Mourvèdre or Shiraz, what are you looking for in terms of taste or style?

*Eben:* Generally a good place to start when looking for taste and style is Châteauneuf-du-Pape. But if you take two extreme examples from Châteauneuf-du-Pape – Château Rayas and Château de Beaucastel – they have no similarities. Château de Beaucastel includes all 13 grape varieties and is very much a terroir wine. Château Rayas uses 100 per cent Grenache and is readily identified with the Château. When you drink a bottle of Rayas, you think of the old vineyard and identify with a wine that is unique. That is precisely what we are trying to do at Spice Route. The French blend for complexity, whereas South Africans, in a lot of cases, blend because they want to fix things.

*Anthony:* In the Rhône a lot of vineyards are mixed with a number of different varieties, and in most cases the winemakers can't even give you a run-down of percentages because it's not important at all. In our case we make wine separately and then look at the separate components to make a blend. We even barrel the wines separately and then we blend the best possible wine we can. Last year we blended Shiraz with Mourvèdre in the vineyard, so it was together right from the start. The wine looks fantastic, but we were lucky that the Shiraz and Mourvèdre ripened together. This year the Mourvèdre was late and field blending wouldn't have worked. When we blend, Shiraz probably forms the main component.

(below) Fairview's famous cheeses.

*Autumn colour*

*Mural*

*Tasting room*

*Ed:* Do different clones affect the taste of Shiraz?

*Anthony:* In the new vineyards we use SH 9C and SH 1, but we are not sure what clones were used in the older vineyards. They were simply the old clones that were readily available at the time. We feel our work in the vineyard and the cellar is more important and I am not sure clones really make a difference in the bottle two years down the line. Maybe a small producer will try for a wine that is site-specific, but I can't really comment on that. We are moving more towards good, clean plant material and site-specific wines.

*Ed:* What about rootstocks?

*Eben:* Fairview is planted mainly on 101-14 because of the clay component in the soil. At Spice Route we use Richter 99 because Spice Route is so dry.

*Ed:* What should your planting distance be?

*Eben:* First, may I tell you what you should not do. You should not try to plant one vineyard in one place, nor should you bulldoze eight hectares of natural forest and plant a vineyard with one clone from left to right. Then you should not try to pick all the fruit in three days and whack it into a beautiful cellar that you have just built with loads of cash. Finally you should not put the wine into great new French oak. There is a good reason for not doing this. Regardless of all the new wood, you will have a wine that is one-dimensional. If you were to compare it to an inexpensive Côte du Rhône, it would taste clumsy. Your wine would be more concentrated, but it would look stupid.

*Ed:* Because it lacks complexity?

*Eben:* Precisely, because it lacks complexity. What you should do is plant a couple of sites of Syrah with different clones and leave at least one tree in the middle of the vineyard.

*Ed:* One what?

*Eben:* Just one tree here or there as an aspect of nature. Our vineyards look like deserts – deserts of vines. Also, if you plant one clone throughout the vineyard, one disease could wipe out the vineyard. In France they will not even plant three rows next to each other with the same clone. The thing to do is to plant different sites with different clones. As far as clones are concerned, we are limited to SH 1, which is the Allesverloren clone, and SH 22, which is the Meerendal clone. Obviously you should plant the virus-free versions. Then there is SH 9 and SH 5, which are Argentinian, and SH 99, which is French. If you plant these imported clones on just vaguely vigorous soils, you will have tomato plants growing everywhere. So the thing to do is to get the Syrah to stress a little bit. In Malmesbury, I would like to push up the densities. If you look at Guigal, for example, he plants to a density of 10 000 vines per hectare. He crushes 50 hectolitres per hectare which translates to seven tons. To my mind, this is still too high. But when you break this down, he harvests 700 grams of fruit per vine. We will typically plant 2450 vines per hectare, and even if we harvest at three tons per hectare, we crop at 1.2 kilograms per vine.

Ed: But how do you work those vines at that density?

Eben: Well, you plant a row width of 1.5 metres and then say one metre in the row. You put the vines on stakes or a customised trellising system for the specific site. You can work the vineyard with four-wheel motorbikes and not compact the soil. The problem is you have to buy a motorbike. In Malmesbury, the farmers farm wheat with huge tractors, so they plant to row widths that are so wide you can play rugby between them. In well-drained poor soils with high planting densities, the vines will naturally get smaller. You will not only have less leaves, but also less grapes. The balances will come down because you have less leaves, and with less leaves you have less respiration so you do not lose as much moisture. The plants are smaller and the berries are smaller, which gives better concentration by far.

Ed: Anthony, do you agree with this planting distance?

Anthony: I think Eben makes a lot of sense and the theory does sound convincing. In South Africa, the argument would be over once someone actually goes ahead and does this in Paarl or Malmesbury. We haven't seen it under our conditions because our conditions are different. I think it is time that it gets done.

Eben: I would just like to add a few more comments on the idea of denser planting because a lot of people resist what I say. They argue that we are single-minded and we want to bring all the French techniques here. Well, it is not about bringing French techniques in to make French wines. It is about bringing French techniques in to optimise ours. We do have dense plantings in South Africa. The first winemaker who planted this way was Peter Finlayson at Bouchard Finlayson. If you look at the shoots growing out of his vines, particularly the thickness of the shoots, the spacing of the shoots and the length of the internodes, it all shows that he is growing grapes for wine production and not grape production. There is a vast difference between producing grapes and producing wine.

Ed: I understand Peter plants at 7500 vines per hectare. But if you have vigorous soils, why not plant three by two metres apart and go the Richard Smart route? Isn't it all about balance in the end?

Eben: I haven't read his book Sunlight into Wine completely, but I understand that he does advocate this. But I am not interested in this type of viticulture because I find that the wines are just too engineered. In Australia, they make a lot of wine from these big over-extracted four-square wines that only have four dimensions. I particularly do not drink these wines as they are not very good with food. As a matter of fact, Australia is changing. They are moving away from these over-ripe, sweet, jammy wines.

Ed: Are you saying the Australians are also moving towards more boutique, artisan-type wineries with more structure in their wines?

Anthony: This is true. They are making more restrained dry wines.

Ed: You mentioned the use of oak. Aren't Rhône-style wines made with second- and third-fill barrels and little new oak?

Reflecting pool

Goat tower

Anthony: Yes, some Rhône-style wines, especially from the south, never see oak at all. Some may see older oak, but I think it depends on the wine. I have some wine that is suited to a sort of medium-aged wood, and some that is suited to new wood. I think one has to look at the material in order to make a decision. There is a danger in buying barrels in November before the harvest is in, but the winemaker has to have an idea of where he wants to go. It doesn't always work that way, as you have to put the wine into the type of barrel that suits it.

Ed: Are there any particular coopers that you work with?

Anthony: There are a couple of favourites but we do mix it up a bit.

Ed: You do that intentionally?

Anthony: Yes, definitely. I wouldn't like to be a cooper-specific winery.

Ed: Eben, do you work on the same principle?

Eben: Yes, I also use a number of coopers. With a seriously concentrated wine from excellent grapes, we can't really over-oak the wine. With top-drawer stuff, it is difficult to really make an oak misjudgement. When you work with more diluted wines from inferior vineyards, you have to be very, very careful. But grapes with less concentration do not necessarily produce bad wine. If you go to Fitou in the Languedoc-Roussillon, they make a fruit-driven style. The wine is lovely and fits the cuisine so well. Just next door we find Corbières with better soils. There they start to use wood and as you go up the Rhône, they use more wood. In the Côte Rôtie, Guigal puts his top wines in 100 per cent new wood for three years.

Ed: I'd like to close. Anthony, do you have a particular philosophy about wine making?

Anthony: I think as we move forward it is going to be our responsibility to work and look at our environment more closely. We have to look at what are we doing in the vineyards, and what our vineyards are going to look like in 50 years time. I am glad to see that there is movement towards organic farming and that farmers are trying to preserve their soils. We still have a lot of work to do because there are a lot of evil practices out there. On the wine-making side, I think there is no greater pleasure than producing a wine that gives someone else pleasure. Our aim and function is to produce the best possible wine we can, and essentially offer good value for money.

Eben: There is a proverb that says, 'We do not inherit the land from our fathers – we borrow it from our children.' I think this is a great quote for people who work in nature. If you look at Burgundy today, with its intense viticultural programme, there are less micro-organisms per square metre there than in the Sahara Desert. The vines are dying. It's the truth, the absolute truth. People like Madame Bize-Leroy, Jacques Prieur and Dominique Lafon are beginning to use organic practices to regenerate the soil. We must ensure that we look after what we have. It would be a disaster if we just plant vineyards like everybody else.

# GRAHAM BECK

## *Pieter Ferreira*

Madame Clicquot's spirit is resting in Robertson, undoubtedly guiding Pieter Ferreira in his quest to make outstanding sparkling wine. Pieter's knowledge of this intricate process is exhaustive and he must be rated as the standout exponent in the Cape. In this interview, Pieter travels through Champagne and Robertson discussing terroir, clones, base wines, beads, blending and disgorgement.

*Editor:* I'd like to open this interview with a discussion on the Champagne region, especially the nature of the *terroir*. I'd also like to know how Champagne compares to Robertson.

**Pieter:** *Well, Champagne is not only blessed with lousy topsoil, but also Heaven below. For the* champenoises, *the world is turned upside down because the* terroir *is built on limestone which is essentially chalk.*

*Ed:* And it's calcareous.

Winter vines

**Pieter:** *Yes. And it's calcareous. It is an interesting area because of the unique natural chalk in the soil. The topsoil is so lousy that farmers often have to cart in soil to establish the vines. But then the roots venture down through the chalk as it cracks and grow particularly well. As the northernmost wine-growing area, Champagne obviously has high rainfall which builds into great underwater reservoirs. They never have to irrigate.*

*In Robertson we are uniquely different. In the context of the world, our soils are the right way round. We have duplex soils with good topsoils built on a sub-base predominately of clay. But within that clay we have limestone. It is a more hardened limestone that we have to break at soil preparation for root penetration, and it is not as porous as the limestone that we find in Champagne.*

*Ed:* Are calcareous soils essential for base wine?

Entrance statue

**Pieter:** *I think there is more to it than that. The* champenoises *had to find varieties that would ripen early in a fairly cool area. Chardonnay, Pinot Noir and Pinot Meunier proved to be successful, and these varieties like calcareous soils. I don't think we have to re-invent the wheel, so we concentrate on these varieties as well.*

*Ed:* But in terms of temperature, we know Champagne has a cool climate. We can hardly regard Robertson as a cool climate area, so how do you manage to grow Pinot Noir and Chardonnay successfully?

**Pieter:** *First, I think I should say that the* champenoises *pray through the growing season for a warm summer. Then they don't have to chapetilise so much. For instance, I visited in 1987. It was a horrible, horrible harvest. During the 10-day harvest period, it rained solidly for nine days. In some years grapes ripen at 10.5 to 11 per cent alcohol. With this in mind, we must*

Aloe

*realise we are completely different. We have to manage sunshine and it is challenging to be in a warmer area. Still, we have some advantages. Because they are early ripeners, we can ripen Chardonnay and Pinot Noir in mid-January. They are not affected by the heat we normally get in February and as such, they ripen virtually in a stress-free environment. The prevailing wind is from the south, not that we have a maritime influence, but we do have a prevailing wind which comes from the coast. With this cool breeze we have consistently warm days with cool evenings.*

*Ed:* What is the ripening period here? How many days do you need from flowering to the ripening stage?

**Pieter:** *First I'd like to mention that there is a general belief in certain quarters that we pick green Chardonnay and green Pinot Noir for our bubbly base wines because we are blessed with so much sunshine. This is totally untrue. Our approach to the vineyard is professional and, as I have said, by managing the sunshine we can control the length of the ripening period. We are also in an area where we have to irrigate and by manipulating our water, we can regulate the ripening period as well. In Champagne the CIVC is the controlling body and it determines when the average flowering period begins in the Champagne region. From that point on they normally count off one hundred days before deciding on the picking period. Here we can ripen in 85 days, but it really depends on the approach to the vineyard. Hanging time is important. We take great care to ensure that we have at least 16 leaves above the fruit in order to provide enough shade and to have sufficient leaves to ripen the fruit. I would comfortably say our average during the past five years has run from 95 to 110 days.*

*(above) Pieter Ferreira inspects the vintage.*

*(right) Cap Classique cellar and tasting room.*

Ed: Do you use Pinot Noir and Chardonnay exclusively for your base wines?

Pieter: Champagne has two main planting areas, the mountains around Reims and Epernay, which forms the start of the Côte de Blanc. Pinot Noir is planted in the high-lying areas and Chardonnay is planted south from Epernay. The valley in the middle around the Marne River is always subject to frost in spring, and there they plant Pinot Meunier, which buds late. Due to restrictions over planting material in the past, we have not been able to get our hands on Pinot Meunier, and we only work with Pinot Noir and Chardonnay at the moment.

Ed: Do you plan to bring in Pinot Meunier in the future?

Pieter: We are looking into it. At the moment, Simonsig is the only estate which has planted Pinot Meunier and I have been tasting the wine on an annual basis. We must not neglect the fact that the more options we have with base wine preparations, the more blending opportunities we have to make a specific style. So we shall definitely plant some Pinot Meunier next season.

Ed: Would you like to talk briefly about rootstocks and clones? How have you gone about your planning and again can you comment on the various rootstocks and clones used in Champagne?

Pieter: This is a fairly complex subject. I think in the last 10 years winemakers have become viticulturists because we have had to find better material. We are plagued with virus-infected material throughout the industry, and it is a bit sad. If you hear of the work that Ernita and other nurseries have done in terms of cleaning up material, we sound like world leaders, but we can't really reap the benefits very quickly. And if we find interesting material from abroad, it takes 10 to 11 years before we can even see the benefits.

In Champagne they are so far north, they only have a handful of clones that ripen properly. I have been to Champagne on a study harvest where we only worked on clonal selections. They have small parcels of different clones in different areas. For example, they are developing Pinot Noir clones with looser clusters because they have problems with botrytis during wet years in some areas. As we have more sunshine here, we should work on clones that deliver smaller berries

Ed: I understand they are still using the BK 5 clone in the main.

Pieter: In the main definitely; however, in Champagne I think they also use almost 12 different Pinot Noir clonal selections. In South Africa we use the BK 5, but we have been looking at newer selections to bring in different flavour spectrums. We have also been looking at different rootstocks that are suitable for complex soils.

Ed: More dwarfing rootstocks?

Pieter: At the moment we plant predominantly on Richter 110. Yes, we are also experimenting with the so-called S 04, which is a French rootstock that can dwarf the vigour of the varietal.

Ed: What about your planting distances? How many vines do you plant per hectare?

Pieter: Our planting distances are roughly 2.5 metres by one metre and in some vineyards 2.2 metres by 1.2 metres, giving us an average of 3700 to 4000 vines per hectare. We aim for between 10 and 12 tons per hectare.

Ed: That feels quite high.

Pieter: Not for sparkling wine. Remember, we don't have a ripening problem and we don't want too much of a varietal

characteristic in the wine. We rely on secondary fermentation to build tertiary aromas from the yeast. If we drop the crop too much I think we will have too much concentration in the wine and the Chardonnay or Pinot Noir characteristics will become too predominant. In Champagne the French are rigid in their method and plant anything from 8000 to 10 000 vines per hectare.

Ed: How do you develop your base wines? Do you depart much from French methods?

Pieter: We must respect the bubble both in the vineyard and in the cellar. In Champagne they have proved there is merit in whole-bunch pressing. The law states they must press in batches of four tons, and they may only draw 2666 litres of juice from each batch. We honour this pressing principle as well. I would like to say we are the only cellar equipped to really work with whole bunches and we can comfortably handle 700 tons in a matter of 10 days.

Ed: Do you pick into bins?

Pieter: Yes. This means that we can select the grapes in the vineyards. The bins can hold 300 kilograms of grapes and we can move the fruit into the cellar within 10 minutes. In the cellar we work on the whole fruit. The fruit bin is tipped onto a flat-bed conveyor, taking the whole bunches to the press for careful selected pressing. The fractions that we recover from the press are very important. We only recover 65 per cent of the juice. On normal wine production we typically take off 72 per cent. Within the 65 per cent, we have two pressings or two fractions. First, we press the quality fraction, which the French refer to as the cuvée fraction, and this could be anything from 500 to 600 litres. With our Chardonnay we take our quality fraction on the amount of juice that runs from the press. We normally cut off at 550 to 600 litres. With our Pinot Noir, we also look at colour. And here we might cut off at 500 to 550 litres for our quality fraction. Then we have a press fraction, which we gently press at 1.5 bars. We keep this fraction separate throughout the vinification process and this gives us another blending

*Maturation cellar*

*Reflections*

opportunity. We can add this fraction should we need to give a more robust characteristic to the wine. We keep the batches from each vineyard separate and end up with 10 or 12 batches of Chardonnay and about the same number of Pinot Noir.

Ed: Do you prefer wood to stainless steel when fermenting?

Pieter: Yes. All the champagnes I like seem to be influenced by a little oak. I think my understanding of what they get from their barrels has given an identity to Graham Beck as well. It is interesting to note that Champagne barrels are slightly smaller than the conventional 225-litre barrique. They only hold 205 litres of wine and the champenoises are only allowed to fill 13 barrels from a 4000-kilogram press. The first 10 are known as the cuvée fraction, the next barrel holds the première taille and the next two hold the deuxième taille. We use 120 barrels in our Cap Classique programme and roughly 12 to 15 per cent are new barrels. The rest are second- and old-fill. We've even got barrels going back to 1992.

Ed: Do you allow your base wines to undergo malolactic fermentation?

Pieter: It's a stylistic decision. I think predominantly eight out of 10 champagnes actually do go through malolactic fermentation because they are very acidic after undergoing alcoholic fermentation. They have to soften the wines. Remember bubbles are like a magnifying glass. I think their malic and tartaric ratios are quite different to ours and they can sustain malolactic fermentation. I don't encourage it. We look for more finesse and elegance, and in the initial stages of our base wine preparation for a firmness of acidity.

Ed: The entire art of the winemaker is to blend. When you blend your Chardonnays and Pinots, what is in your mind and again are you following the champenoises?

*(above) Vineyard and cellar lie below the Klein Karoo hills.*

124

*Pieter:* I think we have about a tenth of the potential blending opportunities. Nevertheless, I think the art is to maintain consistency and style. What I do value is the use of reserve wines and I think the champenoises have taught us the importance of reserve wines in Champagne blends.

*Ed:* How old is your reserve wine?

*Pieter:* Initially we kept separate every parcel that was interesting. But eventually we built up 10, 11, 12 different tanks. In 1995, we decided to develop a global reserve and we put all these disparate wines together. Now our global reserve contains wine from the day we started. We add this wine to each new vintage, and then top it up every year. This keeps our consistency and style. We allow the wine to mature a little bit, and obviously it is kept in stainless steel because we do not want any more wood complexity.

*Ed:* What is your blend between Pinot Noir and Chardonnay? Do you lean more heavily towards Pinot Noir or vice versa?

*Pieter:* Traditionally Champagne contains two thirds red grapes and one third white. Obviously this was our initial point of departure, but the wines developed too much of a strawberry character. We eventually settled on a 50/50 split for our non-vintage style and with the later use of our reserve wine, we have been able to tame the predominant characteristics of either component. Our Blanc de Blanc is 100 per cent Chardonnay made up of three or four different Chardonnays, 50 per cent of which will be the pure champenoise barrel-fermented base wine. We made our Millennium in 1997 with 90 per cent Pinot Noir. We get a bit of a sherbert character, with more of a red wine feeling to it, more structure, more complexity because Pinot Noir tends to give you that. Chardonnay fills in on the finesse or elegance, with a touch of fruit.

*Ed:* Once you have put the base wine into the bottle, how long do you leave it on the lees before disgorgement?

*Pieter:* The period is prescribed. For Cap Classique we only have a nine-month minimum requirement for bottle fermentation. I'll come back to that, I think it is too short. In Champagne it is 12 months, but they have ruled that non-vintage Champagne must remain in the cellar for three years. They can leave it for 12 months on the yeast, and then two years on the cork before release. A number of Champagne houses have opted for two to two and a half years on the lees and then six months on the cork before release once it is three years old. In Champagne they're now passing a law extending the minimum lees contact from 12 to 15 months.

The fermentation period is normally about eight weeks at cool temperatures. In Champagne we know that no autolysis really occurs after nine months because the yeast is not yet in a relaxed mode. After nine months we get a sort of a reverse osmosis when the yeast is in a relaxed mode. It starts giving back amino acids and forming a biscuity character. Here we are also encouraging a minimum period of at least 12 months to 15 months for Cap Classique. At Graham Beck we have a philosophy on minimum yeast contact for our non-vintage wine of 24 months. Our vintage Chardonnay spends five years on the lees because Chardonnay starts its yeast autolysis very slowly. The Pinot is left for three years on the lees. It definitely adds to the complexity and flavour and I think we need to express a little bit of the yeast content.

*Ed:* I have always understood that the size of the bead is vital. What do you do to get the bead really tiny?

*Pieter:* It is a fascinating subject on its own. I think, relatively speaking, the finer the bubble, the more feathers on the tongue. If you have a coarse bubble, it froths out of your ears and out of your nose. I feel the mousse is determined primarily on how we handle the whole bunch and how quickly or slowly we extract the juice. This provides the foundation. We work oxidatively because we want to oxidise the phenols. Phenols have fairly loose tannin structures

and if we oxidise them prior to fermentation we can get rid of them. With fewer phenols, we get less bitterness and a more refined bubble. And then obviously we respect the amount of protein in our base wines. We don't over-fine them with bentonite, or gelatin for that matter. We try for as much protein as possible because protein definitely helps to create the size of the bubble. It creates a better bead and also allows for a lot more consistent bead. When you pour a glass of bubbly, the initial foam is called the crown. If the crown remains, it shows that the wine has more protein. If we remove the protein, we have a thinner wine.

*Ed:* What is the ideal temperature for secondary fermentation?

*Pieter:* I would comfortably say 12 degrees is ideal. We obviously use a very strong yeast in the bottle, known as the prise de mousse, which was developed in Champagne. It is a scavenger or a killer strain. Remember yeast has to work under cool conditions. It has to work in alcohol and under pressure. Cool fermentation allows the bubble to be better impregnated. The longer the wine can remain on the yeast at 12 degrees, the more refined the bubble becomes.

*Ed:* Once you have disgorged, is there a period when one wants to hold the wine before sending it to market?

*Pieter:* Disgorgement is a critical process for the wine, but I feel that remuage is a more delicate process. We use gyropalettes purely because of the volume we do. We do riddle a sample batch by hand because this allows us to manipulate our programme accordingly. At disgorgement we add the liqueur d'expédition. I don't think it will ever make the wine, but it will definitely influence it. Invariably in Champagne, they always talk about the 'house secret' for the dosage. It is usually a little bit of sugar and something else. Some have introduced some Cognac to give a little bit of richness and I've even heard of some adding coffee liqueur. We have tried to develop our own style. We decant the same style of wine that we've had on the lees, then we add sugar and use that as our dosage. There is no doubt in my mind that the wine needs a resting period after disgorgement. A freshly disgorged wine definitely has a different taste to one that's been on cork for at least six months.

*Ed:* So the wine definitely grows in style in the bottle?

*Pieter:* I think cork maturation is just as important as contact time with the yeast. We try for a minimum of three months on the cork prior to release. I would prefer a year. After a year everything has settled and a little bit of cork maturation even enhances the yeast autolysis. We also see more yeasty characters after a year on the cork.

*Ed:* Finally, where do you put your stock in the world of Champagne and what do you see for the future?

*Pieter:* It is an interesting question. I think first of all I've learnt to respect Champagne for what it is. It has created a platform for me to be a unique individual player in the international market. I do believe we can present an alternative to Champagne, but we have to understand the intrinsic values of the process. I think we have developed a platform and now we should try to consistently improve quality yet maintain the style we have developed. Our style has an international flare of flavour that can be a great alternative to Champagne.

# WATERFORD

## Kevin Arnold

Kevin Arnold is a man on a mission. He has recently taken on the challenge of making Waterford a world-class player in the world of wine by creating unique blends with varieties from disparate wine regions. He has an impressive track record to back his quest. In this interview, Kevin shares his views on the components of his blends and the opportunities he can claim from the slopes of the Helderberg.

*Editor:* Waterford is certainly impressive in its scope and vision. With such magnificent slopes on the Helderberg, what are your intentions? What varieties are you planting and where do you see the winery in the future?

**Kevin:** *Well, the Helderberg is one of the prime growing regions in the Cape. What's great about the Helderberg is that we can make terroir-specific wines. Even with my previous experience at Rust en Vrede, I have only touched the tip of the iceberg in terms of quality and style. To this effect we've gone ahead, looked in the crystal ball, and we consider Shiraz to be of paramount importance in the future. We have also considered alternative varieties and we have added Barbera from Italy, Mourvèdre and Grenache from the south of France and Tempranillo from Spain. I guess we will not stop there because at the end of the day South Africa needs to create something very special of its own. To do this we can no longer look at the traditional varieties that have brought us to this point.*

Ed: Are you going to run more with Rhône-style blends?

**Kevin:** *Well, they are my favourites in a sense that if we travel around the world, if we look at drinking patterns, Rhône-style wines are really attracting attention. I believe they are spice-driven wines. I believe they are more leaner in style, yet classic in a sense that they need refinement. Ultimately, I think these are the wines that will be the wines of the future.*

Ed: What are the specific advantages of the Helderberg in terms of *terroir*? What type of soils do you have?

**Kevin:** *The good thing about the Helderberg is that we have a variation. We have both deep red soils and sandstone with rocky areas. We have chosen varieties that do well in the rocky soils and these will complement the traditional varieties, like Cabernet Sauvignon and Merlot, that grow in the easy fertile soils. We hope to create a blended wine that brings to the fore something truly unique.*

*Entrance*

*Courtyard*

Ed: But are you going to stay in the tradition of the Rhône in terms of the mix of wine?

**Kevin:** *No, I don't think that's true. I think terroir around the world needs to be judged and honoured in terms of what has been achieved. South Africa, and more specifically Stellenbosch and the Helderberg, has yet to gain recognition and cannot claim to be called a Rhône or a Bordeaux terroir. The only way we'll succeed in the future is to build a terroir called Stellenbosch. This is vitally important. For too long, we have competed or tried to copy other regions in the world. At the end of the day we need to sell what we have and that is terroir. We have Stellenbosch, we have the Helderberg, and we need to produce wine that is recognised for its terroir-specific characteristics.*

Ed: But specifically when you look at your blends, what will be the mix?

**Kevin:** *I was passionate as a student about Bordeaux as it produces wonderfully dry classic tannic wines which need 15 to 20 years before you can drink them. With that has come my experience in Stellenbosch, and more specifically the Helderberg, where with its different terroir we have grown Cabernet, Merlot and Shiraz to date. Now what I am looking for is a certain element of spice in a wine, which comes from Shiraz and the varieties we are currently planting. Cabernet should still form the backbone, or structure, and then we shall add the other varietals to create spice and finesse. At the end of the day, we hope to create something that is our very own. Wine Spectator recently published its top 100 wines worldwide and it was great to see Rust en Vrede amongst them with a Cabernet/Merlot/Shiraz blend from the Helderberg. That in itself speaks volumes for the future potential of this region. All the varieties I've mentioned have been planted with the exception of Grenache and Tempranillo because we are waiting to get the best possible material. These varieties will be planted within 12 months. The idea is to create a single blend from all our varieties.*

(above) Kevin Arnold.

(above right) View from the tower.

(right) Central courtyard below the Helderberg mountain.

*Ed*: Do you have any preferences when planting your vineyards?

**Kevin:** *I think we have taken a chapter from our European heritage and experience, but we are also looking ahead to the New World countries as well. Viticulturally, California and Australia have similar climates to South Africa. So we use a bit of both worlds. I think we need to look at what is relevant here. After all, we are on the southern tip of Africa, and we need to allow more space for the vines to grow. There is plenty of sunshine, and plants grow with much more vigour here than they do in Europe. Yet there are certain vineyards where we have planted with narrower rows because we feel this suits the variety or the slope. But basically we have an open book in terms of mixing and matching. I think this is the only way to go because there is no blueprint for vineyards on the Helderberg. Sadly, after so many years of research, I honestly believe we are starting from scratch. For me the year 2000 was the start of a new beginning for wines in Stellenbosch.*

*Ed*: If I could just bring you back a moment? When you talk about wide planting, can you give me any specific numbers?

Kevin: Well, we plant from 2.5 to 3 metres between the rows, certainly not more than that since I don't think it's required, and in the rows we plant with a spacing of 0.8, one metre, and in some instances 1.2 or 1.5 metres. I think we are still a little reticent about planting distances, but I think this will come with more and more experience. We do make use of consultants with international experience because I think we

are basically just too conservative to get there on our own. And time is not on our side. If we want to become world players, we need to get in and do things quickly.

*Ed:* What are your crop levels?

**Kevin:** *Well, I think that's one of the problems we've inherited. We are taught that we should only produce six to seven tons per hectare to produce great wine. In a climate like ours, I don't think that's true. I think we can produce from eight to 10 tons and maybe even 12 tons per hectare and still make quality wine. It is something we need to understand. Vines are like people. When people are dressed well, when they eat well, when they are happy, they are really innovative. When a vine is unhappy and not able to do what it needs to do, it may not necessarily produce the best fruit. We have grown up with a very strong European influence of narrow plantings and low crops, supposedly all things that are good for Europe. But remember we live in southern Africa and we need to wear a South African cap.*

*Ed:* If I may just come back to Shiraz? Are you planting on any particular rootstock? And have you gone onto a dwarfing stock or not?

**Kevin:** *We haven't got to the dwarfing stage yet. I think Shiraz is the one variety that will do well on the whole array of different rootstocks because of our different terroirs. We have only just started to get decent material. In time I think we are going to look at many combinations and each region hopefully will come out with what is going to be best for it. At Waterford we have gone with two basic rootstocks for the initial plantings of Shiraz, but as we all know, sadly our material is not 100 per cent virus-free. Within 15 to 20 years, I guess we'll be looking at re-planting and by then we shall have to assess the combinations again.*

*Ed:* Are there any particular clones that you are keen on?

**Kevin:** *There are quite a few new clones in the pipeline. I think we need to look at them, but more importantly we need to look at bringing in more clones. I've tasted some fantastic Shiraz from different parts of the world. I don't think we have touched the surface yet. We need to look beyond what is available to us right know.*

*Ed:* Do you think clones will give you more blending opportunities or do you think that it is more a question of managing the vines than the material itself that counts?

**Kevin:** *That is a tricky one. I think at the end of the day clones do count, but there are very fine nuances in terms of the differences. Where the varieties are planted, how they are looked after, and whether they are picked at the right ripeness is far more important. Also when making the wine, there are influences from yeast selection or barrel maturation. I guess these factors are almost as important as the clones. At the end of the day, vineyard management, picking at the right ripeness and wine-making techniques are going to become very important.*

*Courtyard corner*

*Tower entrance*

*Ed:* Once you have brought the grapes into the cellar, there is obviously a particular style that you have in mind. Could we locate that style in terms of the world of wine?

**Kevin:** *I think an investment in a winery of Waterford's stature means that we should be serious about the style of our wine. One thing that has changed is that we no longer need to wait 15 to 20 years to drink this style of wine. We are creating wines with intensity, with structure and with richness and because of our climate, these wines are going to be drinkable a lot earlier. But I do believe that they need the backbone, the tannin structure and the breeding to be around for a number of years to compete with the big guns.*

*Ed:* I'd like to change gears completely. You mentioned that you are planting vines from Italy and Spain, which is quite unusual. I think there are only a handful of farms that have planted varieties from these regions. You mentioned Barbera, but are you planning to expand with more Italian varieties?

**Kevin:** *I've embarked on this project at Waterford to create a unique and hopefully a successful wine that will compete with other great regions in the world. And to achieve this we need to put together a blend. We chose Barbera because it is a variety that's been grown on an experimental farm and made at Stellenbosch University for the last 10 to 15 years. My yearly judging of these wines indicated to me that this variety produces high natural acids that we often lack. So Barbera was chosen primarily for acid levels. Obviously colour and the intensity it offers are also important, but we are primarily looking at acid from this variety. Other Italian varieties have yet to prove themselves. Although with our climate we need to look at them a lot more earnestly. Italian varieties often offer an array of flavours without the intensity we are so accustomed to, but this is really the challenge of the winemaker.*

*Ed:* Are you not considering Nebbiolo or Sangiovese?

**Kevin:** *Sangiovese and Nebbiolo have been planted in our area as experimental wines for the past 10 to 15 years with such variance in quality from year to year that they haven't been totally convincing. But we should not say when looking ahead that we cannot go that route. I think more growers should be more open-minded towards trying these varieties. It is about looking at the terroir they grow in and not necessarily the style of wines they are making.*

*Ed:* You also mentioned Tempranillo from Spain. Are you going to use this variety as a blending partner as well?

**Kevin:** *Well, I like Spanish wines and I like Rioja blends. I find a lot of similarity with Rioja here in terms of terroir and we've chosen Tempranillo because the Tempranillo combination with Cabernet gives a whole dimension of flavour to red wines. And that dimension I believe can be one of the spice components of the ultimate blend I am trying to put together at Waterford. I travel every year to taste wines from these regions as single varieties and as blends. I have just come back from a London trade fair and I am even more convinced we are on the right track in terms of where we are heading with our vision for a blended wine. There will surely be other varieties which one will look at, but of the eight varieties, six are planted. Whether we use all eight or six initially and refine them down to a smaller number will be seen in the future. But I think this is the real challenge and I am confident we can produce something totally unique.*

*Ed:* So you are becoming almost like the Côte Rôtie with their myriad varieties?

*Kevin: Yes, in a sense I think that's what the Cape is all about. We have such a varied terroir in a sense that if we talk of Stellenbosch as a whole, the south of Stellenbosch is quite different to the north of Stellenbosch. So is east to west and I think we have boringly stuck to common varieties in the past. We need to look beyond that and there is no doubt in my mind that there are still going to be truly great and exciting wines made in the Stellenbosch District from varieties that have not yet been planted here.*

*Ed:* If I can just bring you back? You have mentioned planting eight or nine varieties. Are you really running a Shiraz blend or a Cabernet blend? In other words, what is the starting point?

*Kevin: Well, the starting point got going in 1986 on the Helderberg when I was at Rust en Vrede. We looked at the first combination of Cabernet/Merlot, which I guess was the traditional way to go. I think we were the first producers to introduce Shiraz into the blend when we combined Cabernet, Merlot and Shiraz as a premium quality wine. It had been done for commercial, less expensive wines. Nonetheless it was a first and with the recognition this wine has achieved internationally over the past 10 years, it has proved to me that it is a good solid base to work from. So to answer your question, I cannot say yet whether it will be Shiraz-based or Cabernet-based, but the safe route has been to go the Cabernet route. Shiraz is limited in a sense as to what is available to us in terms of clones, and it is not that exciting. In future plantings we will include more Shiraz. If I were to guess, I would think we would look at something like 70 per cent of the base wine being made up of Cabernet, Merlot and Shiraz, with the other components adding the spices. I am really looking forward to creating the mouth-feel, the texture and what I believe will be a new experience for a consumer of wines from the Helderberg region.*

*Ed:* So essentially the vision for you at Waterford is to create a unique blend that is going to knock the socks off the world?

*Kevin: Well, that is the challenge we've set for ourselves and I think we have the climate, we have the terroir and we have spent the money on the winery, so I have no doubt in my mind that this can be achieved.*

*Ed:* I guess that you are not governed by the laws of Bordeaux or Tuscany so you can create blends that are simply not allowed in these regions?

*Kevin: On my recent visit to a grower's stall at the London trade fair, I told him about the varieties that interested me. He wanted to know where I came from and how I was allowed to grow them. And I think that in itself is an advantage that we have in South Africa. We don't actually realise the potential we have. We have to be more innovative. We have to have people in the vineyards who are passionate about what they are doing. We have to see innovation in the cellars and hopefully find marketing folk who are also passionate about what they are doing. I am not sure whether we have even one or two of these components in place in our industry. I can certainly say from my personal experience that we do not have all three in place. And hence our lack of international recognition, momentum and brand building. They are sadly not there for the benefit of all the growers in the Cape wine industry.*

(right) Entrance shadows.

# Eau-de-Vie

## Brandy Making

The most suitable grape varieties for brandy production are Colombar, Chenin Blanc, Cinsaut, Palomino and Ugni Blanc. As with all products of the vine, the choice of grape is all-important. High acidity and low alcohol are significant factors. The alcoholic strength of the wine should range from seven to nine per cent, with pH values of between 2.8 and 3.2. The wine should also have a low volatile acidity and must contain no sulphur dioxide. In South Africa, however, wines usually have a higher alcohol concentration of 10 to 13 per cent. The main growing areas where soil and climate induce these characteristics include the Little Karoo, Robertson, Worcester and the Olifants and Orange River areas. Parts of Stellenbosch and Paarl produce characters much sought-after for certain styles of blends.

The harvested grapes are lightly pressed, and only the free-run juice, with no off odours, is collected for fermentation into a clean wine. No racking takes place after fermentation, as this would eliminate valuable nitrogen compounds. All wines destined for distillation have to pass strict standards set by the government Brandy Board. After distillation, the spirit produced also has to undergo inspection before approval is given for it to be placed in oak casks. There it will rest for the minimum three-year ageing period, before it can legally be called brandy. The first distillation is done as soon as fermentation is completed since the wine is not protected by sulphur dioxide, which has an adverse effect on the copper of the still. This distillation increases the alcoholic content to about 28 per cent, and is called 'low wine'. It contains volatile substances, including esters and aldehydes which are carried over from the wine. A residue is also produced containing water, non-volatile substances, salts, and sugars if the wine is not fermented dry.

The low wine is brought back to the pot still at a later stage and re-distilled. Only the 'heart' of the distillation is collected for ageing. The 'heads' and 'tails' are separated at the start and towards the end of distillation, since these fractions contain substances that do not contribute to good character in the final spirit. The collected fraction ends up with a strength of 68 per cent, but throughout the distillation the strength may not exceed 72 per cent. In any event, a higher percentage is not likely to happen in a pot still. The colourless, near neutral spirit hardly resembles brandy as we know it. Once the heart is approved by the Board, it is reduced in strength with neutral, de-ionised or distilled water to a strength of 60 per cent, which is considered the optimum strength while the spirit is in the oak cask.

*Van Ryn brandy cask*

*Viceroy brandy cask*

## Maturation 6

While the brandy is in the 300-litre cask (the law states that the cask cannot exceed 340 litres), a remarkable transformation takes place. Visually it picks up some colour from the wood, but this can vary from cask to cask. The major change, however, is in the aroma and taste. During the time spent in the cask evaporation takes place. In the course of one year, a single cask can lose as much as nine litres, and over three years this can amount to 36 bottles of brandy. Over a 10-year period as much as 30 per cent is lost. The lost portion is romantically termed 'the angel's share', and the longer the time in wood, the more concentrated the character. The brandy will not remain in wood for more than 20 years, as this serves no further beneficial purpose. The brandy is then removed from the cask for preservation in stainless steel or glass containers.

Pot-still brandy is the key to all South African brandy, and to qualify as a brandy, the less expensive brands must contain 30 per cent of this product by alcohol content. The balance is non-aged spirit distilled from wine in continuous or patent stills that produce a very neutral but soft-charactered product. This blend is the basic brandy of South Africa. Its colour is achieved by the addition of caramel, as with all the world's great spirit brands, be they cognac, whisky or rum.

The better-quality brands usually contain higher proportions of pot-still brandy, which may have aged longer in oak, and an increasing number of brands are now aged for five years. Once the blend has been determined in the tasting room, it is assembled in the cellar, and finally reduced in strength for bottling. The lowest this strength can be is 38 per cent, and the usual strength is 43 per cent.

In South Africa, bureaucrats use odd terminology to describe the wine and brandy used in the brandy-making process. They use the terms 'rebate wine', 'rebate brandy' and 'distilling wine'. Their terminology is unfortunate from a consumer's point of view, because the terms appear to be negative.

'Rebate wine' is the wine destined for distillation into pot-still brandy.

'Rebate brandy' is pot-still brandy approved by the Board and aged in oak, and the rebate is granted on 'the angel's share', hence the strict excise control.

'Distilling wine' is the wine produced for distillation in continuous stills into highly rectified wine spirit. Again, every aspect is controlled by the Brandy Board.

# HISTORY

The Dutch had long been traders with the Charentais of La Rochelle and it was no surprise that brandy played an integral part in the new settlement at the Cape. All brandy, however, was imported and sold at exorbitant prices.

Brandy is recorded as having first been distilled in the Cape in 1672, 20 years after the arrival of Jan van Riebeeck. Apparently, the distillation was carried out by an assistant cook of the Company's ship, Pijl. He used the Charentais method of double distillation with very rudimentary equipment. It was undoubtedly consumed without any maturation. The good cook started a tradition of crude and inferior brandy in the Cape which lasted for almost 250 years.

A boost to brandy production came with the first British occupation in 1795. It then gained momentum after the colony was annexed by Great Britain in 1806. The annexation brought new settlers and visitors to the Cape who demanded better brandy. Since Cape brandy had such an unpleasant taste and could only be swallowed with a 'shudder', this demand led to a surge in imported brandy. The poor quality of Cape brandy was largely due to the practice of fermenting wine with the husks and dregs after the first juice was taken off. Although this practice did extract the maximum amount of juice from the grapes, it also meant that a large percentage of odious material was left in the wine. Due to the primitive distillation methods, it persisted into the final product. These early products were given colloquial names such as Kaapse Smaak, because of the bad taste, and Cape Dop, because husk means 'dop' in Dutch. The settlers set new standards of taste which local brandy producers attempted to achieve, and these developments came under the direction of Governor Sir John Cradock and then Lord Charles Somerset. Regrettably, the spirit was strong, the flesh was weak, and brandy remained evil.

In the early days on the Reef, flamboyant entrepreneur Sammy Marks invited René Santhagens, a young French cavalry officer who had worked in the Cognac distilleries of France, to open a distillery at his factory east of Pretoria. The young man arrived at the Cape in 1887 with his own copper stills and then transported them north by ox wagon.

The distillery became an instant success, but the outbreak of the Anglo-Boer War in 1899 killed this lucrative business and in 1902 the British colonial authorities revoked Marks' licence.

Santhagens returned to France for a brief spell, and arrived back at the Cape in 1903. Appalled by the abominable quality of Cape brandy, he made it his life's work to upgrade the quality to French standards.

In 1905 Santhagens collaborated with the Marais brothers to form a co-operative, the Golden Lion Distillery. The building was designed with French flair by Santhagens' wife, Jeanne. Today it houses the distillery of the Van Ryn Wine and Spirit Company. By 1907 annual production of the Golden Lion Distillery averaged 750 000 litres. Santhagens was now in a position to fulfil his dream of making a spirit comparable to Cognac and he purchased the farm Oude Molen in 1909. There he established the distillery that today houses a museum dedicated to his memory.

Santy, as Santhagens became known, established the principles for wine selection, copper pot still distillation, and maturation in small French oak casks. These principles formed the basis of Act 42, passed in 1909, and this legislation led to the appointment of a Board of Reference to interpret the law and classification of spirits. Eventually this Board became the government Brandy Board.

Considerable developments followed and well-known names like Collison, Van Ryn, the Castle Wine & Brandy Company and the Paarlsche Wijn en Brandewijn Maatsschappij Beperkt came into being. The formation of the KWV further helped to establish quality brandy production, and after various attempts to stabilise the market, it set down strict regulations in 1924. These regulations prescribed the Charentais method of double distillation. All stills that did not conform to the regulations were 'destroyed' by excise officials. This accounts for the many old copper stills now decorating the verandas of homes, not only in the Cape, but upcountry as well.

The great distilleries introduced highly efficient continuous stills to produce pure spirit that could be blended with three-year-old, oak-matured, pot-still brandy. All production came under the control of the Brandy Board. South Africa earned the reputation for producing some of the world's best brandies. Oude Meester set the trend by winning many international awards, and at the Half-Century Wine Exhibition in London, it was awarded the accolade of 'The World's Best Brandy'. It was brandies of this quality that really turned South Africans into the major brandy consumers that they are today.

The quality of South African brandy also attracted some of Europe's most famous brandy makers to the Cape. Bols was introduced in 1955, and in 1960 the great House of Martell honoured Ronnie Melck by licensing Stellenbosch Farmers' Winery to produce a local product under its brand name.

*(right) Recently restored original mural in the main hall of Uitkyk's historic manor house.*

*(far right) Working copper still at the Van Ryn Wine and Spirit Company.*

*(left) Old copper still.*

## Eau-de-Vie

Historians disagree on when and where distilling was first discovered, and for centuries the wonderful secrets of *aqua vitae*, water of life, were limited to a privileged few. In the 13th century, Arnau de Vilanova and Raimundo Lullio of the University of Montpellier published their testamentum on distilling spirit from wine. They thought they had discovered the fifth element, the elixir of life, and after air, water, fire and earth, they saw it as the origin of life itself. Later, the farmers of the Charentes distilled their surplus wines in pot stills to preserve them, and in the process created a thriving export market. The farmers named their product eau-de-vie, and the nearby port of La Rochelle did a thriving business to customers across the English Channel.

War intervened and the port of La Rochelle was blockaded. More and more casks of eau-de-vie piled up in the warehouses. After the war the merchants of La Rochelle opened their warehouses with trepidation, convinced that time must have ruined their water of life. Instead a miracle had occurred. Their colourless, rough eau-de-vie had been transformed into a rich, golden liquid, beautifully smooth and round, and rich in taste and aroma. It was the miracle of maturation, and the beginning of the great story of brandy.

# The Great Distilleries

'Every cloud has a silver lining', so the saying goes. This adage is true for South African brandy, for despite declining sales due to high excise duties, brandy producers are using the lull to further improve quality. South African brandy has proved its consistent high quality not only through the success of its international sales, but also at the International Wine and Spirit Competition held annually in London. During an 11-year period, South Africa has won the trophy for the 'Best Brandy Worldwide' no fewer than six times.

South Africa has not only recorded success with the quality of its products. In 1983 KWV 20-Year-Old won the Trophy for the 'Best Package' overall at the competition. At that stage there was no award for the best brandy. This trophy, introduced in 1984 for the 'Best Brandy Worldwide', was won by Camus Cognac. Sponsorship lapsed until 1989 when Domecq took over as a regular sponsor and the trophy went to Cognac Napoleon again from Camus in that year. Domecq continued its sponsorship until 1996. In 1997 Oude Meester took over the sponsorship and South African producers have been victorious in the following years:

| | | |
|---|---|---|
| 1990 | KWV 20-Year-Old | Domecq Trophy |
| 1991 | KWV 10-Year-Old | Domecq Trophy |
| 1995 | Sydney Back Brandy | Domecq Trophy |
| 1999 | Oude Molen VOV 14-Year-Old | Oude Meester Trophy |
| 2000 | KWV Imoya VSOP Cape Alembic Brandy | Oude Meester Trophy |
| 2001 | Oude Molen VOV 14-Year-Old | Oude Meester Trophy |

In the years South Africa did not win, South African brandies have still been placed in the final 'taste off'. South Africa's continuing success in producing high-quality brandy stems largely from the fact that wine is specifically made for distillation, as happens in Cognac and Armagnac. Brandy in many other parts of the world is generally made from wine rejected for consumption as wine. Even the pure grape spirit produced in South Africa is often made from grapes grown for that purpose. Moreover, the South African Brandy Board ensures that wine produced specifically for distillation adheres to strict quality standards. The Department of Customs and Excise has, however, increased duties to such an extent that it has had a detrimental effect on the sale of brandy within South Africa.

In the mid-1980s, the KWV consolidated its brandy production at its Worcester premises. The Worcester facility now uses 120 traditional South African brandy pot stills, two large French alembic stills and two monster, six-column continuous stills. The first alembic still was installed in 1992 and production from this still is being matured in small oak for 10 years. The first release of this brandy will be sampled in 2002 with eager anticipation. Due to depressed sales, the KWV has been able to take pot stills out of production and alter them to be more in line with the alembic stills which have proven to produce better brandies. The KWV has also been able to insulate most of the stills, which has conserved energy and saved on costs.

The reduction in volume has also meant that only the very best wine is selected for pot-still brandy. Now that the 'surplus' system has been discontinued, only wines meant for distillation, either pot still or continuous, are used. No unwanted, discarded wine or wine of dubious quality is obliged to be distilled. This

*Headquarters of the Van Ryn Wine and Spirit Company.*

*Distillery of the Van Ryn Wine and Spirit Company.*

*Some of the 120 brandy pot stills at the KWV Worcester facility.*

means all winemakers are more quality-driven than ever before. Any sub-standard wine is distilled into non-potable alcohol.

The KWV has experimented with a wide range of oaks from as far afield as the United States and Russia, but the traditional wide-grained Limousin oak from France is still considered the best. The warmer maturation conditions in the Cape when compared to France also mean that a brandy aged for 10 years in South Africa is equal in 'age' to about a 15-year-old brandy in France. The KWV only sells its 10- and 20-year-old brandies on the local market, but does produce some superb brandies for export. Evidence of its success is the world-renowned Imoya VSOP Cape Alembic Brandy. Launched in New York in 1999, it had an immediate rave reception and set a new standard for South African brandy on the international scene. In 2000 it won the trophy at the International Wine and Spirit Competition for the 'Best Brandy Worldwide' against incredible competition. Made from Chenin Blanc, Riesling and Colombar, Imoya VSOP is double distilled in copper pot stills and aged for five, eight, 10 and 20 years before being blended and packaged in its superlative black, frosted flask. It is also backed by very imaginative marketing. Imoya can mean 'wind' or 'breath' and both are cleverly used in the international marketing of the Imoya VSOP Cape Alembic Brandy.

The KWV is not alone in the drive for quality. Distillers Corporation was concerned with absolute quality from its inception in 1945. After one year of production, Distillers Corporation received the highest praise from the Syndicate de la Distillerie Agricole in Paris for the purity of its distilled alcohol. The report concluded: 'It is not practically possible to achieve a better analysis.' Distillers Corporation installed its first pot stills in 1945 and only five years later received a gold medal for its brandy at the Half Century Empire Wine Show held in London. In 1958 Distillers was the first in South Africa to replace its five-column continuous still with a six-column still in order to produce the finest spirits for blending with its pot still production. In 1967 the company then installed a six-column still at its Worcester distillery. In 1969 plans for a merger with SA Distilleries began and were concluded in 1970. The great brandy names of Castle Wine and Brandy, E. K. Green, Van Ryn's and Collisons eventually became part of Distillers Corporation, providing the company with products dating back to the turn of the century. More recently, Distillers has improved and extended its maturation facilities at the Van Ryn Distillery in Vlottenburg, introducing a number of well-aged brandies to the market. Distillers also entered the Estate Brandy market after launching its 10-year-old Uitkyk Estate brandy in 2000. Uitkyk Estate's Brandy is double distilled in 2000-litre pot stills heated over open flame. This bottling is considered particularly interesting since it is distilled from Cinsaut, Cabernet Sauvignon and Clairette Blanche. The young brandy is matured for nine months in new Limousin French oak before going into second-fill barrels for the rest of its 10-year maturation period. Stellenbosch Farmers' Winery, now part of Distell, is the other major brandy marketer in South Africa. It has upgraded its Goudini distillery to keep pace with the ever-improving quality of South African brandies. Nederburg now has a superb pot-still brandy distilled from wine containing Sauvignon Blanc lees for extra special character. The brandy is aged in the *solera* process.

*(left) KWV's Charentais still in Worcester.*

*(right) KWV's famous 10-year-old brandy.*

# Boutique Distilleries

After a good deal of lobbying, a legislative amendment in 1990 made provision for the distillation of Estate and Husk Brandy. The Liquor Products Act now allows four types of brandy in South Africa: husk brandy (marc or grappa), pot-still brandy, brandy and vintage brandy. In November 1993 a further provision was passed to certify the use of the term 'Estate Brandy', defined under the Wine of Origin scheme.

Cape Wine Master, Carel Nel of Boplaas, quickly took advantage of the change in legislation to satisfy his ambition for distilling brandy. At the end of the three-year minimum maturation period, Nel launched an estate brandy onto the market in 1995. His brandy was the first to carry an Origin Certification. Using Colombar, one of the traditional grapes of Cognac, he allowed the wine to undergo malolactic fermentation, and to lie on its lees to enhance the body of the final product before double distillation. Carel Nel has one of the original Santhagens stills.

Distillation of brandy was first recorded in 1851 on what is now Backsberg. When the late Sydney Back learned that the law was to be changed again to allow distillation on the property, he went to France to meet with leading Rémy Martin expert, Robert Léauté. Sydney then imported and installed a completely automated, computer-controlled, 5-hectolitre pot still from the largest manufacturer in Cognac. Using only Chenin Blanc, he made the wines using the Cognac method to give an alcohol of nine to 10 per cent, without any sulphur addition. The wine was kept on the lees at low temperature and then distilled with the same lees. The first release was aged for the three-year minimum in Limousin oak, and later won the Domecq Trophy at the International Wine and Spirit Competition for the best brandy in 1995. As older brandies become available, older blends will be made.

Achim von Arnim was also quick off the mark with his Fine de Jourdan, a pot-still brandy distilled from the final pressing, the *deuxième taille,* of his Chardonnay and Pinot Noir, used in the making of his Cap Classique. Achim's process follows the traditional practice of Champagne. The double-distilled spirit is then aged in Limousin oak for three years.

The explosion of small independent wineries in the Cape has also been emulated in the brandy area. We have already seen the establishment of small-scale producers; now independent blenders are coming into the market. Together they are producing some interesting product and they are listed below by area.

### Wellington – Paarl
In 2001 Roger Jorgensen released his 1995 Claridge Pot-Still Brandy, made from Colombar and aged on Chardonnay lees before going to the still. After distillation, the new brandy was reduced to cask ageing strength with low calcium water from a spring on the farm. Prior to bottling, the same water will be used to bring the brandy to bottling strength. Claridge Pot-Still Brandy is handsomely packaged in tall, classic clear glass with the Claridge

crest silk-screened on the shoulder. The brandy is also vintage dated. About a third of each year's production is reserved so as to eventually bottle an eight-year-old brandy.

The KWV has also produced Pinotage brandy on its Laborie Estate, which it uses exclusively to fortify a Pineau de Laborie, also made from Pinotage.

Rolf Schumacher of Oude Wellington began distilling in 1999, using Chenin Blanc and Clairette Blanche. The brandy will be three years old in 2002, but may be held until five years old. In the meantime, the cellar has been producing a grappa made from Cabernet Sauvignon and Chenin Blanc husks.

Another vintage pot-still brandy from Wellington is made at Upland Estate. There Dr Edmund Oettlé not only produces wine, but has also constructed his own pot still. He has set out to, as far as possible, mimic a Cognac. Whereas others might want to produce a brandy with a distinctive South African character, the one time veterinarian and his electrical engineer wife, Elsie, have opted for the Cognac route. Distilled from wines made from Chenin Blanc, Riesling and some Colombar, the brandy is bottled at 38 per cent. The first release was only 150 cases, but the next vintage should exceed 1000 cases.

### Stellenbosch
Avontuur, on the Helderberg between Stellenbosch and Somerset West, is now also a feature on the Brandy Route. Packed in a classic flint bottle, the brandy is aged five years and distilled in a copper pot still, mainly from Chenin Blanc.

Giorgio Dalla Cia of Meerlust, originally a distiller by trade, has pioneered grappa production in South Africa. In 1996 Meerlust launched two top-quality grappas, one distilled from the classic Champagne combination of Chardonnay and Pinot Noir, and the other from the classic Bordeaux blend of Cabernet Sauvignon and Merlot.

Tokara, at the top of Helshoogte, is where G.T. Ferreira has perched his sensationally-sited cellar where he is not only making wine, but is also distilling brandy. The first blend is a Backsberg look-a-like Cognac. An alembic still was put into use and the distillation was made from Chenin Blanc. Initial samples give every impression of yet another world champion in the making. The brandy, however, will probably be aged for five years before release, so patience is required.

At the other end of the Simonsberg is Uitkyk, where for more than 10 years estate brandy has been produced. This remains one of the winelands' best-kept secrets. The wine for distillation was blended from the estate's own Cinsaut, Cabernet Sauvignon and Clairette Blanche, and distilled in Cognac-type stills fired with an open flame. The brandy was matured in new Limousin oak for nine months, then matured in second use for the rest of the 10 years. Uitkyk's brandy is bottled at 38 per cent and attractively packaged in tall, clear, classic brandy bottles.

### Klein Karoo
After all his years producing 'witblitz' and liqueurs, Danie Grundling of Grundheim will bring a pot-still brandy to the market in 2002. Made from Colombar and Hanepoot, which gives an exquisite character, it is sure to create an enthusiastic following. Only half of each year's production will go to blending and bottling until sufficient six-year-old stock is available to launch and maintain a supply of six-year-old 100 per cent pot-still brandy.

Die Poort winery near Herbertsdale produces various brandies, including a pot-still brandy made from Colombar grapes aged for three years and bottled at 43 per cent. A very palatable brandy is also made from apples.

Joseph Barry Brandy is produced at the Barrydale Co-operative, established in 1940 specifically as a distillery. Barrydale Co-op only began bottling wine in 1976, but throughout its history it has produced brandy for sale to merchants. In 1994 the cellar decided to age a portion of its production for bottling. Distilled from Colombar and Ugni Blanc, both traditional varieties used in Cognac, Joseph Barry, labelled as a 5-year-old, has already received international recognition for its fine quality. First production is 5000 cases. The brandy is attractively packaged and bottled at 40 per cent.

The Kango Co-operative in Oudtshoorn produces a number of brandies, one of which is distilled from Hanepoot and labelled accordingly. Limerick is a 3-year-old blended brandy and Valkenier, another blend, has some 5-year-old in the blend.

Mons Ruber near Oudtshoorn has put its vintage stills into operation to produce a pot-still brandy from Hanepoot at a very attractive price. Mons Ruber also produces a 'witblitz' which is very popular in its 200-ml bottle.

### Independent Blenders

First has been Marbonne, named by Stefan Smit after the family farm. The composition originates from the research done on distillation by the Brandy Research Institute at Nietvoorbij. Stefan's blend of his particularly dry style of brandy carries no age statement, although the blend contains brandies of considerable age. Stefan has now installed his own still for future production.

Paul Grinstead created Hamlin House, a blend of three superior pot-still brandies aged three, five and 14 years into 'one' brandy. It is beautifully packaged in a black bottle with gold printing that resembles an upside-down Olympic torch. The Hamlin House crest carries a flaming torch with the legend 'Knowledge, Pride, Integrity'. Hamlin House has also added an Old Reserve (OR) Brandy. Old Reserve is aged for 11 years in a slightly lighter style and bottled in imported French antique green bottles.

Rietrivier Wynkelder near Montagu has bought in brandy and created its own blend sold under the 'John Montagu' label. Both a three- and a five-year-old brandy are available.

Whitby Distillers in Elgin have quietly been distilling a wide range of distillates for more than a decade. Dave Acker is the technical fundi behind this private distilling venture. Acker is a Natal sugar industry-trained man with many years of versatile distilling experience in Scotland, former Rhodesia and the Cape. Besides gin and whisky, Whitby has produced brandy for various wholesalers, and is currently distilling a brandy that will be launched by the Robertson Winery in 2003 or 2005. Robertson Winery produced Colombar, a rebate wine of particular quality. This wine was then double distilled by the specialists at Whitby and returned to Robertson for ageing. Cellar samples promise that it could be one of South Africa's great brandies in the making.

### The Brandy Route

The Brandy Route was established in 1997 by the Stellenbosch-based South African Brandy Foundation, in an attempt to open the South African brandy world to tourists. Initially the route had seven members covering all types and styles of brandy distillation. The distilleries range from minute operations to distilleries with a massive scale of production. Foundation venues were: the Van Ryn Brandy Cellar at Vlottenburg near Stellenbosch; the Oude Molen Brandy Museum in Stellenbosch, which regrettably disappeared as Gilbeys withdrew from the town and closed its primary

production units; Backsberg Estate in Paarl; the Paarl Rock Brandy cellar in Paarl, which also closed to the public although brandy is still being produced; Cabrière Estate in Fanschhoek; Olof Bergh at Goudini Road near Worcester; and the KWV Brandy Cellar in Worcester.

Uitkyk joined the route as soon as it launched its 10-year-old. Recently Avontuur has joined, as have Louisenhof and Claridge. A second brandy route, associated with the Klein Karoo's 'Route 62', will be up and running by 2002. This will include Barrydale, Boplaas, Kango, Grundheim and possibly the Rietrivier Wynkelder.

*(left) Giorgio Dalla Cia with his Grappa still at Meerlust.*

*(far left) Grappa still.*

*(below) Backsberg's automated, computer-controlled, five-hectolitre pot still.*

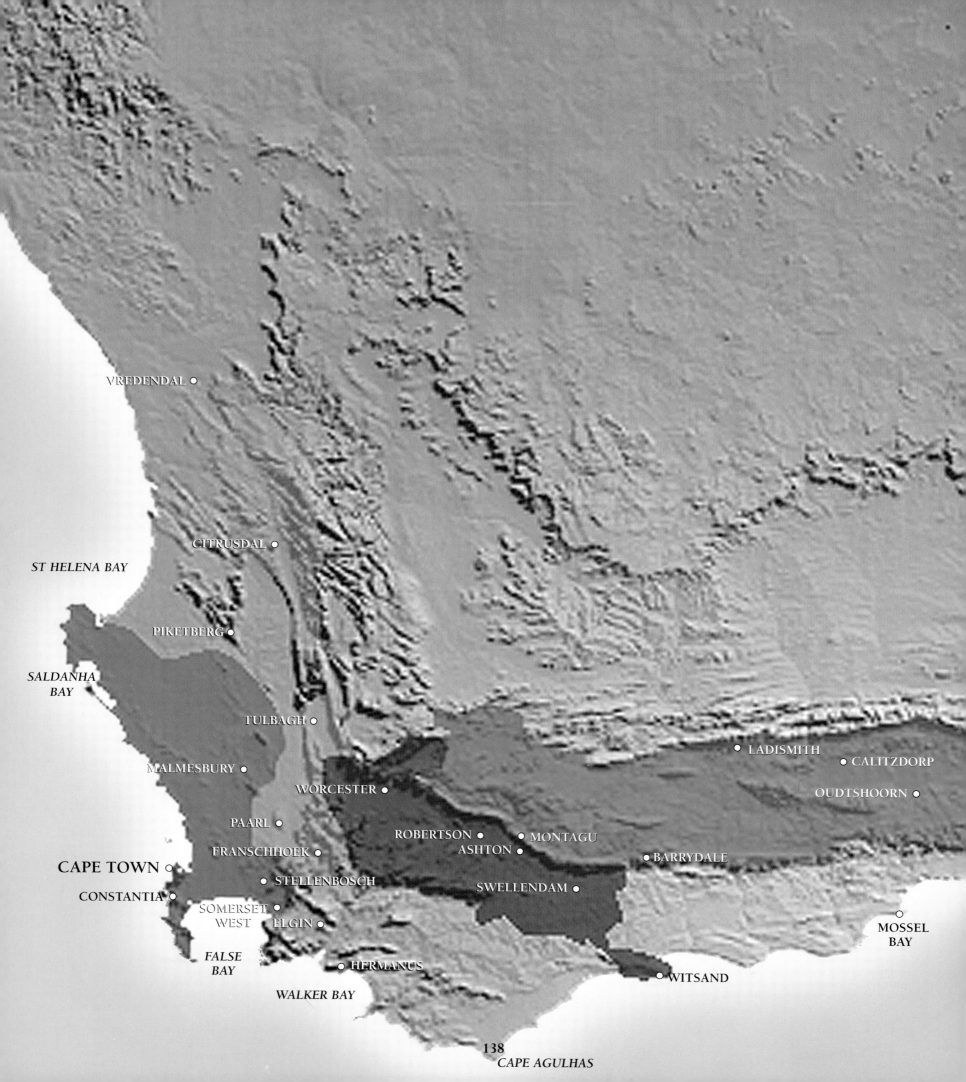

VREDENDAL ○

ST HELENA BAY

CITRUSDAL ○

PIKETBERG ○

SALDANHA
BAY

TULBAGH ○

LADISMITH ○

CALITZDORP ○

MALMESBURY ○

OUDTSHOORN ○

WORCESTER ○

PAARL ○

ROBERTSON ○       ○ MONTAGU

FRANSCHHOEK ○       ASHTON ○

CAPE TOWN ○       BARRYDALE ○

CONSTANTIA ○       STELLENBOSCH ○       SWELLENDAM ○

SOMERSET
WEST       ELGIN ○

MOSSEL
BAY ○

FALSE
BAY

HERMANUS ○       WITSAND ○

WALKER BAY

138

*CAPE AGULHAS*

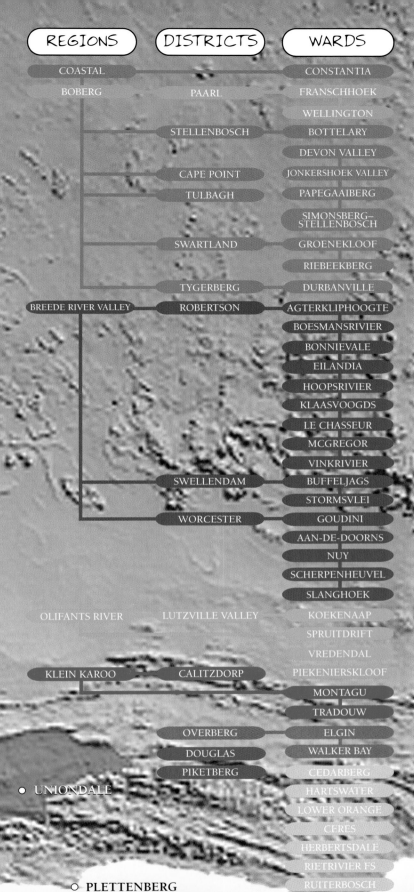

| REGIONS | DISTRICTS | WARDS |
|---|---|---|
| COASTAL | | CONSTANTIA |
| BOBERG | PAARL | FRANSCHHOEK |
| | | WELLINGTON |
| | STELLENBOSCH | BOTTELARY |
| | | DEVON VALLEY |
| | CAPE POINT | JONKERSHOEK VALLEY |
| | TULBAGH | PAPEGAAIBERG |
| | | SIMONSBERG–STELLENBOSCH |
| | SWARTLAND | GROENEKLOOF |
| | | RIEBEEKBERG |
| | TYGERBERG | DURBANVILLE |
| BREEDE RIVER VALLEY | ROBERTSON | AGTERKLIPHOOGTE |
| | | BOESMANSRIVIER |
| | | BONNIEVALE |
| | | EILANDIA |
| | | HOOPSRIVIER |
| | | KLAASVOOGDS |
| | | LE CHASSEUR |
| | | MCGREGOR |
| | | VINKRIVIER |
| | SWELLENDAM | BUFFELJAGS |
| | | STORMSVLEI |
| | WORCESTER | GOUDINI |
| | | AAN-DE-DOORNS |
| | | NUY |
| | | SCHERPENHEUVEL |
| | | SLANGHOEK |
| OLIFANTS RIVER | LUTZVILLE VALLEY | KOEKENAAP |
| | | SPRUITDRIFT |
| | | VREDENDAL |
| KLEIN KAROO | CALITZDORP | PIEKENIERSKLOOF |
| | | MONTAGU |
| | | TRADOUW |
| | OVERBERG | ELGIN |
| | DOUGLAS | WALKER BAY |
| | PIKETBERG | CEDARBERG |
| | | HARTSWATER |
| | | LOWER ORANGE |
| | | CERES |
| | | HERBERTSDALE |
| | | RIETRIVIER FS |
| | | RUITERBOSCH |
| | | SWARTBERG |

UNIONDALE

PLETTENBERG
BAY

# 7 Vignerons

Over the past few years, expansion in the winelands has been phenomenal. New cellars are springing up with remarkable regularity. This chapter is an exhaustive exposition on an ever-changing subject. All cellars are governed by the Wine of Origin legislation, implemented in 1973. First, the legislation defined the meaning of an estate as a property, which may be made up of one or more farms that share the same climate and ecology and are farmed as a unit with production cellars. Second, the legislation defined the boundaries of all production units. A Ward is defined as a small homogeneous area that is normally within the boundaries of a District. A District is a geographic demarcation and a Region is a combination of districts or parts of districts, or it can be a completely separate area.

Like all bureaucratic decisions, the legislation developed incrementally. The Regions, Districts and Wards were demarcated on existing geographic boundaries, and not on soil or climate. As a result, there is no clear way to understand why any particular area would lie in a particular Region or District. For example, Paarl lies in the Coastal Region although it is 50 kilometres inland, while the Hemel en Aarde valley, which is situated only two kilometres from the coast, does not.

The following cellars, estates, co-operatives and wineries are listed alphabetically. Their location is listed for easy reference to the regional map.

## Regions of the Winelands

The logical way to demarcate areas would be on the basis of *terroir*, but as the mountain ranges and rivers in the Cape have such an immediate effect on the surrounding areas, this leads to a bureaucratic nightmare.

Rainfall is heavily influenced by the mountain ranges that differentiate the Little Karoo and Breede River regions from the coastal area. For example, Stellenbosch may receive more than 800 millimetres of rain per year, while Robertson may typically receive less than 300 millimetres of rain per year. The Olifants River Region is also very dry and heavily dependent upon irrigation. The possibility exists that boundaries may be created on the basis of rainfall, but this would not really provide any more information than the current system.

The winemakers differentiate areas by the phenology of the vines. Clearly, Constantia is a later-ripening area than Stellenbosch, and if one were to compare the phenology tables on pages 36 and 37, one would find that Robertson is approximately one to two weeks earlier than Stellenbosch, depending on the variety. Franschhoek, however, a Ward in the Paarl District, is later than Stellenbosch. The distance from the sea does not give a clear indication of when the important phenological stages will occur. The phenology, under normal conditions, is more readily influenced by climate, and ripening conditions are especially dependent upon the cool south-easterly breezes that tend to funnel through the valleys. If one were to discuss phenology in general terms across the regions, then one could argue that ripening would first begin along the West Coast in the Olifants River Region, and this stage would become later and later as one moved west across the Cape. This is a generalisation, however, as the grapes in different Wards will ripen at different times due to their own special climatic conditions.

Measuring the mean temperatures across the Regions does not provide much information either, as Regions that are considered warmer in summer usually have colder temperatures during winter or at night. Thus a milder area will not differ much from an area that has quite considerable temperature fluctuations. One can only refer to ripening conditions and climate to understand properly where Cabernet Sauvignon would be better suited to the soil, than Pinot Noir for instance.

*Map.* Courtesy of Council for Geoscience, Pretoria.

## AAN DE DOORNS CO-OP
Worcester

This co-op was established in 1955 with 35 members, and takes its name from the many thorn trees that grew on the banks of the Nuy River. The first grapes were pressed in 1956, and a total of 4715 tons were crushed. Today the co-op crushes 18 000 tons and has 54 members. It bottles a small proportion of its production, and the balance is delivered in bulk to merchants. During the preparation of the 1997 vintage, winemaker/manager, Alwyn Mostert, went to the aid of a cellar worker who had been overcome by carbon dioxide while cleaning an open tank, and they both died. A sad loss to the industry.

## AFRICAN WINES AND SPIRITS
Stellenbosch

In 1902 Robert Fuller Bertram purchased High Constantia, and for many years excelled in the making of fine red wines. After his death in 1942, his successors continued to make fine reds and excellent fortified wines, moving to Devon valley in 1959. In 1972 Bertrams was purchased by Gilbeys, which developed the property and winery. After Gilbeys decided to consolidate its South African interests by doing away with its primary production units and disposing of a number of brands, a group of marketing men established African Wines and Spirits. They took a number of Gilbeys brands, including Bertrams wines, sherries and brandies, Alphen, Craighall, Mondial and the internationally known Cinzano sparkling wines and vermouth. Immediately one of their inherited brands of brandy, Bertrams VOV 14-year-old, won the trophy for the 'Best Brandy Worldwide' at the International Wine and Spirit Competition. The company's wines are all easy drinking and made to meet the popular palate.

## AGTERKLIPHOOGTE
Robertson

Twenty-four members established the co-op in 1965, when they crushed 4500 tons. With substantial cellar alterations in progress, the cellar now crushes some 6000 tons. The bulk goes to merchants, with a small amount bottled under its own labels.

## AGUSTA WINES
Franschhoek – Paarl

Haute Provence was purchased by Count Riccardo Agusta in 1997 from Peter Younghusband. Agusta merged Haute Provence with La Provence, a farm originally established by Huguenot immigrant, Pierre Joubert. Despite its roots, a 1999 European Court ruling prevented the use of the French name on a South African wine; hence the Agusta name, which is probably still better associated with helicopters and high-speed motorcycles. Nevertheless, the good count intends to have it equally well-known for his wine. Agusta hired the highly talented winemaker John Goschen and constructed a state-of-the-art cellar in 1998. But before Goschen could fully utilise the cellar, he was tragically electrocuted while assisting in its completion. Agusta is now home of the highly popular Angels Tears and to date has produced some stunning Chardonnays that have attracted international attention.

## ALLESVERLOREN ESTATE
Swartland

The Malan family has owned Allesverloren since 1870. The farm was divided up by successive generations, and the homestead, on about 200 hectares, now makes up the farm. Fanie Malan is the current owner with son Danie in charge of the wine making. Currently 160 hectares are planted to vines and 30 additional hectares will be planted to vines by 2004. The most planted variety is Cabernet Sauvignon followed by Shiraz. Six port varieties are currently planted on the farm and the popular Late Bottled Vintage Port accounts for 20 per cent of local market sales for fortified dessert wines.

## ALTO ESTATE
Stellenbosch

Hennie Malan bought this property in 1919. The Malans did not have the technical expertise available today, but realised that the type of soil and its west-facing vineyards would be best for red varieties. They planted Cabernet Sauvignon, Shiraz and Cinsaut for a blend they called Alto Rouge. The wine was an instant success. It was exported in casks to London from 1923 until 1956 and has remained a firm favourite both at home and abroad. Piet du Toit took over the responsibilities in the cellar in 1957 and eventually handed over to his son Hempies in 1983. In 2000 Hempies moved to Annandale and the new winemaker is Schalk van der Merwe. The most planted vines at Alto are Cabernet Sauvignon followed by Merlot, Cabernet Franc and Shiraz. Alto will continue to produce two red wines and a new Cape-style port. This will be made from Shiraz, which is no longer being used in the blend.

## ALTYDGEDACHT ESTATE
Durbanville

The property was granted to Elsje van Suurwaarde in 1698, as her husband, an officer of the Dutch East India Company, was not allowed to own land. The farm was then called De Tygerbergen, and supplied fresh produce to the Dutch East India Company. Situated on the outskirts of Durbanville, Altydgedacht has one of the longest histories of continuous wine making. The first wines were sold from the farm in 1730. The Parker family have owned Altydgedacht since 1852. Oliver and John Parker took over the running of the farm from their mother, Jean, in 1984. In 1985 Altydgedacht became a registered estate and began bottling its own wines. The estate presently produces a range of five red and three white wines. Its most notable red wine is a Barbera, which is currently the only Cape wine made from this Italian grape. An unusual and popular red wine is Tintoretto which is a 50/50 blend of Shiraz and Barbera that are fermented together. Altydgedacht's Gewürztraminer is still one of the few to be bone dry in the true Alsace style. Altydgedacht is 415 hectares in extent and 130 hectares are planted to vines.

## AMANI
Stellenbosch

Mark Makepeace bought this 35-hectare farm in 1995. He built a showpiece cellar and named the farm Amani, which means 'peace' in Swahili. The label design is unique, inspired by African artist Credo Mutwa's striking hieroglyphics. Amani's first wines were released in 1997. The current range includes Merlot, Chardonnay, Sauvignon Blanc and a wooded Chenin Blanc.

## AMBELOUI WINE CELLAR
Hout Bay

Financial executive and wine enthusiast Nick Christodoulou bought a plot in Hout Bay to build a family home. He eventually built a cellar beneath the house to accommodate his passion for making a Champagne-style wine. Using traditional methods, Christodoulou now produces about 400 cases of hand-crafted Cap Classique.

## ANNANDALE
Stellenbosch

Hempies du Toit, formerly of Alto, has taken on the daunting task of developing this neglected farm. Annandale, registered in 1688, is one of the oldest farms in the Stellenbosch district. Wines from the farm could have been produced as early as the 1700s. Presently, Annandale has 45 hectares planted to vines with 15 hectares still in development. Cabernet Sauvignon is the most planted variety, followed by Merlot, Shiraz and Cabernet Franc. Only two red wines will be bottled and, in time, a port.

## APPELSDRIFT WINERY
Robertson

Kobus van der Merwe is the winemaker and manager of this new venture controlled by Wouter de Wet. A few years ago, Wouter bought a farm and soon discovered that it was a perfect site for the production of high-quality wine grapes. Over the past three years he has planted varieties that include Cabernet Sauvignon, Merlot, Shiraz and Chardonnay. Instead of building a cellar on the farm, he decided to buy Clairvaux Cellar, situated on the outskirts of Robertson. The cellar is being rebuilt and the first vintage will be vinified in 2002.

## ASHANTI
Paarl

Ashanti is derived from a Swahili term meaning 'thank you'. Established in 1997 by a group of international shareholders with Manfred Schoeni at the helm, the estate is exporting successfully to Belgium, the United Kingdom and to its sister restaurant, Ashanti Dome in Shanghai. A new cellar built in time for the 1998 harvest produces 30 000 cases from 95 hectares set in the Klein Drakenstein area of Paarl. The estate also features the Il Cesale restaurant which serves Cape Mediterranean cuisine.

## ASHBOURNE
Walker Bay – Overberg

Single-vineyard Chardonnay and Pinot Noir premium-priced wines are produced from ideal sites by Hamilton Russell Vineyards. For more information, see also Hamilton Russell Vineyards.

## ASHTON CO-OP
Robertson

This co-op, established in 1962 with 65 members, has grown to 94 members. The co-op draws grapes from 1300 hectares. It crushes 24 500 tons and bottles 10 000 cases. The bulk of the wine is delivered to merchants.

## ASHWOOD WINES
Franschhoek – Paarl

Ashwood is a *négociant* winery that provides bottling services for other wine producers. New cellars in Simondium produce about 70 per cent of production for export. The owners also have an interest in developing a nursery business to supply plant material.

## AUDACIA WINES
Stellenbosch

Johannesburg-based insurance whiz Trevor Strydom has given this old property a new life. Since the purchase of this Stellenbosch estate in 1996, Strydom has had a steady development programme and at long last the maturing winery is producing some very acceptable wines.

## AVONDALE
Paarl

In 1996 Vital Health CEO John Grieve and his wife Ginny purchased Avondale, situated below the towering Klein Drakenstein mountain. The farm, established in the early 1800s, has been beautifully restored. Although 60 hectares have been planted, Avondale only produces 4000 cases. So far, Avondale has released some outstanding Cabernet, Shiraz and Sauvignon Blanc, and an unusual sweet fortified 'Muscat du Cap'.

## AVONREDE
Paarl

John and Christine Enthoven purchased this small property on the Paarl side of the Simonsberg in 1995. A minute production was kept for their own consumption until the recent launch of their Konigshof Noble Red. The wine is a Bordeaux-style blend with a Cape character.

## AVONTUUR ESTATE
Helderberg – Stellenbosch

Horses and vines, combined with Avontuur's Victorian cellar, provide a magnificent vista on the western slopes of the Helderberg mountains. Tony Taberer, a tobacco baron from Zimbabwe, bought Avontuur in the late 1970s and replanted the farm to classic grape varieties. Dynamic winemaker, Lizelle Gerber, made a statement with her 1999 vintage, her first at Avontuur, gaining recognition for her Sauvignon Blanc and Dolcetto wines at the Singapore 2000 Wine Challenge in very good company. Avontuur also won a Gold for the same Sauvignon Blanc at the prestigious Michelangelo competition and Golds for the 1999 Noble Late Harvest and Avontuur Bordeaux-style blend, Baccarat. Sixty hectares are planted to Cabernet Sauvignon, Chardonnay, Pinotage, Merlot and Sauvignon Blanc. Avontuur has released a Premier range in addition to seven white wines, including a Méthode Cap Classique, and eight red wines. Avontuur can also boast an excellent five-year-old pot-still brandy that is served on the Blue Train.

## AXE HILL
Calitzdorp – Klein Karoo

In 1990 Cape Wine Master, Tony Mossop, bought Axe Hill in order to satisfy his desire to make a 'proper' port. This one-hectare property can certainly lay claim to being the smallest commercial vineyard in South Africa. Tony has planted Touriga Naçional and Tinta Barocca and in 2001 he is adding a further portion of Souzão. Traditional Portuguese methods for making this port are the order of the day and the total crop of six tons is hand-picked and crushed entirely by foot. A winner of the Grape 2000 Packaging Award, Axe Hill Cape Vintage Port is elegantly packaged in a 500-ml bottle.

## BACKSBERG ESTATE
Paarl

Sydney Back, the doyen of South African winemakers, passed away in 1996, after celebrating 60 vintages at Backsberg. Sydney began working on the farm as a schoolboy. In 1945 he won the General Smuts Trophy as Champion Winemaker. He produced the country's first inexpensive semi-sweet wine, and won the first 'Superior' rating after the introduction of the Wine of Origin system in 1973. He was the Diners Club 'Winemaker of the Year' in 1986, and at the 1995 International Wine and Spirit Competition, his 1986 Chardonnay received the Cape Wine Academy Trophy for the best South African white wine. He was twice South African Champion Winemaker, and was honoured by the KWV in 1996 for his contributions to the Wine and Spirit industry. When most people would have thought of retiring, Sydney started distilling brandy, and his first release was awarded the Domecq Trophy for the best brandy. In the same year the Cape Wine Masters selected him as their 'Personality of the Year', and in November 1995 he was made a member of the Brandy Guild of the South African Brandy Foundation. Sidney's son, Michael Back, together with winemaker Hardy Laubscher, have taken this estate into the new millennium with up-to-the-minute efficiency. One hundred and sixty hectares are planted to Chardonnay, Cabernet Sauvignon, Merlot, Pinotage, Barbera and Sangiovese. The range includes seven white wines, including a Méthode Cap Classique, and six red wines.

## BADSBERG CO-OP
Worcester

The Badsberg Co-op, established in 1951, crushed its first grapes in 1952. The co-op, with 26 members, crushes 15 000 tons from 855 hectares. Most of the production is delivered in bulk to merchants, but some is used in Pernod Ricard's Long Mountain range of wines. Badsberg is best known for its fortified Hanepoot.

## BAREFOOT WINE COMPANY
Stellenbosch

Cathy Marshall has an impressive record, having worked in cellars in Saint Emilion, Oregon and California. She has finally decided to become a *négociant* after doing duty at a number of the Cape's well-known cellars. She is currently crushing 20 tons, but this figure could soon double. Top of the range is a 1999 Shiraz. She has also released a Pinot Noir and Pineau des Charentes.

## BARRYDALE CO-OP
Klein Karoo

Despite its name, this winery is also a long time producer of fine brandy after originally being established as a distillery in the early 1940s. Wine making was eventually added and in 1985 the co-op began to bottle some of its production under the Tradouw label. In the past, Barrydale's brandy had only been delivered to merchants. Now its pot-still production is matured for five years in small oak and bottled under the Joseph Barry label. This transformation has brought forth some international recognition. Today 45 members deliver some 4000 tons of grapes.

## BARTHO EKSTEEN WINES
Overberg

After putting Wildekrans firmly and successfully on the wine map, Bartho Eksteen has launched his own wines. Sauvignon Blanc remains his passion and he presently bottles a very good example of this wine. His first Shiraz, from the 2000 vintage, has still to make its debut, but his enthusiasm for this variety should be well rewarded.

*(below) Autumn colours at Klein Constantia.*

## BEAUMONT WINES
Overberg

Raoul and Jayne Beaumont live on this historic farm in Bot River which served as an outpost for the Dutch East India Company in the 1700s. Raoul decided to revitalise the old wine cellar in 1993, and made a small batch of Pinotage from an 18-year-old vineyard. In December 1995 he appointed Niels Verbrug as winemaker. Their flagship wines in the future will be Pinotage and a wooded Chenin Blanc made from 30-year-old vines.

## BELLVUE ESTATE
Stellenbosch

Situated on Bottelary Road, this Stellenbosch estate has been producing wine for many years. Bellvue pioneered the world's first Pinotage when in 1959 the Morkels of Bellvue created a sensation at the Cape Wine Show by taking the prize for the best wine on show with this relatively unknown variety. This wine, launched under the Lanzerac label, made up part of the world's first ever Pinotage to enter the wine market. In the following years, the Morkels' wine was sold in bulk to merchants. Now in a joint venture with KWV, the pick of Dirkie Morkel's production is being bottled for export. The new venture has produced spectacular wines with Pinotage at centre stage. Tumara, a New World, Bordeaux-style blend, has grabbed attention and Bellvue is also producing a significant amount of Malbec.

## BERGKELDER, THE
Stellenbosch

The Bergkelder was opened in 1968. Through a marketing partnership, it handles the quality wines for a range of estates spread across the winelands. This venture has slowly toned down since many cellars have decided to promote themselves independently. Today Allesverloren, Jacobsdal, Rietvallei, Theuniskraal and Fort Simon wines are still marketed by the Bergkelder. The cellar produces its own range of wines under the labels Fleur du Cap and Stellenryck. The actual cellar is built into the Papegaaiberg and has first-class facilities for visitors and sales.

## BERGSIG ESTATE
Worcester

Bergsig is one of the Cape's largest estates, producing 3000 tons from 250 hectares. The estate has been owned by the Lategan family since 1843. Over the years various family farms were consolidated by 'Prop' Lategan. Bergsig's winemaker is De Wet Lategan, and the estate is a founder member of Cape Vineyards, a consortium of Worcester co-ops that concentrates on exports. Bergsig produces a wide range of wines, with its Edel Laatoes consistently highly rated. The 1997 Late Bottled Vintage Port is also worth seeking out. There are 12 whites and four reds bottled under the Bergsig label. In recent years it has made a name with its reds, including Cabernet Sauvignon and Pinotage.

## BERNHEIM
Paarl

Owned by the Schwulst Family Trust, Bernheim produces about 60 tons and some 4000 cases of predominantly red varieties. Whimsical stories are behind the sentimental names, and rustic production has remained the norm at this establishment. Bottling, corking and labelling are all still done by hand. An old concrete water tank is now the tasting room, appropriately named 'Dop and Dam'.

## BEYERSKLOOF
Stellenbosch

Five hectares are planted to Cabernet Sauvignon and Merlot on this small property owned by Beyers Truter and partners, Johann and Paul Krige. Beyers equipped the cellar on a minimal budget. He found a grape press in Robertson that was being used for sheep food and he paid for it with two cases of wine, even though it

was incomplete. The press is now working perfectly. Top of the range is a Cabernet Sauvignon/Merlot blend, which is presently sourced from the farm and specially selected bought-in grapes. Only the Beyerskloof Bordeaux-style blend and a particularly good Pinotage are bottled under this popular label. An impressive 70 000 cases are currently bottled.

## BILTON WINES
Stellenbosch

Simon van der Stel granted the farm Bonte Rivier to Willem Jansz van de Wêreld in 1694. After a chequered history, the Bilton Trust bought Bonte Rivier in 1957 and Mark Bilton is now the owner of 400 hectares on the slopes of the Helderberg. To date, 64 hectares are planted to Cabernet Sauvignon, Merlot, Shiraz, Pinotage and Sauvignon Blanc. A further 40 hectares are planned to include Mourvèdre, Petit Verdot and Roobernet. The old wine cellar, built in 1824, was restored in 2000 and Mark released his first vintage, a 1998 Merlot in that year. Currently Merlot and Cabernet Sauvignon are the only wines on the market.

## BLAAUWKLIPPEN FARMERS MARKT
Stellenbosch

First granted in 1682 to German immigrants, Blaauwklippen was purchased in 1971 by Graham Boonzaier, who totally revitalised the property and appointed winemaker Walter Finlayson. Walter was replaced by Jacques Kruger in 1989 and Blaauwklippen, with a production of 35 000 cases, has an excellent record of success. Its Zinfandel, in particular, has been the leading label for this variety in the Cape over the past decade, and has even achieved success in California. Now more than three centuries later the property is once more in the hands of German owners, Farmers Markt and Landhandel GmbH. According to the group's chairman, Blaauwklippen was purchased to expand and give additional dimension to the group's beverage interests. The recent purchase of a brandy pot still from Oude Molen hints at a multiple change in direction. To date, 70 hectares are planted to Zinfandel, Shiraz, Cabernet Sauvignon, Chardonnay and Sauvignon Blanc. A further 25 hectares are in the pipeline. The range consists of seven white and seven red wines. A feature of the property is a collection of horse-drawn vehicles, leading to the names of the blended wines Landau and Cabriolet.

## BLOEMENDAL ESTATE
Durbanville

Bloemendal is owned by Jackie Coetzee. The farm is situated in the Durbanville area and Jackie produces 4500 cases from 146 hectares. Known for its Cabernet Sauvignon, the farm also produces a commendable Merlot and a couple of good white wines.

## BLOUPUNT WINES
Klein Karoo

The Hoffman family began this venture with two hectares of Chardonnay. After significant growth, the farm is producing 4000 cases, and another 3.5 hectares of Merlot, Chardonnay and Ruby Cabernet are in the planning stage.

## BLUE CREEK
Stellenbosch

Piet Smal puts quality first on this five-hectare smallholding in the Blaauwklip valley. Production remains at 1000 cases of polished Cabernet Sauvignon, with Pinotage and Merlot expected to follow.

## BODEGA
Paarl

Julianne Barlow, with help from brother Jeremy Squire, has taken over this 14-hectare property on the Joostenberg Vlakte. Eugene van Zyl helps with the wine making and viticulturist Paul Wallace with the vineyard. Cabernet Sauvignon and Merlot are the only

wines bottled on the property and they are sold under the Beaconsfield label in the United Kingdom.

## BOEKENHOUTSKLOOF
Franschhoek – Paarl

Boekenhoutskloof is named after the Cape beech and remains one of the oldest farms in Franschhoek. Its homestead, dating to 1784, has been immaculately restored. The farm is situated far up the valley, close to the source of the Franschhoek River. The unique label with seven chairs represents the seven partners in this venture. Winemaker Marc Kent has produced sensational wines, especially his Syrah which has received international acclaim. The estate can also boast about its outstanding Cabernet, Pinotage and Sémillon. Its second label, named Porcupine Ridge, pays homage to the many porcupines that frequent the property.

## BOLAND WINE CELLAR
Paarl

The Boland Wine Cellar, established in 1947, was the product of an amalgamation of various co-ops. Fifty years later, its success in both local and international competitions reflects the great strides this company has made. The Boland Wine Cellar has now become a company under the name Boland Vineyards International, with 114 shareholders. Production runs to 20 000 tons and the company has strong marketing ties with Holland and Germany where it participates in a joint venture with German wine-marketing group WIF. Its consumer-friendly wines are highlighted by Bon Vino Dry White in a 500-ml screw-top bottle which has twice gained gold at Veritas. The wine-making team recently won 'Winemaker of the Year' at the 2001 International Wine and Spirit Competition.

## BON COURAGE ESTATE
Robertson

Bon Courage is owned by André Bruwer, who together with his son Jacques makes the wine on this model farm. The estate has a gabled tasting room and underground cellar where the much-acclaimed Cap Classique, Jacques Bruére, Brut Millennium is produced. In 1990 Jacques was Diners Club 'Winemaker of the Year' for a Gewürztraminer Special Late Harvest and this wine continues to be one of the flagship wines. The 1999 Shiraz, made in a Rhône style, is also particularly good. A total of 200 hectares is planted to vines with a further 10 to 15 hectares on the drawing board. New varieties will include Petit Verdot and Touriga Naçional.

## BONFOI ESTATE
Stellenbosch

Originally linked to the Bergkelder, Bonfoi has not produced wine since 1994. Johannes van der Westhuizen has rejuvenated this 200-hectare estate, planting Cabernet Sauvignon, Shiraz, Chardonnay, Merlot and Sauvignon Blanc. First release is a Cabernet Sauvignon.

## BONNIEVALE CO-OP
Bonnievale – Robertson

Bonnievale Co-op was established in 1964. Its attractive façade, together with tasting and sales facilities, was added in the early 1980s. The co-op is a specialist Colombar and fortified wine producer, with 60 members producing 13 000 tons. A new red wine making facility came into production with the 2000 vintage and members have planted substantial quantities of red varieties, with Shiraz dominant. Large volumes are exported in bulk, while locally bottled Kelkiewit and Kelkierooi are very popular.

## BOPLAAS
Calitzdorp – Klein Karoo

Boplaas is 80 kilometres from the sea and lies directly in line with two gaps in the Gamka mountains. These gaps channel cool afternoon breezes, creating better ripening conditions which are perfect for quality grape production. Grapes have been grown on Boplaas for wine and brandy production for over 150 years, and brandy was exported to London as far back as 1860. With the recent changes in legislation, Boplaas has returned to distilling, producing a Boplaas Pot Still Brandy and a Carel Nel Reserve. The farm has been a leader in the production of drier ports along the lines of those of Portugal. The current owner is Cape Wine Master, Carel Nel. Carel has added Touriga Naçional and Touriga Francesca to the range of varieties grown for fine port production. Seventy-five hectares are planted to port varieties, Cabernet Sauvignon, Pinotage, Merlot and Sangiovese. Boplaas bottles six white natural table wines and six red.

## BOSCHENDAL
### Franschhoek – Paarl

The farm was originally granted to Jean le Long, one of the first Huguenots to arrive at the Cape. In 1715 the farm was sold to Abraham de Villiers. The family developed the vineyards and an impressive farm complex. In 1812 Paul de Villiers completed a Flemish-style homestead for his wife. The De Villiers family was forced to sell Boschendal in 1879 due to the collapse of the wine export market to Great Britain. A few years later Boschendal was one of 30 farms bought as a Rhodes Fruit Farm. Boschendal was purchased by the Anglo American Corporation in 1969, and was painstakingly restored by renowned architect, Gabriel Fagan. The manor house, now a museum, is furnished with period pieces and a fine collection of Ming porcelain. The estate stretches over 3500 hectares, but only 350 hectares are planted to Sauvignon Blanc, Chardonnay, Merlot, Cabernet Sauvignon and Shiraz. There are still plans to plant a further 30 hectares and Viognier will be included in the new plantings. The winery at Boschendal was upgraded during 1995 and 1996, and a new red wine cellar has been developed. Boschendal is known for its innovation and experimentation, and two of the most notable examples are a Boschendal Blanc de Noir, and a wooded Sauvignon Blanc blend, Grand Vin Blanc. An impressive range runs to 12 white wines, including a Méthode Cap Classique, and five reds.

## BOSCHKLOOF WINES
### Stellenbosch

Dr Reenen Furter has developed this 25-hectare property in one of the prime vineyard areas of Stellenbosch. The wine making is done by Reenen, and his son-in-law Jacques Borman oversees the technical side whenever he can take a couple of hours off from his responsibilities at La Motte. Fifteen hectares are currently planted to Cabernet Sauvignon, Merlot, Chardonnay and Shiraz. Another three hectares will be planted to Shiraz and Cabernet Franc. Boschkloof wines are complex and well structured.

## BOTHA WINE CELLAR
### Worcester

The co-op was established in 1948 with 17 members. By 1950 a cellar was built and today it crushes 20 000 tons. To celebrate its fiftieth anniversary, special packaged magnums were released. The arrival of Dassie Smith in 1997 has upped the overall standard. Today 56 members deliver about 24 000 tons of grapes.

## BOTTELARY CO-OP
### Stellenbosch

Bottelary Co-op was established in 1946 by eight farmers. In the early 1970s winemaker Danie Zeeman produced creditable wines. After his departure due to ill health, the co-op continued to develop, and in the 1990s merged with four other co-ops to form Stellenbosch Vineyards. Stellenbosch Vineyards introduced 'flying' winemakers and a more modern, accessible style of early-drinking wines. Nearly 40 members deliver 11 000 tons of grapes from 1000 hectares.

## BOUCHARD FINLAYSON
### Walker Bay – Overberg

Peter Finlayson and Paul Bouchard bought this property in 1990. The Hemel en Aarde valley is one of the coolest areas in the Cape and particularly suited to Pinot Noir production. Bouchard Finlayson crushed its first vintage in 1991 and the grapes for these wines were sourced from the Elgin area. Since 1993 Bouchard Finlayson has harvested grapes from its domaine. Plantings of Pinot Noir account for almost 50 per cent of total planting, and Bouchard Finlayson must be rated as one of the most innovative farms in South Africa. Vines are planted in five rows 1.1 metres apart, with spacing at one metre in the row, to give 7500 vines per hectare. Every sixth row is left open so that a tractor can spray. Most pruning in South Africa is done on a short spur of about two buds, with four spurs on each arm. Bouchard Finlayson have opted for two canes on each arm with about eight buds on each cane. Innovation in the vineyards has translated to wines of critical acclaim. Bouchard Finlayson's Tête de Cuvée Galpin Peak Pinot Noir is outstanding. The range also includes Galpin Peak Pinot Noir, three Chardonnays, a Pinot Blanc/Chardonnay blend and a Sauvignon Blanc.

## BOUWLAND
### Stellenbosch

Johann and Paul Krige along with Beyers Truter of Kanonkop and Beyerskloof fame have re-run the recipe with their investment in this Bottelary property. Development started in 1997 and 120 hectares are already planted mostly to Pinotage with a bit of Merlot and Cabernet Sauvignon. The first vintage Cabernet Sauvignon/Merlot was crushed from bought-in grapes from surrounding farms and the mouth-filling Pinotage is already selling in 20 countries.

## BOVLEI WINERY
### Wellington – Paarl

Bovlei is one of the earliest co-ops established in the Cape, dating back to 1907. It is unusual in that it has a 60 red to 40 white ratio. A wide range of wines are produced for the local and export market. Today there are 56 members who deliver about 8000 tons. Bovlei is also one of four partners in the Wellington-based Cape Wine Cellars.

## BOWE JOUBERT
### Stellenbosch

This 150-hectare farm, situated on the highest part of the Vlaeberg on the old Polkadraai Road, was first granted in 1695. In 2000 the Jouberts sold 75 per cent of the land to Bahamian entrepreneur, Alphonso Bowe. In 1995 Bowe had also purchased a large farm in the Worcester area and replanted to classic varieties. The yields there now find their way to the upgraded Stellenbosch farm. The Stellenbosch property sells its wine in bulk to Longridge. Major replanting is underway to change the mix to 60 per cent red and 40 per cent white varieties. Wines are destined for export to hotels and restaurants in the Bahamas and United States.

## BRANDVLEI WINERY
### Worcester

The Brandvlei Co-operative was formed in 1955, however, the rising Brandvlei embankment threatened flooding of the cellar's original site. This meant winemakers were forced to rebuild a modern cellar safe from the nearby river's rising waters. They did so in time to receive grapes from the 1975 vintage. Today the cellar has 32 members and crushes about 20 000 tons of grapes. About 4000 cases are bottled under its own label, with the balance going in bulk to merchants. About 90 per cent of the production is white.

## BREDELL J.P. WINES
### Helderberg – Stellenbosch

The name Bredell has long been associated with port and Anton Bredell matches his style as closely as possible to the Portuguese. Bredell Wines is considered the largest privately owned port operation in the world with an annual production of 1800 tons. Its port has been judged the South African Champion Port at the annual South Africa National Young Wine Show, and the Cape Vintage Reserve was awarded a five-star rating by *Wine* magazine and *John Platter South African Wines*. Bredell is not only producing port under the Bredell and Helderzicht labels, but also some dry red wines, including a Pinotage and a Pinotage/Shiraz blend under the Sinai Hill label. One of these wines, the 1998 Merlot, won a trophy at the prestigious International Wine and Spirit Competition.

## BRENTHURST
### Paarl

Josi Jordaan backed into this boutique winery with his first vintage in 1994. With just five hectares planted to Cabernet Sauvignon, Merlot, Cabernet Franc and Petit Verdot, production will remain at 5000 cases. In the February 2000 issue of *International Wine Magazine*, the 1996 Brenthurst Cabernet Sauvignon/Merlot blend was rated amongst the top-scoring South African wines in very good company.

## BUITENVERWACHTING
### Constantia

The farm was originally part of Simon van der Stel's Constantia estate. In 1793 the farm, then known as Bergvliet, was sold to Cornelis Brink who changed its name to Buitenverwachting. Buitenverwachting has had many owners, and of them all, Ryk Cloete, the brother of Hendrik Cloete of Constantia fame, was the most successful. In 1981 Richard Mueller bought Buitenverwachting, and it was only a matter of time before the farm became the showpiece it is today. Lars Maack is a director and co-owner with Christine Mueller. He has developed this property into a dynamic but low-key business. A large new cellar was built, the historical homestead and other farm buildings were restored, and a tasting venue and restaurant were built. Jean Daneel was appointed as winemaker, and the first 100 tons of grapes were crushed in 1985. Since 1993 winemaker Herman Kirschbaum has produced an excellent range of red and white wines that includes Christine, a Bordeaux-style blend, a Cabernet Sauvignon, Chardonnay, Sauvignon Blanc and one of the Cape's top quality Rhine Riesling wines. A quality Méthode Cap Classique is also in the range.

## CABRIERE ESTATE
### Franschhoek – Paarl

In 1694 land in Franschhoek was granted to French Huguenot settler, Pierre Jourdan, and named Olifantshoek. Jourdan renamed his new farm Cabrière after the French village Cabrière d'Aigues where he was born. In 1982 Achim von Arnim bought 25 hectares, including the original cellar. The estate is well known for its Cap Classique wines. Achim purchased a further 15 hectares on the slopes of the Franschhoek mountain, where he built a most attractive cellar into the mountain. Here he produces his 'still' Pinot Noir red wine. The Haute Cabrière Chardonnay/Pinot Noir, made as a 'still wine', more than doubled production in 1996 to 10 000 cases because of the demand and total production now stands at 30 000 cases. A novelty is Petit Pierre Ratafia, a Chardonnay aperitif fortified with pot-still Chardonnay brandy, with an alcohol content of 20 per cent.

## CALITZDORP CO-OP
### Klein Karoo

As with most wineries in Calitzdorp, port is a feature at this cellar and for many years the Ruby Port was considered not only a very good example of this style but also excellent value for money. Alwyn Burger, winemaker for just over a decade, has recently released a 1997 Late Bottled Vintage Port – his first – using only traditional Portuguese grape varieties. The wine

has been as well received as the fortified muscadel wines have always been. Today 66 members deliver 3000 tons, including Cabernet Sauvignon, Merlot, Chardonnay and Sauvignon Blanc.

### CAMBERLEY WINES
Stellenbosch

Camberley is a small boutique winery situated at the top of Helshoogte. John Nel has two and a half hectares planted to Cabernet Sauvignon and Merlot. A further five hectares, planted to Merlot, Cabernet Sauvignon, Cabernet Franc and Shiraz, have been leased on a neighbouring farm. Currently the Nels vinify a 1999 Cabernet Sauvignon/Merlot blend and a Merlot of the same vintage.

### CAPE BAY (NEWTON JOHNSON WINES)
Overberg

Cape Wine Master Dave Johnson started Cape Bay as a *négociant* brand in 1991 for export. In 1996 Dave bought a property in the Hemel en Aarde valley for his winery. The choice wines are bottled under the name Newton Johnson Wines. Grapes for Cape Bay wines are sourced from the Breede River valley. The Cape Bay range includes five white wines and three reds which are all highly commendable. The Newton Johnson range is distributed locally from the Johnson property.

### CAPE CHAMONIX WINE FARM
Franschhoek – Paarl

Chamonix is one of the larger farms in the Franschhoek valley. Chris Hellinger, owner of this lovely property on the higher slopes of the Franschhoek mountains, must be delighted with his achievements. Winemaker Peter Arnold has excelled in getting the very best from the vineyards. An award that

must be mentioned follows the 1999 Chardonnay du Monde Competition held in Paris. Chamonix's 1997 Chardonnay Reserve was the only South African wine to be awarded a Gold Medal out of 882 Chardonnays entered from 31 countries. Only 16 Gold Medals were awarded by 88 international judges over a period of three days. Chamonix is planted to 50 hectares of Chardonnay, Sauvignon Blanc, Cabernet Sauvignon, Merlot, Pinotage and Pinot Noir. The vineyards will be increased by another six hectares over the next few years. Six white wines, including a Méthode Cap Classique, and four reds will be bottled eventually.

### CAPE POINT VINEYARDS
Cape Point

Owned by Sybrand van der Spuy, this endeavour has three different vineyard sites. Its older vines are situated below Chapmans Peak on the Atlantic side of the Constantiaberg, where mostly white and Pinot Noir grapes are planted. Cabernet Sauvignon and Shiraz are appropriately planted on Redhill above Simon's Town. Close to Fish Hoek, about 35 hectares are planted, but should soon reach a total of 50 hectares. In 2000 winemaker, Emmanuel Bolliger, surprised the cognoscenti by winning the Jan Smuts Trophy as 'Grand Champion' for his Sauvignon Blanc.

### CAPE VINEYARDS
Rawsonville – Worcester

This is a joint venture between a number of Breede River producers who source wine, mainly in bulk, from their own and other cellars for export. Additionally, they bottle under the labels Rawson's and Andrew Bain, the latter named after the famous Scottish pioneer and road builder,. Andrew Geddes Bain.

*Buitenverwachting manor house and vineyards.*

### CAPE WINE CELLARS
Wellington – Paarl

Cape Wine Cellars is owned by South African Dried Fruit Holdings. It is mainly an export operation and moves considerable quantities to Europe and the Far East under the Limiet Vallei and Kleinbosch labels. The wines have now also been launched locally. Under the experienced palate of Jeff Wedgwood, wines are sourced from the Boland Wine Cellar in Paarl and the Wellington co-ops of Bovlei, Wellington and Wamakersvallei. Names like Morning Mist and Twist Niet are becoming well known and export sales have reached a remarkable 400 000 cases, the main brands being Kleinbosch and Cape Safari ranges.

### CARISBROOKE
Stellenbosch

Owned by senior counsel Willem Pretorius, whose single wine, a Cabernet Sauvignon, from his six-hectare vineyard is highly rated.

### CEDERBERG CELLARS
Olifants River

These vineyards, planted at 1100 metres above sea level, are at a higher altitude than any other wine estate in the Cape. Owned by the Nieuwoudt family since 1835, the farm began harvesting table grapes in the mid-1960s and by the early 1970s, wine grapes were added. David Nieuwoudt, an Elsenburg-trained winemaker, took over the farm in 1997 and has been creating successful wines ever since. Cederberg Cellars earned a spot among South African Airways' selection, a Veritas Double Gold Award, a runner-up position in the Wine Chenin Challenge and other distinctions. At present vines cover 23 hectares, with plantings of mainly white varieties and some Pinotage, but winemakers plan to expand by another 15 hectares with Merlot and Shiraz. Other than wine, the farm offers wonderful weekend retreats with self-catering cottages in a rugged mountain setting.

## CILMOR
Worcester

Owned by the Cilmor Trust, this heavily invested, monster winery and very large vineyard of 700 hectares produces only for export in a venture with Sonop.

## CLARIDGE WINES
Wellington – Paarl

Roger Jorgensen was a strawberry farmer in England before coming to South Africa in the mid-1980s. He produced his first Chardonnay in 1991, which was snapped up by the export market. Jorgenson produces 15 000 cases from 17 hectares and 90 per cent is red. In 1994 he launched his pot-still five-year-old brandy, distilling Colombar on Chardonnay lees. Four Claridge red wines are made and one white. Recently Jorgenson formed a company called 'The Pinotage Chardonnay Cabernet Pudding Wine Company' which gives a different slant to a second label. The full name appears on every label as a brand name.

## CLOS DU CIEL
Stellenbosch

Previously owned by John and Erica Platter, this small 1.6-hectare property has now been acquired by Peter Aschke. André Morgenthal has been entrusted with the wine making. A Chardonnay Reserve will be released during 2001 and two red wines, a Pinot Noir and a Shiraz/Cabernet Sauvignon blend, should be released in 2002.

## CLOS MALVERNE ESTATE
Stellenbosch

Seymour Pritchard bought Clos Malverne in 1970 and gradually replanted his vineyards to Pinotage, Cabernet Sauvignon, Merlot and Shiraz. Until 1986 he sold his grapes to a producing wholesaler in Stellenbosch. By the year 2000 Pritchard wanted 70 per cent of his cellar production to be Pinotage. One year later he is already at 60 per cent, developing a dynamic export market. Since his son, Llewellyn, was appointed to develop sales on the local market, locals are now delighted that Clos Malverne's wines are more widely distributed. Three red wines, Pinotage, Cabernet Sauvignon and Auret, are listed in Disney's New Animal Kingdom Restaurant in Florida.

## COGMANS CO-OP
Montagu – Klein Karoo

This co-op was previously the Soetwyn Boere Co-op. It has been prevented from using the Cogmans name on its wines, as the name is the property of Zandvliet. Originally founded in 1941, it now has 40 members who deliver 6000 tons.

## COLERAINE WINES
Paarl

This Irish-named cellar in Paarl indicates the proud ancestry of owner, Kevin Kerr. Focusing solely on red wines, talented young winemaker Graham Weerts grabbed attention with his first release of a 1999 vintage Shiraz. The vineyard has 30 hectares producing about 4000 cases. Its Fire Engine Red is a regular drinking wine named in honour of a 1940s engine, which is still in service with the local brigade and used frequently for fighting the area's mountain fires.

## CONSTANTIA UITSIG
Constantia

David McCay has a private cricket oval on his property. The farm is planted to 35 hectares with another five in the pipeline. There are no plans to build a production cellar on Constantia Uitsig, and its wines are made at the Steenberg wine cellar. Wine director André Badenhorst is responsible for developing Constantia Uitsig into a major attraction. Two of Cape Town's best restaurants, a delightful café and an attractive wine shop are all situated here. Pride of place in the range is a Chardonnay Reserve, a Sémillon Reserve and a Sémillon Noble Late Harvest. A good Cabernet Sauvignon and a Cabernet Sauvignon blend are also produced. The total range consists of six whites and three reds.

## CONTREBERG WINES
Darling – Swartland

Alex Versfeld hooked up with Neil Ellis on this farm situated in the Groenekloof Ward of the Swartland. Forty-five hectares are planted to Sauvignon Blanc, Cabernet Sauvignon, Shiraz, Merlot and Pinotage. An additional 15 hectares must still be developed. The grapes are all vinified by Neil Ellis at Oude Nektar in the Jonkershoek valley. The Groenekloof label Sauvignon Blanc is one of the best available in South Africa.

## COPPOOLSE FINLAYSON
Stellenbosch

This winery, situated in the Brackenfell industrial area, is technically considered to be in the Stellenbosch District. Nevertheless, it is ideally positioned to draw high-quality grapes from the surrounding areas of Durbanville, Paarl and Stellenbosch. Coppoolse Finlayson is equally well positioned to deliver to the Cape Town docks, and most of its production is destined for export. Owners are Rob Coppoolse of Holland, local wine-making guru Walter Finlayson and Viv Grater. Their Sentinel is considered in the high-quality range, as are their Cape Salute, Mount Disa and others.

## CORDOBA
Helderberg – Stellenbosch

Cordoba was purchased in 1982 by Jannie Jooste. Over the past 14 years the farm has been redeveloped under the expert guidance of Jan Coetzee. There are currently 30 hectares planted mainly to Cabernet Franc, Merlot, Cabernet Sauvignon and Shiraz. A further 11 hectares will be planted high on the slopes of the Helderberg, and Cabernet Franc is bound to remain the featured variety. Chris Keet has been winemaker since 1994. In 1996 Cordoba released a Sauvignon Blanc and a Chardonnay, followed in 1998 by its reds. Cordoba's soils have yielded excellent Cabernet Franc grapes producing superb quality wines. Cordoba's Crescendo is 70 per cent Cabernet Franc. Merlot has been bottled since 1994 and an experimental Shiraz was vinified in 1997. The range now consists of two reds and one white. There is a second label, Mount Claire, which consists of a good red and a good white.

## DARLING CELLARS
Groenekloof – Swartland

If there were a prize for the most improved cellar in the Cape, Darling Cellars would qualify. Originally established as the Mamreweg Co-operative in 1949 with 29 members, it has transformed into a company with 22 shareholders, undergoing massive restructuring with new wine-making facilities under the leadership of winemaker Abe Beukes. Changes are also well underway to remove the Ward of Groenekloof from the Swartland District where Darling Cellars is currently located. Production is 500 000 cases, half red and half white. The top-of-the-line wines are sold under the Onyx range. The Groenekloof range features surprisingly good quality, and Flamingo Bay is considered amazing value for money. The Lagoon Rosé is also a smash hit.

## DE DOORNS WINE CELLAR CO-OP
Hex River Valley – Worcester

This co-op exports table grapes as well as making wine. It was one of the wineries established with a distillery by the Deciduous Fruit Board during the Second World War to handle fruit and grapes that were prevented from being exported. In 1968 it was taken over by 50 farmers and became the De Doorns Wine Cellar Co-op. It now has 225 members and crushes some 25 000 tons.

## DE FRANCHI WINES
Stellenbosch

For a long time fine quality grapes were delivered to SFW and Koelenhof Co-op from this Monterosso property. Now the first-generation Italian descent De Franchi brothers have branched out and built a fine Tuscan-styled winery where they crushed their first vintage in 2000. They will still deliver some of their crop to SFW and their own initial production will be about 2000 cases. Wines could be released under the Monterosso label.

## DE HEUVEL ESTATE
Tulbagh

This estate has total family involvement, owned and operated by Antonio Bianco and his sons. The small 15-hectare vineyard produces 2500 cases, but plans are in progress to increase production.

## DE MEYE
Stellenbosch

Owned by the Jan Myburgh Family Trust, this cellar was named De Meye after a Dutch river close to where the Mybugh's forefathers originated. The vineyard covers 65 hectares, concentrating mainly on red varieties such as Shiraz, Cabernet Sauvignon, Cabernet Franc, Merlot and some Pinotage. The only white grape variety planted here is Chardonnay.

## DE TOREN
Stellenbosch

Owners Emil and Sonette den Dulk, who fled the Johannesburg business scene, have an unusual winery that was once a small slaughterhouse. They replaced the previous gantry arrangement by installing a pressure tank that moves wine around the winery without employing any pumps. Instead, they rely simply on pressure and gravity. The cellar's name, De Toren, comes from the tower-like structure that houses the contraption. De Toren's first wine was dedicated to combining Bordeaux's five traditional varieties into a blend named Fusion V, which proved to be an absolutely splendid debut wine.

## DE TRAFFORD WINE
Stellenbosch

David Trafford runs a boutique winery on three hectares, and at present produces 3000 cases of wine. David has not wavered from his old-fashioned methods of wine making. His first vintage was produced from grapes that were not harvested according to sugar content, but entirely on taste. He only uses natural yeasts and perhaps the only deviation from traditional wine making is that the grapes are not crushed by foot. Known particularly for his Cabernet Sauvignon, he recently released a small quantity of 1998 vintage Shiraz to great acclaim. The 1999 De Trafford Chenin Blanc won the Cape Chenin 2000 Challenge.

## DE VILLIERS WINES
Paarl

Villiers de Villiers, together with winemaker Dominique Waso, are working wonders on this 90-hectare farm in the Nantes valley. Plantings include Cabernet Sauvignon, Merlot, Cabernet Franc, Chardonnay and new blocks of Viognier. Presently the range consists of three whites and five reds.

## DE WET CO-OP
### Worcester

This co-op was established in 1946 and celebrated its 50th anniversary by upgrading its cellar which was previously geared mainly for white wine. The winery now handles 30 per cent red. The 50-member co-op receives 18 000 tons and since 1978 has bottled a portion of its production. It has an interesting port made from Shiraz matured on Nevers staves.

## DE WETSHOF ESTATE
### Robertson

Danie de Wet abhors too much toast flavour in wooded wines. His benchmark is Corton Charlemagne and this vision has certainly put Robertson's white wines firmly on the map. De Wetshof can claim to have the country's highest lime content in its soils, giving a high fixed acid content to the wines. The estate currently has 160 hectares planted to Chardonnay, Sauvignon Blanc, Pinot Noir, Cabernet Sauvignon, Merlot and Sémillon. A further 45 hectares will be developed over the next three years. Recent accolades include an award for its 1998 Edeloes Noble Late Harvest for 'Best Botrytis Dessert Wine Worldwide' at the 2000 International Wine and Spirit Competition. His 1999 Chardonnay d'Honneur was also well received at the 2000 Chardonnay du Monde held in Paris. Demand for De Wetshof wines continues to grow, and a second label, Danie de Wet, has been developed. There are currently ten white wines in the De Wetshof range and the reds are still awaiting their debut.

## DE ZOETE INVAL ESTATE
### Paarl

De Zoete Inval is one of the five original farms granted to French Huguenot settlers. Robert Frater bought De Zoete Inval in 1878 and the farm has been in the Frater family ever since. Gerard Frater is in charge of the vineyards and brother Robert the wine making. There are five white wines bottled and five red. Exports are going well to four countries, including the UK.

## DEETLEFS ESTATE
### Rawsonville – Worcester

Situated on the lower slopes of the Du Toits Kloof mountains near Rawsonville, this estate has belonged to the Deetlefs family since 1822. Present owner, Kobus Deetlefs, has had remarkable success with his wines, which are not only exported to eight countries, but are also flying high on British Airways. Currently 100 hectares are planted to Sémillon, Pinotage, Cabernet Sauvignon and Shiraz. A further 20 hectares still need to be developed. Since 1997 Kobus has consolidated a range that includes a Sémillon with a Reserve label in certain years. His dry 1998 vintage Chenin Blanc was rated 'Best Dry Unwooded Chenin Blanc' in the 1999 Chenin Blanc Challenge.

## DELAIRE
### Stellenbosch

Hanging off the Helshoogte pass, Delaire has magnificent views and more importantly good vineyard soils. There have been dramatic changes since Agrifarm International (Pty) Ltd bought the property in 1995. The cellar has been upgraded and vineyards replanted. In 1997 Bruwer Raats started as winemaker after stints in California, Bordeaux and Tuscany. Delaire has 22 hectares planted to Cabernet Sauvignon, Sauvignon Blanc, Merlot and Chardonnay. A further two hectares are planned. Three white and three red wines make up the range and a second Green Door label is used in the restaurant on the property. Delaire has been recognised both at home and abroad. *Decanter* nominated its 1997 Chardonnay as 'The Best New World White Wine', and the 1998

vintage Chardonnay won a Gold at the 1999 Michelangelo International Awards.

## DELHEIM WINES
### Stellenbosch

Delheim produces 80 000 cases of wine. The wide range includes Cabernet Sauvignon, Shiraz, Gewürztraminer and an early-release Pinotage rosé. The Heerenwijn, Goldspatz Stein and Spatzendreck Late Harvest all have great followings, as does the Noble Late Harvest. This property is co-owned by Hans Hoheisen and Spatz Sperling. A pillar of the wine industry and a dynamic character, one of Spatz Sperling's most important contributions to the Stellenbosch winelands was the founding of the Stellenbosch Wine Route in 1971. Although Spatz is still active, his son, Victor, is now responsible for the vineyards while his daughter, Nora, is in charge of marketing.

## DELLRUST
### Stellenbosch

Rustenberg is owned by Albert Bredell, brother of port fundi, Anton. As the name 'Rustenberg' is already in use, the new name for this venture stems from a combination of the family name 'Bredell' and the name of the farm. The farm lies in a prime area with lots of potential, and the most popular wine is an easy-drinking dry red made from the old work-horse variety, Cinsaut, and a port variety, Tinta Barocca. Production is almost 900 tons, with a healthy 65 per cent red to white balance.

## DEVON HILL ESTATE
### Stellenbosch

This hill-top winery overlooking the entire Devon valley has undergone various changes since it first came into production in 1997. Originally Swiss financed, it is now again Swiss-owned by Capamis (Friends of the Cape) (Pty) Ltd, with Jean Voger as a hands-on CEO. The vineyard is planted to 55 hectares of Merlot, Cabernet Sauvignon, Pinotage and Sauvignon Blanc. Former KWV winemaker Kosie Möller is under a five-year contract as the estate's wine-making consultant.

## DIAMANT
### Paarl

Since 1992 Niel Malan has been making wine on this family farm. The grapes are pressed traditionally with bare feet and its red blend is produced from aged bush vines.

## DIE KRANS
### Calitzdorp – Klein Karoo

Die Krans dates back to 1890 when the farm was bought by the Nel family. The current cellar was built in 1964. The original farm was divided between brothers Chris and Danie, with Danie naming his section Boplaas, and Chris retaining the original name. In 1979 it was the first farm to be registered as an Estate Wine Cellar in the District. The 1997 Vintage Reserve Port won the Peter Schulz Port Challenge in 1999. The Jerepiko and muscadel wines are also excellent. Its ports are exceptional in the new, drier style of the Cape. Cape Wine Master Boets Nel is the winemaker and Stroebel Nel is the viticulturist.

## DIE POORT
### Klein Karoo

Jannie Jonker has developed this property since it was purchased by his father in 1957. Today the vineyards extend over 80 hectares. After obtaining a quota, Jannie built a cellar and the first vintage was crushed in 1963.

## DIEMERSDAL ESTATE
### Durbanville

The name of this property comes from the surname of Captain Diemer. He married the widow of Hendrik Sneeuwind who had been granted the land in 1698. Diemersdal has been in the Louw family for over 100 years. Owner Tienie Louw is committed to dry-land farming. Vineyards now cover 180 hectares, with 80

per cent red and 20 per cent white. The reds have a good reputation. Wines are exported by SAVISO and exports now make up most of Diemersdal's production.

## DIEMERSFONTEIN WINE AND COUNTRY ESTATE
### Wellington – Paarl

This 180-hectare farm is owned by David and Sue Sonnenberg. The winemaker is Bertus Fourie, who won the Paul Sauer Trophy at the South African Young Wine Show as a Pinotage Class Winner. At present, only red wines are produced.

## DIEU DONNE VINEYARDS
### Franschhoek – Paarl

Dieu Donné was acquired by the Maingard family in 1986. Stefan du Toit has been the winemaker since 1996. As red wine is Stefan's speciality, Dieu Donné is producing commendable Merlot as well as Cabernet Sauvignon. Thirteen white wines, including a Méthode Cap Classique, and five red are available. Dieu Donné won a Double Gold for its 1997 Merlot at the Michelangelo International Awards in 1999.

## DISTELL
### Stellenbosch

Developed through the merger between Stellenbosch Farmers' Winery and Distillers Corporation, Distell has become one of South Africa's leading wine and spirits producers. On Monday, 19 March 2001, it was officially listed on the Johannesburg Stock Exchange. With assets of R3.8 billion, a turnover of R4.6 billion and headline earnings of about R278 million, Distell is by far the leading producer of wines, spirits and alcoholic fruit beverages in Africa. It employs more than 5500 people at 58 depots throughout South Africa and maintains a robust network of international agents throughout the world. Distell has over 300 products, including international award winners such as Amarula Cream liqueur, and Nederburg and Fleur du Cap wines. It owns the country's top-selling premium brandies such as Klipdrift, Oude Meester, Mellowwood and Flight of the Fish Eagle. Its flagship brands include Bacardi, Gordons Gin, Old Buck Gin and Three Ships Whisky. It is the leader in the AFB market with top selling brands Hunters, Savanha, Bacardi Breezer, Bernini, Crown and Esprit. Famous cellars that now form part of the Distell group are Nederburg, the Bergkelder, Plaisir de Merle, J.C. le Roux, Monis, and the Lusan group which is an acronym for Le Bonheur, Uitkyk, Stellenzicht, Alto and Neethlingshof. Other famous wine names like Stellenryk, Zonnebloem, Château Libertas, Tassenberg and Cellar Cask are also part of the Distell line.

## DISTILLERS CORPORATION AND OUDEMEESTER GROUP
### Stellenbosch

Distillers Corporation (SA) Limited was established in 1945. Now part of Distell, the company was quick to embark on a series of mergers and take-overs. For example, it grasped ownership of the Drostdy Winery in Tulbagh, home to the largest privately owned sherry maturation cellar in South Africa. The Oude Meester Group was established in 1965 after mergers with more than 40 companies. In 1970 the Oude Meester Group merged again with Distillers Corporation, and its asset register includes such distinguished old names as the Castle Wine and Brandy Company, E.K. Green, Van Ryn Wine and Spirit Company and Henry C. Collison. The group also owns Western Province Cellars, a national retail chain with an extensive list of brands. Its better-known brandies include Oude Meester, Richelieu, Klipdrift, Limousin, Paarl Rock, Viceroy, Flight of the Fish Eagle and Commando. Its flagship wines form the Stellenryck Collection and other brands include Fleur du Cap, J.C. le Roux sparkling wines, Pongracz, Here XVII, Drostdy sherries, Drostdy Hof natural wines, Witzenberg, Cellar Cask, Kupferberger and Grünberger. In 1968 the Bergkelder was built on the southern slopes of the Papegaaiberg with an underground cellar forged into the mountain. The Group consolidated all its sparkling wine production on the former Bertrams site in Devon valley. The group also produces Gordons Gin, Bacardi Light Rum and distributes prestigious Scotch whiskies. Amarula Cream, a liqueur made from the African wild fruit called marula, is also a proud product of the corporation, having won multiple awards and proving to be a success on the international market.

## DOMEIN DOORNKRAAL
Klein Karoo

This farm is owned by Swepie le Roux, and his son, Piet, is the winemaker. The farm is situated near De Rust in the Klein Karoo, and produces 3000 cases from 24 hectares. The wines produced by Domein Doornkraal are predominantly white, but it also produces a Jerepiko and a tawny port. Three fortified wines, each given a military rank, Majoor, Kaptein and Luitenant, are also popular with customers.

## DORNIER WINES
Helderberg – Stellenbosch

Born in Germany and a resident of Switzerland, Christoph Dornier is an internationally exhibited artist. Since 1955 he has acquired three neighbouring farms in the Keerweder valley on the Helderberg. The R100 million investment includes the old Stuttaford homestead on Stellenrust, home to a cellar, conference facility and open-air courtyard concert venue. Its maiden 2001 wines were made in the neighbouring cellars. Noble varieties are planted on the 70-hectare farm, and there are plans to grow to 100 hectares by 2003, featuring mainly red varieties and Sémillon.

## DOUGLAS GREEN BELLINGHAM
Franschhoek – Paarl

Bellingham became a household name after Bernard Podlashuk purchased the property in 1943. He produced the first dry rosé in the late 1940s, and a dry white wine in the early 1950s. He pioneered the production of the varietal Shiraz label in 1955, and the popular semi-sweet Johannisberger, which sold in the unmistakable Bellingham flask. Graham Beck bought Bellingham in 1991. He appointed Charles Hopkins as winemaker and Charles has been closely involved with the redevelopment programme. Bellingham crushes grapes from 110 hectares of newly planted vineyards, and also draws grapes from other vineyards in the Coastal Region. The rejuvenated winery has added a highly rated Chardonnay, a Sauvignon Blanc, and a blend of the two, called Sauvenay, to its range. Bellingham's Cabernet Franc is also highly rated. Bellingham will now be vinified by Jaco Potgieter, who is also responsible for Douglas Green at Wellington. Jaco will be purchasing fruit and wine for both the Douglas Green Saints label and Bellingham wines, which has long-standing suppliers of high-quality grapes for its Premium Big Six range. Charles Hopkins will still be consultant for the Bellingham wines. The Bellingham Premium Range will remain, as well as old favourites from the 1950s: Bellingham Johannisberger, Bellingham Dry Rosé and Bellingham Premier Grand Cru. Bellingham's production of its well-established wines is about 350 000 cases. The label Douglas Green was launched in 1940 and for some years Douglas Green bottled wine made by the KWV. Now wines from selected producers are bought, blended and aged in the Wellington cellars. The Saints range of three white wines and two red continues to charm wine lovers locally and overseas, and a ruby port is also sold under the Douglas Green label.

*L'Ormarins below the Groot Drakenstein mountain.*

## DOUGLAS WINERY
Douglas – Orange River

Douglas is a district of its own in the Northern Cape on the Orange River. Established in 1968, it amalgamated with the Prieska Co-operative in 1996 to form the Griqualand West Co-operative that is now GWK Ltd with 2000 shareholders. In a productive year, the winery can handle up to 6000 to 7000 tons. Efforts are being made to improve quality and marketing, but 2001 has resulted in a difficult vintage. More than 20 labels make up its range.

## DRIE BERGE
Montagu – Klein Karoo

This wine wholesale business, owned by Paul Jordaan and situated some three kilometres from Montagu on the road to Koo, was originally set up as a wine farmers' licence in the early 1950s by Paul's father. It was converted to a wholesaler in 1969.

## DROSTDY WINERY
Tulbagh

The Drostdy Winery in Tulbagh takes its name from De Oude Drostdy, one of the finest examples of the work of architect Louis Michel Thibault. The building was opened in lavish style in 1806. Since then it has been severely ravaged by storm and fire, and was virtually destroyed by an earthquake in 1969. It was totally restored by the National Monuments Council, and is now home to Drostdy Cellars (Pty) Limited, a member of the Oude Meester Group of companies and makers of Drostdy sherries and Drostdy-Hof wines.

## DU PREEZ ESTATE
Rawsonville – Worcester

Fresh on the market with its 1999 vintage, this estate has 130 hectares of vineyard. It is moving more towards red varieties now as more plantings are planned. Grapes were previously delivered to a local cellar. The estate is owned by the Du Preez family and Hennie du Preez is making the wine after taking over in 1995.

## DU PREEZ WINE
Stellenbosch

Winemaker Jan du Preez uses various cellars to produce his wines under the names Twin Oaks, Migration and others.

## DU TOITSKLOOF WINE CELLAR
Worcester

A 12-member co-operative established in 1962, Du Toitskloof presently grows close to 700 hectares of vineyard. Plans to replant prime sites with red varieties will take this stellar cellar into a new dimension. Its goal is to produce quality wines at reasonable prices and this approach has already seen remarkable sales success locally and, more recently, on the export market. Under the leadership of Philip Jordaan since 1983, this winery consistently strives for distinction, as reflected by numerous awards collected locally and internationally. New wines are eagerly awaited with enthusiastic younger winemakers to assist the upcoming generation of red wines.

## DURBANVILLE HILLS
Durbanville

This is a joint venture between South African Wine Cellars and a group of established Durbanville wine growers that includes Altydgedacht, Bloemendal and Nitida. Their production is upwards of 5000 tons under the experienced control of Martin Moore. Extremely efficient with a minute staff, the space-age winery launched a stunning range of white and red wines, all reflecting the high quality of the area.

## EAGLEVLEI WINES
Stellenbosch

Owned by Steve and Jean Wier, and André and Tessa van Helsdingen, the partners have decided to produce red wines. About seven hectares yield 1500 cases, but the 50-hectare property has room for more development. Already another three hectares of Cabernet Sauvignon have recently been planted. The maiden vintage from 1997 saw a very stylish Cabernet Sauvignon, and in 1998 a Pinotage was added to the repertoire. A Merlot blend is also certain to follow.

## EIKEHOF
Franschhoek – Paarl

The Malherbe family bought the farm in 1903. Owner Tielman Malherbe's son, Francois, is the winemaker. Eikehof's first Sémillon, a 1992 vintage, was made from 95-year-old vines which are still in production. Forty-three hectares are planted predominantly to Cabernet Sauvignon, followed by Sauvignon Blanc and Sémillon. New plantings include Merlot, Chardonnay and Shiraz. Three white and three reds are produced and the Shiraz 2000 is still awaiting release.

## EIKENDAL VINEYARDS
Stellenbosch

Swiss public company A.G. Für Plantagen purchased two properties in 1982 and combined them to form Eikendal Vineyards. Jan Coetzee was the consultant on all the practical aspects of the winery and the replanting of the vineyards. The winemaker/general manager is Josef Krammer, and in 1991 he was joined in the cellar by Anneka Burger and Leonard O'Rein. The latter won the 2000 Patrick Grubb Scholarship which allowed him to work a vintage in the United States at Stimson Lane Vineyards. Eikendal, a very low-key but excellent winery, has grown slowly but surely in stature since its first wines were released in 1984. In the September 2000 issue of *Gault Millau*, Eikendal vineyards were mentioned with acclaim. In the last decade Josef has really excelled, producing a Cabernet Sauvignon Reserve, Merlot, Chardonnay and recently a Cabernet Sauvignon blend.

## ELEPHANT PASS VINEYARDS
Franschhoek – Paarl

The name is apt, as this corner of the Franschhoek valley was criss-crossed by herds of elephant in days gone by. Peter and Ann Wrighton own the farm as well as Guldenheuvel, the farm next door. Jean Daneel, one of South Africa's premier winemakers, is currently making an excellent Merlot, a Chardonnay Reserve and a good blended white wine called Celebration.

## EXCELSIOR ESTATE
Robertson

Originally part of the Zandvliet Estate, Excelsior was hived off in the late 1800s by Jacobus de Wet for a son. In the 1950s Excelsior became well known for its high-quality muscadel Jerepikos. The current owners, Stephen and Freddie de Wet, farm about 250 hectares of vines, of which 60 per cent is red. So far, production is primarily exported to British supermarkets, but they intend to create more wines featuring their own labels.

## EXCELSIOR WINERY
Vredendal

Stoffel Stoumann together with his sons farm this 100-hectare boutique winery near Vredendal. The farm is planted predominantly with white varieties and some Cabernet Sauvignon, Shiraz, Pinotage, Merlot and Ruby Cabernet.

## FAIR VALLEY
Paarl

Fair Valley is one of the first farm-worker empowerment ventures in the Cape. The 17-hectare farm is being developed by the Farm Workers' Association and is headed by seven officers elected by members who make up the Fairview staff. Winemaker Awie Adolph produced a Chenin in the Fairview cellar from bought-in grapes for Fair Valley's 1999 vintage. In 2000 he also produced a Pinotage. All of the wines have been exported to the United Kingdom. Besides development of the vineyards, a winery, some homes and other farming endeavours are being planned.

## FAIRVIEW
Paarl

Charles Back bought Fairview in 1937. After his death in 1954, he was succeeded by his son Cyril. Charles Back, Cyril's son, became winemaker at Fairview in 1978. Charles is unconventional, and certainly an innovator. In 1986 he was the first to make a traditional Gamay Nouveau by carbonic maceration. Among his unusual blends is a Cinsaut/Zinfandel that won the Dave Hughes Trophy in 1996 for the best South African red wine at the International Wine and Spirit Competition. In 1996, Anthony de Jager joined Charles in the cellar. Fairview has 112 hectares planted to vines and Charles anticipates planting a further 40 hectares to Rhône varieties Shiraz, Mourvèdre, Carignan and Grenache. Viognier was planted in 1993, with the wine's first release in 1998. The Fairview Cyril Back 1997 Shiraz was awarded a Gold Medal at the UK *Wine* magazine's 2000 International Wine Challenge. This is the largest competition in the world and Fairview won awards for the full complement of wines entered. Fairview is also famous for its cheeses, producing the largest range in South Africa.

## FLAGSTONE
Cape Town

Bruce Jack has established his winery in the Cape Town Waterfront development with existing cold storage facilities that were originally used for the fishing industry. He's been able to produce innovative wines by acquiring grapes from prime areas throughout the Cape. Production has now reached 20 000 cases. With highly unusual labels, the wines have become instant hits. Future development will be to restore a tunnel that once led prisoners from their inland jail to work on the breakwater. Look for Flagstone labels with names such as Dragon Tree Cabernet/Pinotage, Chapman's Chance, Heywood House, Two Roads Chardonnay and Noon Gun.

## FLEERMUISKLIP WINES
Lutzville valley

This co-op was established in 1962 with over 100 members who deliver 30 000 tons. Originally named Lutzville Vineyards, it changed its name to Fleermuisklip, after a rock where early explorers in the region took shelter. The rock has now become a national monument. The diamond-rich West Coast gives its name to the Diamant sparkling wine. This area was previously considered good enough only for bulk wine production, but great strides have been made to upgrade the quality of the vineyards and wine. The bulk of production goes to merchants, but the co-op has bottled ever-increasing quantities since 1978.

## FLEUR DU CAP
Stellenbosch

The Fleur du Cap range is produced by the Bergkelder. Fleur du Cap is named after a building designed by Sir Herbert Baker where the Bergkelder has its 'Mother Block' vine plantations. The grapes for Fleur du Cap wines are sourced from prime sites in the Coastal Region. A more innovative approach to wine making is evidenced in the more recently produced 'Unfiltered Collection'.

## FORRESTER VINEYARDS
Helderberg – Stellenbosch

In 1993 Ken and Teresa Forrester bought Scholtzenhof, an historic farm on the Stellenbosch-Somerset West road. The farm suffered from severe neglect and they immediately started restoration work on the buildings. The vineyards were in a better condition and Ken decided to make his own wine. He also opened a restaurant. Ken's first Chenin Blanc, made from very old vines, was released in 1995. Forrester Vineyards wines are now made by restaurant partner and well-known winemaker, Martin Meinert, at his Devon Crest Winery. The range has gone from strength to strength. Besides Chenin Blanc, which is wood and bottle-aged, there is also an easy drinking Petit Chenin, two Sauvignon Blancs and two red wines. The Grenache/Syrah blend is a first in South Africa, and the Merlot/Cabernet has good potential.

## FORT SIMON ESTATE
Bottelary – Stellenbosch

High up in the Bottelary Hills, Dr Simon Uys built a fort as his entertainment area. The late Dr Uys had worked in Namibia near Grootfontein, where the Duwisib Castle had left strong impressions on him. After retiring from his practice, his memories of the castle became a model for his own colonial fort. His sons, Rennier and Petrus Uys, decided to add a winery to the property that continued with their father's theme. An ultra modern winery is now housed within the fort surrounded by a medieval moat, drawbridge, turrets and plenty of stonework. Grapes used to be delivered to the Bergkelder. Now wines are being made by Marinus Bredell. Fort Simon's Merlot has seen Double Gold at Veritas and its Merlot/Pinotage blend has also been well received. The Chardonnay is regularly top class.

## FRAAI UITZICHT 1798
Robertson

Pharmaceutical specialist Axel Spanholtz gave up Sweden and Germany for his Valhalla, which he found in the Klaas Voogds valley near Robertson. With his partner, Mario Motti, he set about restoring the nine-hectare property whose vineyards and long-forgotten

cellar were established in 1798. Hence the odd name Fraai Uitzicht 1798. With a lot of help from the locals and wine expertise from Pieter Ferreira, the grapes are now being hand-crafted, using the best oak, to create fine reds. The focus is on Shiraz, Cabernet Sauvignon and a Merlot that is featured in the 2000 range. This winery is the first to use the Klaas Voogds Wine of Origin designation.

## FRANSCHHOEK VINEYARDS
Franschhoek – Paarl

Originally established as a co-operative in 1945, change has come to this cellar in the Franschhoek valley, where 85 shareholders have recreated themselves into Franschhoek Vineyards Ltd. Deon Truter and Driaan van der Merwe crush 4200 tons under the cellar's La Cotte and Franschhoek labels. Fourteen whites and six reds are being marketed successfully at home and abroad to Great Britain, Holland, Belgium, Germany and Japan.

## GILGA
Stellenbosch

Gilga is made by Overgaauw winemaker Chris Joubert. Appropriately named after a Persian legend, this Shiraz has already attracted quite a following.

## GLEN CARLOU
Paarl

This 108-hectare farm, originally called 'Skilpaadjie', was established in 1985 by Walter Finlayson. The property is now jointly owned by Walter and his son David, together with Hess Holdings Switzerland. Donald Hess has other wine interests in Chile, California, Argentina and Australia. David Finlayson has been winemaker since 1996. Glen Carlou's most sought-after wines are its Chardonnay and its Bordeaux-style blend Grand Classique. Glen Carlou's Merlot and Pinot Noir are also showing great promise.

## GOEDE HOOP ESTATE
Stellenbosch

Goede Hoop farm, on the western slopes of the Bottelary hills, was bought by Petrus Johannes Bestbier in 1928. It was a mixed farm producing some sweet fortified wine. Johan Bestbier took over the management of the farm in 1961 and developed it into a predominantly red wine farm. His son, Pieter, now owns the farm, with 80 hectares planted to vineyards. Pieter is also the winemaker, producing Cabernet Sauvignon, Shiraz, Pinotage and the ever-popular Vintage Rouge Bordeaux-style blend.

*Winter vines at Vergelegen.*

## GOEDVERTROUW ESTATE
Overberg

This 250-hectare property near Bot River was bought by Arthur Pillman in 1984. The Pillmans started planting vineyards in 1985 and their first wine, a 1990 Chardonnay, was a good first effort. Arthur released his first Pinot Noir in 1995. The 1995 crop of Sauvignon Blanc was eaten by ribbok that came down from the mountain due to the drought, and a fence has been erected to ensure that this will not happen again. The Pillmans have eight hectares planted to Pinot Noir, Chardonnay, Sauvignon Blanc, Cabernet Sauvignon and Pinotage. A further two are planned. Three whites and two reds are bottled.

## GOEDVERWACHT ESTATE
Bonnievale – Robertson

The estate is owned by brothers Jan and Thys du Toit, and for years it has supplied all its production to the merchants. In 1993 the estate bottled a Colombar under its own label depicting the blue crane, South Africa's national bird. In 1995 the cellar was upgraded and winemaker Jan du Toit now produces Colombar, Chardonnay and Sauvignon Blanc. Machine harvesting ensures that the grapes are picked at the optimum stage of ripeness. While few folk rush to plant new Colombar vines, Du Toit has done exceptionally well with his Colombar exports to Germany and Holland. Future plans are to use new plantings of Cabernet and Merlot in a red blend.

## GOUDINI CO-OP
Worcester

This was the second co-op to operate in the Worcester area. It was established in 1948, near the Goudini Spa, with 25 members and crushed 6000 tons for its first vintage in 1949. Now 42 members deliver 20 000 tons which include a growing quantity of red varieties. The co-op has collected an impressive range of awards, and exports to British and European markets. The cellar produces its wines under the Umfiki label, which means 'newcomer'. The Sémillon/Chardonnay blend, basically a nouveau, is good value for money.

## GOUDVELD ESTATE
Free State

One of the Free State's two wineries, Goudveld is named after the world's richest gold fields in nearby Welkom. The Alers family run the 18-hectare vineyard and produce
4000 cases of wine. Their private collection of cycads is reputed to be the biggest in the country and seedlings are for sale. Soewenier, a Pinotage, is a local favourite red wine, and Goue Nektar, a sweet fortified Hanepoot, is a sworn lifesaver in their freezing winters. Recent additions include single varietals from Pinot Noir, Ruby Cabernet and Chardonnay.

## GOUE VALLEI WINES
Olifants River

The vineyards are tucked away in the foothills of the Cedarberg. The name Goue Vallei means 'golden valley', and comes from the nearby orchards of oranges and the wonderful local display of spring flowers. Most of the area is irrigated from the Olifants River. The co-op was established in 1957 and installed its own bottling line, selling its production in bottles, which was unusual for a co-op. No longer a co-op, it is now Goue Vallei Wines (Pty) Ltd, with about 100 growers delivering about 8000 tons of mostly white, but with growing quantities of red. There are 15 growers in the new cool-climate ward of Piekenierskloof where altitudes are 480 to 750 metres above sea level. Colourful packaging is being upgraded to meet international needs.

## GRACELAND VINEYARDS
Helderberg – Stellenbosch

Red wine is produced at this boutique winery owned by Paul and Sue McNaughton. With a refreshingly different approach to labelling, the McNaughtons have succeeded in producing quality wine to live up to the packaging. The Three Graces of Greek mythology, Charm, Joy and Beauty, were chosen for the neck labels of their elegant bottles. The first vintage was in 1998, with the release of a Cabernet Sauvignon and Merlot. Rod Easthope has succeeded Martin Meinert as consultant winemaker. The first Shiraz was harvested in 2001 and will be released in a few years.

## GRAHAM BECK WINES
Robertson and Franschhoek – Paarl

Graham Beck purchased Madeba Farm in 1983. He was already the owner of Highlands Stud in the Madeba valley. Immediate upgrading of vineyards and replanting began. The first cellar was specifically built for Méthode Cap Classique in 1990 and in 1991 the first Graham Beck Brut was produced. A second cellar was built in 1992 specifically for red and white still wine. In 1990 Graham Beck bought Union Wine which owned Bellingham Farm in Franschhoek and the Bellingham brands. In 1991 Union Wine was amalgamated with Douglas Green Paarl to form Douglas Green Bellingham (DGB). In 1996 Graham Beck secured 100 per cent ownership of DGB and then in 1997 combined all his wine interests together. Then came a surprise move when in 1999 he sold 80 per cent of the shares in DGB to the management. This sale, however, excluded the cellars in Robertson and Bellingham. The Robertson cellar falls under the direction of Pieter Ferreira who joined in 1990. Charles Hopkins is in charge at Bellingham, where Graham Beck Coastal Wines are now made.

## GRANGEHURST WINERY
Helderberg – Stellenbosch

Jeremy Walker converted his squash court on this small property into a winery. He is a boutique red wine specialist. In 1992, his first crush, he produced the South African champion wine, winning the General Smuts Trophy for a Cabernet/Merlot blend. All grapes supplied to the winery come from nearby non-irrigated vineyards. Jeremy crushes 135 tons and produces 9000 cases of wine. Difficult to find, Jeremy's wines are deservedly much sought after. In 1996 he built an underground barrel cellar to accommodate 300 barrels. A new label, Nikela, has been added as a special blend of Cabernet Sauvignon, Pinotage and Merlot. Jeremy has recently acquired 13 hectares near L'Avenir, close to Stellenbosch. Planting of the new vineyards will begin in 2001.

## GROENE CLOOF ESTATE
Swartland

This property near Darling was purchased in 1994 by Johan van den Berg. By 1997 he had upgraded the vineyards and built a cellar where Cabernet Sauvignon, Pinotage and Chenin are produced. New plantings of Cabernet Sauvignon, Merlot, Shiraz, Cinsaut and Chardonnay are expected. In 2001 the estate won *Wine* magazine's 2001 Pinotage Championship.

## GROENELAND
Stellenbosch

Kosie Steenkamp owns this 188-hectare farm which lies just off the Bottelary road. Cabernet Sauvignon dominates the planted area of 151 hectares. Currently KWV International markets a Shiraz and Cabernet Sauvignon to Europe.

## GROOT CONSTANTIA ESTATE
Constantia

Groot Constantia is the Cape's most historic estate. In 1685 Simon van der Stel, governor of the Cape, was granted this large tract of land on the eastern side of Table Mountain. The house itself is considered one of the best examples of 17th-century architecture. Groot Constantia changed hands many times until Hendrik Cloete bought it in 1778. He revitalised the neglected farm and by 1783 had begun exporting his wines, especially a sweet wine called Constantia, to Europe to great acclaim. Unfortunately, the Cloetes did not record the grape varieties that were used, nor how they made the wine. A number of bottles of this luscious wine were found in the Duke of Northumberland's cellar in England in the early 1980s. The wines were auctioned and some were returned to the Cape, proving to be as remarkable as ever. The Cloete family owned Groot Constantia for more than 100 years, and eventually sold the estate in 1885 to the colonial government. On June 22, 1993 Groot Constantia Estate saw the beginning of a new era after the government created the Groot Constantia Trust. The aim of the Trust is to produce quality wines, and to use the profits to protect and maintain this treasure for future generations. In 1999 Bob de Villiers became winemaker with Roger Arendse as his assistant. Roger was the first recipient of a Patrick Grubb bursary for cellar workers, a bursary that is keenly contested. Boete Gerber was appointed as winemaker in 2001 after Bob moved to Klawer winery. Groot Constantia remains a prime historic estate, marketing Sauvignon Blanc, Cabernet Sauvignon and Merlot to the local market and abroad to 12 countries.

## GROOT EILAND WINERY
Goudini – Worcester

This cellar pressed its first grapes in 1961. Today it has 17 members who deliver about 11 000 tons from 600 hectares planted almost exclusively to white grapes. Groot Eiland is undergoing a major quality upgrade and more red varieties are being planted. Packaging is also being improved. The cellar's name is derived from the fact that most of its members' farms are surrounded by the Molenaars River when it is in full spate. Slightly more than 10 per cent of production is bottled for export and the bulk is sold to local wholesale merchants.

## GROOTE POST VINEYARDS
Darling – Swartland

Father and son team, Peter and Nick Pentz, are third- and fourth-generation dairymen whose forefathers arrived at the Cape in 1742. The increasing urban sprawl of Cape Town finally forced them to move their prize Holstein dairy herd to the cool Darling hills. The area proved to be an ideal location, especially in helping them to abide by an ancestral request that the farm must always have Table Mountain in view. Without ever thinking of making wine, they bought Groote Post in 1972. Two decades later, the Pentz family commenced a 10-year programme to plant 120 hectares to vines. They built a modern cellar in time for the 1999 vintage and production will be limited to 350 tons. First release was a Sauvignon Blanc followed by Chardonnay, Chenin, Merlot and Pinot Noir.

## GRUNDHEIM WINES
Klein Karoo

Danie and Susan Grundling have provided fortified wine to wholesalers for years and their distilling licence dates back 50 years. Apart from their wine and witblitz, they offer all kinds of fruit preserved in witblitz, liqueurs, local produce and old-fashioned remedies. The fascinating labels are copies of wall paintings discovered under the wallpaper when the homestead was restored. The unique tasting room was once a stable, and has clay walls and a reed ceiling. A particularly good Red Muscadel is made and a brandy maturation cellar has been completed.

## HAMILTON RUSSELL VINEYARDS
Walker Bay – Overberg

Tim Hamilton Russell has been a thorn in the side of officialdom for many years. When he purchased property near Hermanus in 1975, he came up against a great deal of unnecessary, archaic bureaucracy, and raised many objections. These objections led to some changes, the most important being the termination of the production quota system and the minimum price structure. A thorny issue that remains, however, is the redrawing of boundaries of the areas of origin to reflect climatic rather than administrative differences. Tim queries the fact that Paarl, which is far inland, is classified as being within the 'Coastal' Region while Walker Bay, which is virtually on the sea, is not. Tim had found the coolest area possible, and at the time established the Cape's most southerly vineyards to grow Pinot Noir and Chardonnay. Hamilton Russell Vineyards is situated in the Hemel en Aarde valley only two kilometres from the Indian Ocean. Planting started in 1976. There are now 52 hectares planted to Pinot Noir and Chardonnay. Peter Finlayson was appointed as winemaker, and in the 1980s Hamilton Russell Vineyards certainly produced the Cape's best Pinot Noir. In 1991, Tim Hamilton Russell succeeded his father and Storm Kreusch was appointed winemaker. Storm changed the style of the Pinot Noir, with great success, and used no filtration for the wine. New winemaker Kevin Grant has been in charge since the 1995 vintage.

## HARTENBERG ESTATE
### Stellenbosch

This estate was known as Montagne until Gilbeys Distillers and Vintners took over the property in the mid-1970s. Hartenberg was sold to Ken Mackenzie in 1986 and is currently owned by Fiona Mackenzie and Tanya Brown. A new team, headed by marketing director James Brown and winemaker Carl Schultz, has changed Hartenberg's image completely. The estate has always been known for its Shiraz and Weisser Riesling. The range now includes Merlot, Cabernet Sauvignon and Zinfandel. Hartenberg is unique because it produces the only Pontac wine in South Africa.

## HARTSWATER WINE CELLAR
### Northern Cape

Hartswater is the most northerly of the Cape's cellars, with some growers actually situated across the Vaal River. Established in 1977, it receives grapes from some 70 growers on the Vaalharts irrigation scheme. Now owned by Senwes Limited, Hartswater undertook upgrades in 2000 to improve quality required for the ever-growing export market. The range of wines includes Hinterland and Elements.

## HAVANA HILLS
### Tygerberg

This mountain-top winery on the West Coast above Melkbosstrand is home to winemaker Nico Vermeulen. The owner is Cape entrepreneur, Kobus du Plessis, who has 'always' wanted to make wine. He got his chance in Helshoogte, but considered the winery too small and confined. Therefore from scratch, he developed this massive undertaking high in the Tygerberg hills with the intention to grow Havana Hills into one of the world's great wineries. While 43 hectares of plantings mature, more grapes are being purchased from high-quality vineyards in Malmesbury and Durbanville. With input from famous French winemakers, this cellar is set on course to achieve the owner's ambitions and leads the vast development of other vineyards in this area. Already, the cellar's maiden 1999 vintage has produced spectacular Shiraz and Merlot.

## HAZENDAL ESTATE
### Stellenbosch

The estate is named after first owner Christoffel Hazenwinkel, who was granted this land in 1704. The Bosman family owned the farm from 1851 to 1994. The property is now owned by Mark Voloshin, chairman of the Marvol Group. He has spared no time restoring the 66 hectares of vineyards which are being replanted with more red varieties. The farm buildings have also been beautifully renovated into a country hotel, and the old wine cellar, a national monument, is the tasting venue. The first vintage was produced in 1996. Ronell Wiid has been winemaker since 1998. In 1999 she won the prestigious Diners Club 'Winemaker of the Year Award' with the 1998 Hazendal

Estate Shiraz/Cabernet Sauvignon blend. At present seven white wines are bottled, including a beautifully packaged Méthode Cap Classique, and two reds.

## HELDERBERG WINERY
### Helderberg – Stellenbosch

Helderberg Winery pressed its first grapes in 1906. Today it is one of the four foundation members of Stellenbosch Vineyards Limited. Bricks were carried from Firgrove Station in horse-drawn wagons, and early power was generated by the winery's own steam engine. Today the cellar boasts modern wine-making equipment and stainless steel tanks. Much of the recent production has been sent to British supermarkets.

## HELDERKRUIN WINE CELLAR
### Helderberg – Stellenbosch

Bought by Ben du Toit in 1968, Helderkruin was originally part of one of the oldest farms in the Groenrivier area. Ben's son, Niel, is now the owner. In 1998 he started building a wine cellar. Currently the farm is planted to 100 hectares of Cabernet Sauvignon, Merlot, Pinotage, Sauvignon Blanc and Chardonnay. There are also new plantings of Petit Verdot and Malbec. Winemaker Koos Bosman won the 1999 South African Young Wine Championship with his 1999 vintage Pinotage. Helderkruin also produces a special workers' Cape Vintage Port that benefits philanthropic projects chosen by the farm staff. Five white wines are bottled, including a Phyllis Hands Méthode Cap Classique to honour her contribution to the wine industry over the past three decades.

## HERMANUSRIVIER
### Walker Bay – Overberg

Grapes for the production of 300 cases are sourced by owner/winemaker Rudolf Rosochacki from friends' vineyards. His wines sell under the name of Vivamus, which is derived from the family crest.

## HIDDEN VALLEY WINES
### Stellenbosch

An interesting working partnership has evolved between Hidden Valley's Dave Hidden and Grangehurst's Jeremy Walker. Dave Hidden now owns 23 hectares of vineyard in Devon valley. He has also purchased another 28 hectares on the higher slopes of the Helderberg mountain where the Hiddens plan to build a home, and in time a winery. Viticulturist and winemaker Johan Grobbelaar runs the vineyards to internationally recognised organic farming standards. Since 1997 Jeremy Walker has made the wine. The 1997 vintage Hidden Valley Pinotage was not only winner of *Wine* magazine's 'South Africa's Top Pinotage Competition', but also won a Gold Medal at the UK *Wine* magazine's International Wine Challenge.

## HIGH CONSTANTIA.
### Constantia

With support from financier David van Niekerk and advice from winemaker Bob de Villiers, this 14-hectare vineyard leases small parcels of its land. Red grapes are predominantly grown with 12 per cent reserved for Chardonnay. Its first releases were Cabernet Franc, Cabernet Sauvignon and a Chardonnay.

## HILDENBRAND ESTATE
### Wellington – Paarl

In 1982 petite dynamo Reni Hildenbrand, an architectural interior designer by profession, emigrated to South Africa with her husband. Sadly, he was killed in a motor accident. Reni decided to follow their dream and buy a farm in the winelands. In 1991 she bought Rhebokskloof, one of the oldest farms in the Wellington area. The vineyards consisted of about three hectares of Chenin Blanc bush vines, less than a hundred olive trees, and a few neglected buildings. Reni planted 17 hectares of vineyard and an additional two are still planned. The main varietal remains Chenin Blanc, still as bush vines,

followed by Chardonnay, Sémillon, Cabernet Sauvignon, Shiraz, Barbera and Malbec. Reni made a successful debut in 1999. Her 1999 vintage unwooded Chardonnay was awarded a 'Diploma di Gran Menzione' at Vin Italy 2000 against impressive competition.

## HOOPENBURG WINES
### Stellenbosch

This relatively new wine farm, situated on the old Paarl Road, is owned by Ernst Gouws and a German partner. Winemaker Ernst will continue to buy in grapes for Hoopenburg wines until 2002, when the vineyards will be in production. Just under 37 hectares are planted to Merlot, Chardonnay, Cabernet Sauvignon, Shiraz and Pinot Noir. Hoopenburg's Chardonnay was awarded a Gold Medal at the 1999 Chardonnay Du Monde Competition held in Beaune, France. The same Chardonnay was chosen as the best South African Chardonnay at Prowein in Düsseldorf, Germany.

## HUGUENOT WINE FARMS
### Wellington – Paarl

Established in 1884, this privately owned wholesaler is still alive and well. The cellar blends, bottles and distributes wines and spirits from its Wellington address.

## INGWE
### Helderberg – Stellenbosch

This is a venture heavily influenced by famous French names with backing from Alain Mouiex and wine making by Etienne Charrier. Both also have involvement with Winecorp and Graham Knox, but this is their own venture. Wines at the moment are made at Havana Hills, where their touch also has an influence. Ingwe wines have been launched with Chardonnay and Sauvignon Blanc, but it is cellar samples of the reds that make noses and palates excited.

## INTERNATIONAL WINE SERVICES – PACIFIC WINES

Headquartered in the United Kingdom, this 'flying' winemaker operation produces close to three quarters of a million cases a year blended to suit UK palates at cellars in Stellenbosch, Wellington, Worcester and Robertson. A whole host of labels is used to supply various UK retailers and include Apostles Falls, Fontein, Plantation, Rylands Grove and others.

## JACARANDA ESTATE
### Wellington – Paarl

This is a small operation, making 300 cases from 2.8 hectares of vines. Jan Tromp bought Jacaranda in 1988 and built his cellar in an old concrete water reservoir. Jan specialises in Chenin Blanc and makes a great Jerepiko.

## JACOBSDAL ESTATE
### Stellenbosch

Cornelis Dumas is a specialist Pinotage producer on his farm that overlooks the Kuils River. He is now assisted by son Hannes. Pinotage is the most planted variety but there are also plantings of Chenin Blanc, Sauvignon Blanc, Cabernet Sauvignon and Merlot. In fact, Jacobsdal is on the very edge of the viable wine-producing area before the soil gives way to the sand of the Cape Flats. One hundred hectares are planted mostly to bush vines. At present, Pinotage is bottled under the Jacobsdal label and the wine is marketed by the Bergkelder.

## JEAN DANEEL WINES
### Franschhoek – Paarl

Jean Daneel has drawn his bow, finally setting up his own *négociant* business in Franschhoek. He has converted an old stable into a small cellar where he crushes 40 tons of mainly red varieties. He also makes wines in other cellars for their owners. Expansion plans include vineyards on both the East and West coasts and also in the mountains near Barrydale. Jean's first flight includes a magnificent Merlot, confirming his pedigree as Diners Club 'Winemaker of the Year'.

He has also produced a Cabernet Sauvignon/Merlot blend and a Chenin/Sauvignon Blanc blend that have been snapped up by buyers in the European market.

## JONKHEER FARMERS' WINERY
Bonnievale – Robertson

This wholesale wine and spirit business in Bonnievale is owned by the Jonker family. It celebrated its 75th anniversary in 1995. The Jonkers keep up with world trends and use organic farming methods. They are one of the largest producers of fortified muscadels in the area, and have done well in various competitions, including a gold for their Bakenskop Muscadel at the 1995 International Wine and Spirit Competition. Major improvements to cellars, production equipment and especially vineyards will show in future improved quality.

## JOOSTENBERG WINES
Paarl

Joostenberg is owned by the Myburgh family and steered by Philip Myburgh Senior. Since 1999 he has been joined by his sons: Philip attends to the vineyards and Tyrrel makes the wine. The Myburghs have farmed this property for over 120 years. Mixed farming has always been the norm, but now the dairy has been converted to a winery. Instead of selling their grapes, they are now making their own wine. The Muldersvlei Market is part of their operation where, besides selling their wine, they market outstanding pork and serve country-style meals.

## JORDAN VINEYARDS
Stellenbosch

When Ted Jordan bought this farm, his son Gary was studying for his Geology degree and helped on the farm whenever possible. Gary and his wife Kathy joined Ted in 1985, and together they became the first husband-and-wife wine-making team in the Cape Winelands. The farm crushed its first vintage in 1993, and from that first vintage Jordan wines have been exceptional. Success has become the norm, together with recognition from British wine writers such as Jancis Robinson and Tim Atkin. Tim Atkin is on record arguing that Jordan Chardonnay is on a par with some of the world's greatest white wines from Burgundy, California, Australia and New Zealand. The 1999 vintage Chardonnay also won a Gold Medal at The International Challenge Du Vin held in Burgundy in 2000. Vineyard plantings have been increased to 101 hectares of Merlot, Chardonnay, Sauvignon Blanc and Shiraz, and further development is still envisaged. Production currently stands at 45 000 cases in 2000 and the goal is to reach 60 000 cases by 2003.

## JOUBERT-TRADOUW WINERY
Barrydale – Klein Karoo

This is one of the oldest farms in the Klein Karoo. It has traditionally had grapes in its mix of fruit and dairy and grapes were previously delivered to the Barrydale Co-op. The winery is owned by the Joubert Family Trust, with wine making by Meyer Joubert whose father, Kobus, is the long-standing chairman of the KWK. The 30-hectare vineyard is currently planted to 80 per cent red, and California-experienced Meyer is determined to produce attention-grabbing, high-quality wines. First releases were the 1999 and 2000 vintages of Cabernet/Merlot and Chardonnay. The potential is certainly there.

## KAAPZICHT ESTATE
Stellenbosch

Kaapzicht, owned by Steytdal Farms, became an estate in 1984 and the first bottling of Kaapzicht wine took place that year. Since then, vineyard plantings have been upgraded and now include classic red varieties. The estate is one of the largest in the Bottelary hills. It has 135 hectares planted to vines with a further 12 hectares on the drawing board. Production is currently 60 per cent white and 40 per cent red. The range of wines has increased considerably to 10 whites and 18 reds. Winemaker Danie Steytler has introduced 'Cape View' as a second label, and a third for The Netherlands. Kaapzicht has won numerous awards, including the ABSA and *Wine* magazine's Pinotage Champion 2000 Award for the Kaapzicht 1998 Steytler Pinotage. At the Michelangelo 2000 competition, Steytler Pinotage 1999 won a Double Gold and was Champion Wine. The Kaapzicht Kaaprood 1996 won the UK *Wine* magazine's award for the best wine out of 120 entries.

## KANGO CO-OP
Oudtshoorn – Klein Karoo

Originally established as a tobacco co-op, Kango added wine when the Union Wine Cellar in the area closed down and grape growers needed a cellar. In 1974 the co-op started production, and a year later the first wines were bottled under the Rijckshof label. Rijckshof was an 'ostrich palace' that has now been demolished. The 60 members are spread over a wide area, and despite the hot, arid climate of the Karoo, some of the vineyards are in cool spots high up in the Swartberg mountains. From these sources have come the grapes that have produced the co-op's award-winning Sauvignon Blanc.

## KANONKOP ESTATE
Stellenbosch

In the early 20th century Kanonkop was owned by the Sauer family and wine farming began in the early 1930s under Paul Sauer. The farm is now owned and run by his grandsons, Johan and Paul Krige, and wine guru Beyers Truter has been winemaker since 1981. Kanonkop was one of the first farms to establish Pinotage vineyards. Although Beyers is associated most with Pinotage, recognition on the international stage has come for his Paul Sauer Bordeaux-style blend. This wine has twice won the Pichon-Longueville Comptesse de Lalande Trophy for the best blended red wine at the International Wine and Spirit Competition. Beyers first won the award in 1994 for the Kanonkop 1991 Paul Sauer and again in 1999 for the 1995 Kanonkop Paul Sauer. In 1991 Beyers also won The Robert Mondavi 'International Winemaker of the Year Award'. With 100 hectares planted to red varieties, Kanonkop has consolidated its range to just four labels and must be an odds-on favourite in the race to produce South Africa's first icon red wine. Kanonkop wines are currently being marketed to 39 countries abroad.

## KANU WINES
Stellenbosch

Kanu Wines are owned by Hydro Holdings, the same owners as Mulderbosch. The Kanu cellar in the Stellenbosch Kloof area was little known as Goedgekloof and produced the wine for the original Spier. Now totally revamped and modernised, it produces outstanding wines under the talented care of Teddy Hall, who turned to wine making somewhat late in life. His talent was proved not only by winning *Wine* magazine's Chenin Challenge in 2000, but also by being placed second and fourth with other entries. He is producing some outstanding varietal wines, including Cabernet Sauvignon, Merlot, Chardonnay and Sauvignon Blanc.

## KHANYA WINES
Durbanville

Nico Vermeulen, now firmly settled in the cellars of Havana Hills, is making a small amount of super quality wines. His Khanya wines began in various other cellars, but the transfer to Havana Hills seems to have only improved their quality. So far a stunning Cabernet/Merlot blend and a Sauvignon Blanc have been released. Khanya means 'shine' in Xhosa. Nico's wines will surely shine.

## KLAWER CO-OP
Olifants River

The co-op was formed in 1956 with a membership of 80 and the winery was built to receive grapes the following year. At one time Klawer was a large producer of distilling wine, but has bottled a selection of fortified and natural wines since the early 1970s. It won gold at the 1986 International Wine and Spirit Competition for its off-dry Colombar. The co-op handles over 27 000 tons and is now making red wines from Pinotage, Cabernet Sauvignon, Merlot and Shiraz. Now firmly established in the export arena, quality and packaging have improved to meet the demands.

## KLAWERVLEI ESTATE
Stellenbosch

Klawervlei was purchased in time to produce its first wines from the 1995 vintage. The farm is owned by Austrian-born Hermann Feichtenschlager, who with his wife, Inge, is committed to producing organically grown grapes and making wine as eco-friendly as possible. The 114-hectare property has some 35 hectares under vineyard. Hermann is the winemaker and wines are predominantly for export.

## KLEIN CONSTANTIA ESTATE
Constantia

Klein Constantia has a remarkable history that began with the first plantings by Simon van der Stel. The farm originally produced dessert wines that were sought after in the courts of Europe. Dougie Jooste bought this neglected property in 1980 and together with his son, Lowell, immediately set about restoring it. He replanted and extended the vineyards and built a wine cellar. Winemaker Ross Gower joined Klein Constantia in 1983, and from the first vintage he has ensured that Klein Constantia remains one of the Cape's top producers. Distinctive variations in *terroir* exist because the variance in elevation above sea level rises from 72 metres on north-facing slopes to 440 metres on south-facing slopes. Later-ripening varieties such as Cabernet Sauvignon are planted low down and Sauvignon Blanc and Chardonnay can reach full potential under cool growing conditions higher on the slopes of the mountain. At present, 75 hectares are planted to vineyards, with no suitable ground for further expansion. Ross Gower's special talent was proved immediately when Klein Constantia won the Johann Graue Memorial Trophy for the champion South African dry white wine with a 1986 vintage Sauvignon Blanc. More recently Klein Constantia's 1998 Sauvignon Blanc and 1997 Shiraz both won Gold Medals at the 1999 International Wine Challenge held in London. In addition, Klein Constantia has achieved icon status with its Vin de Constance, which is modelled on the famous Constantia sweet dessert wine of the 18th century.

## KLEIN GUSTROUW
Stellenbosch

The farm has 16 hectares of vineyard and all the white wine is delivered to a local merchant. Chris McDonald is concentrating on producing a rich, well-oaked red blend of Cabernet Sauvignon and Merlot. Total production will be 1500 cases.

## KLEINE DRAKEN
Paarl

Previously known as Zandwijk, Kleine Draken changed its name to eliminate any confusion with any other producer. Kleine Draken is South Africa's only kosher winery and is run along the strictest 'kosher le pessach' lines throughout the year. The farm is situated below the Taal Monument on Paarl mountain. It was purchased by a Jewish company, Cape Gate, in 1983. Besides supplying local demand, a good deal of the 8000-case production is exported.

## KLEINE ZALZE
Stellenbosch

Three farms make up this enterprise. First, 30 hectares of vineyard, situated just south of Stellenbosch, are planted to premium grape varieties. Second, 200 hectares are situated near the Berg River in Wellington, consisting of old bush vines and new clone material. The third property, a new acquisition, is Boskloof, situated near Cape Agulhas with its particularly cool climate. Twenty hectares are already planted to vines and Kleine Zalze can now claim to own the most southerly vineyard in Africa. The new Kleine Zalze venture started in 1996 when the first farm was bought by Jan Malan and his brother-in-law, Kobus Basson. Willem Loots was appointed as cellarmaster in July 1999. The Kleine Zalze Vineyard Selection Range is being bottled with a new dark green label and there is also the Kleine Zalze range. In total, Kleine Zalze bottles five whites and seven reds. Accolades are rolling in, with the 1998 Kleine Zalze Shiraz winning a Double Gold at the 2000 Michelangelo International Wine Awards. The 1998 Kleine Zalze Cabernet Sauvignon won a Gold at the 2000 Monde Sélection Concours International Des Vins, Bruxelles, and the same wine won a Gold at the 2000 Singapore International Wine Challenge.

## KLOOFZICHT ESTATE
Tulbagh

Roger Fehlmann is an individualist who does not believe in modern methods in his vineyards and cellar. The popular Alter Ego is a Cabernet Sauvignon/Merlot blend, Alternative is a Chardonnay, and A Breed Apart is a fortified dessert wine. The property is currently up for sale.

## KOELENHOF CO-OP
Stellenbosch

The 80 members of this co-op are spread as far afield as Constantia, Stellenbosch, Durbanville and Wellington. Most of the wine is delivered in bulk to merchants, with only a very small portion being bottled under the co-op's name.

## KLOOVENBURG
Riebeek Berg – Swartland

This family-owned property last made wine in the 1950s and has since delivered its grapes to the Riebeek Co-op. The results of a small experimental amount of wine, produced in 1997, led Pieter du Toit to restore the farm cellar and go back into production. Early production was in the Riebeek cellar, but now a portion of the grapes from the 130-hectare vineyard will be made in the farm cellar. Seventy per cent of plantings are red and the 1998 Shiraz is a stunner. Pinotage and Chardonnay will follow.

## KNORHOEK
Stellenbosch

The Van Niekerks have long owned Knorhoek and delivered high-quality grapes to various cellars. When Hansie van Niekerk wanted to have wine under his own label, his old school pal Kobus Basson of Kleine Zalze provided cellar space until the Knorhoek cellar was completed. A portion of the property was sold to businessman David King, leaving 130 hectares of top-quality grapes for the Knorhoek cellar. Further plantings have been made as far away as Cape Agulhas in a joint venture with Kleine Zalze. Initial Cabernet Sauvignon and Pinotage are amongst the best the Cape produces.

## KOELENHOF WINERY
Stellenbosch

As with many of the co-ops, Koelenhof has become a company with its members now making up 75 shareholders. The cellar draws grapes from as far afield as Constantia, Stellenbosch, Durbanville and Wellington. It does contract wine making for numerous wineries and *négociants*. Some 5000 cases of wine are made under the cellar's own label.

## KWV
Paarl

On December 2, 1997 the KWV converted into a company after operating as a co-op for 80 years. It now conducts its business as a group of commercial companies with KWV Group Limited as the holding company. The shares of the group are held mainly by wine farmers. On August 1, 1995 the KWV founded KWV International to handle its total marketing drive, mainly into the export arena. The administrative and regulatory functions previously performed by the KWV are now the responsibility of the Wine Industry Trust. The Department of Agriculture is the current co-ordinater of establishing the Wine Trust. The KWV is well known for its high-quality brandies. In recent years its natural wines, particularly Cathedral Cellars, its premium label, have garnered more international awards than any other South African producer. With the launch of its Perold label in 2000, KWV International has established itself in the league of top-quality performers. This has been recognised by many of the world's industry commentators and underlined by Zelma Long during her opening address at the 2001 Nederburg International Auction, despite some curiously negative gripes from some local commentators. The Perold label will only be awarded to outstanding wines of a particular vintage. If a vintage does not produce a wine of sufficient quality, the label will not be used. The first release was an outstanding Shiraz from the 1996 vintage. Thus the KWV's various ranges are topped by the Perold label, with the flagship range being Cathedral Cellars. Robert's Rock is named after the giant chunk of granite on Paarl Mountain and includes the award-winning Roodeberg. Other ranges include Cape Country, Bonne Esperance, Pearly Bay and Kaaplander. 'New World' ventures include Red Vale, Cape Dutch and Mission Hill. The KWV also has some exciting joint marketing ventures with various cellars, including Riebeek, Slanghoek, Barrydale, McGregor and Botha. It also represents certain estates on some markets and these include La Borie, its own estate, Backsberg, Neethlingshof, Stellenzicht, Saxenburg and Môreson. The KWV's brandies won the trophy for 'Best Brandy Worldwide' at the International Wine and Spirit Competition in 1990 with a 20-year-old, in 1991 with a 10-year-old and in 2000 with Imoya VSOP. In 1999 the VOV 14-year-old was made from KWV distilled brandy. This record cannot be remotely matched by any other country, let alone another company. The KWV's Van der Hum and Van der Hum cream have done particularly well on the international market. Its head office, La Concorde, is a landmark in Paarl, as are its massive cellars across the railway line. The company has one of the world's largest brandy distilleries at Worcester. It also owns distilleries at Upington and Vredendal. It has a juice concentrating plant in Upington and a 25 per cent shareholding in Ceres Fruit Juices. The company has a distribution and marketing subsidiary in the UK, Edward Cavendish and Sons (ECS), established in 1976. In Germany, the KWV holds the majority interest in the highly respected liquor company, Eggers and Franke of Bremen, with whom it has done business since the early 1930s. Dr Willem Barnard is managing director and Lourens Jonker is chairman. Vernon Cavis is managing director of KWV International.

## L'AVENIR ESTATE
Stellenbosch

Marc Wiehe bought L'Avenir in May 1992. He built the cellar in 1993 and hired Francois Naudé as winemaker. Francois has won the Perold Trophy for 'Best Pinotage' twice, once for the L'Avenir 1994 and again with the 1996 vintage at the International Wine and Spirit Competition. He has also been nominated a few times among the top 10 Pinotages in the Pinotage of the Year Competition. L'Avenir's 1999 Pinotage was the only Pinotage to receive a Double Gold at the Veritas 2000 Awards. In March 2001 L'Avenir won a Gold Medal for

its 2000 Chardonnay at the Chardonnay Du Monde competition in France. This was a great achievement since only 19 gold medals were awarded out of 897 entries from 35 countries. Not surprisingly, the most planted variety at L'Avenir is Pinotage, followed by Cabernet Sauvignon, Sauvignon Blanc, Chardonnay and Chenin Blanc.

## L'EMIGRE WINES
Stellenbosch

L'Emigré, originally Morgenzon, was bought by Alfred Gentis in the early 1920s. The current range of seven wines, made by Frans Gentis and his son Emile, includes a good Shiraz. He also makes port from traditional Portuguese varieties. Seventy-nine hectares are planted to vineyards, and the upgrading of varieties has been ongoing for the past decade. Only five per cent of the crop is bottled, with the balance going to wholesalers. Sixty per cent of the wine produced is red and the balance white.

## L'ORMARINS ESTATE
Franschhoek – Paarl

Jean Roi was granted the property in 1694. It was later owned by the De Villiers family who built a T-shaped home. This building is the oldest surviving building in the Cape winelands and is now occupied by the farm manager. The old wine cellar now houses attractive casks depicting the hand-carved coats of arms of many of the original French Huguenot families. In 1811 Isak Jacob Marais built the L'Ormarins homestead and planted 115 000 vines. L'Ormarins was bought by Dr Anton Rupert in 1969 and the farm is now owned by his son Anthonij Rupert. The current winemaker is Wrensch Roux. L'Ormarins is known for its Bordeaux-style blend, Optima. The Cabernet Sauvignon La Maison du Roi was the only South African wine to win Gold at the 1996 International Wine Challenge in Bordeaux. An impressive range of wines with four reds and six whites are bottled. Anthonij established Sangiovese and Nebbiolo vineyards some years ago and two Italian-style red wines are being made at L'Ormarins. A limited release of a 1998 Terra Del Capo Sangiovese has already been released to specialised Italian restaurants and a few selected wine shops. A 1999 Terra Del Capo will be released in the second half of 2001. Still in barrel, this is an impressive, beautifully structured wine. A luscious Nebbiolo will probably be released within the next year.

## LA BOURGOGNE
Franschhoek – Paarl

Michael Gillis is a pioneer in bringing Sémillon, the Cape's most planted vine earlier this century, back to the notice of wine lovers. He has been successful with his Joie de Vivre Sémillon, made by Franschhoek Vineyards Co-op, with some grapes from 50-year-old vines. His second wine is a Sémillon/Muscat d'Alexandrie blend. Michael is a member and former chairman of the Vignerons de Franschhoek.

## LA BRI
Franschhoek – Paarl

In 1997 Rob Hamilton bought this lovely property from Michael Trull. Michael and his wife Cheryl founded the Vignerons de Franschhoek and certainly put what was once a sleepy hollow firmly on the wine, food and tourism map. Rob has now replanted 10 hectares of vineyard with Cabernet Sauvignon, Merlot, Shiraz, Chardonnay and Sémillon. Driaan van der Merwe of Franschhoek Vineyards makes the wine. The Chardonnay/Sémillon blend is not only an unusual blend for South Africa, it is interestingly different and a really good wine. Two white wines are bottled and three reds.

## LA COURONNE
### Franschhoek – Paarl

Franschhoek can be desperately unlucky for talented young winemakers. First there was the death of John Goshen at Agusta Wines, and then in 1999, talented youngster from La Couronne, Spike Russell, was killed in a motor accident. Testimony to his talents were the Cabernet and Bordeaux-style blend he produced in 1999. Owner Miles Oates has splendidly luxurious accommodation and a quality, continental restaurant at La Couronne. He also produces a good Chardonnay and Sauvignon Blanc.

## LA MOTTE ESTATE
### Franschhoek – Paarl

Huguenot Pierre Joubert bought this property in 1709 and named it La Motte after his home in France. The Rupert family bought the farm in 1970 and La Motte is now owned by Dr Rupert's famous mezzo-soprano daughter, Hanneli Koegelenberg. La Motte is one of the largest properties in the Franschhoek valley. Currently 104 hectares are planted to Cabernet Sauvignon, Sauvignon Blanc, Shiraz, Merlot and Chardonnay. A further five hectares are in the pipeline. Jacques Borman started making wine at La Motte in 1984, and does not pander to fashion quirks. A regular visitor to the top châteaux in France, Jacques enthusiastically admits that he is inspired by top French wines. La Motte Millennium, a Bordeaux-style blend, received international recognition when the 1991 vintage won a Gold Medal at Vinexpo in France in 1995. This exceptional wine also won a Gold Medal at Intervin in the United States.

## LA PETITE FERME
### Franschhoek – Paarl

John Dendy Young and his family own this farm. In 1993 their first vintage was made by neighbour Francois Malherbe. In 1995 Mark Dendy Young converted part of the restaurant's bakery into a cellar. In May 1996 the restaurant was gutted by fire, but luckily the cellar and the vineyards escaped unscathed. Mark has been making wine since the 1996 vintage. There are now 10 hectares established to Sauvignon Blanc, Merlot, Chardonnay and Shiraz. A further five hectares are being developed. La Petite Ferme produces a particularly good Chardonnay and Blanc Fumé.

## LA ROCHE DU PREEZ
### Stellenbosch

Jan du Preez has established his cellar in Vlottenburg and sources his grapes from the Coastal Region. In 1992 he created the La Roche du Preez collection of wines in memory of his Huguenot forefathers. The range includes a Sauvignon Blanc, a Cabernet Sauvignon/Merlot blend and a Chardonnay Reserve.

## LABORIE ESTATE
### Paarl

In 1691 Laborie was established by French Huguenot, Jean Taillefert. In recent decades Laborie has been redeveloped and restored as a leading wine estate producing natural wines, sparkling wines and Alembic brandy. The curiosity is Pineau de Laborie, made from Pinotage grape juice fortified with Pinotage brandy. Production is about 35 000 cases, of which 70 per cent is red and the balance white.

## LADISMITH CO-OP
### Klein Karoo

The co-op is situated at the foot of the Towerkop mountain in the Swartberg range. In 1939 the Ladismith Co-operative Winery and Distillery was formed with 95 members. The distillery was the main source of income for many years, and the area was known for its high-quality brandy. A recent major upgrade of the distillery and the purchase of distilling wine from many other cellars has considerably increased quality production. The young spirit

produced is sold to merchants for ageing and eventual blending into its own brands. Today the 130 members are scattered as far apart as Laingsburg to Riversdale, and Amalienstein to Anysberg. The cellar crushes 10 000 tons, but only 4000 cases of wine are bottled, with an amount going to Switzerland in bulk, due no doubt to the influence of Swiss winemaker André Simonis. Towerkop Aristaat is a favourite Chardonnay/Colombar blend.

## LAIBACH VINEYARDS
### Stellenbosch

Laibach was considered by many as a 'bargain buy' when it was purchased in 1994 by Friederich and Loni Laibach who had retired from their German manufacturing business. They are now regular commuters between their homes in Italy and the Simonsberg, where 40 hectares of vineyards have been replanted. Wine making is under the consultancy of Weinsberg graduate Stefan Dorst. Seventy-five per cent is planted to red varieties, producing a total of some 17 000 cases. As would be expected, Laibach produces outstanding reds, Chardonnay, Chenin Blanc and Sauvignon Blanc.

## LANDAU DU VAL WINES
### Franschhoek – Paarl

In 1986 Basil and Jane Landau bought the La Brie property. It is an original Huguenot farm, but they have used their own name to avoid confusion with an existing wine named La Bri. The property, first farmed in 1689, has been totally restored by the Landaus. Their wines were made by the late John Goshen and now production is overseen by Jean Daneel. The 17-hectare vineyard only produces some 500 cases of Sémillon and Sauvignon Blanc. The Sémillon is made from vines dating back more than 90 years.

## LANDS END WINES
### Elim

This is a far-reaching project of a group of enthusiasts who have established, so far, 35 hectares of vineyard on three separate properties near Agulhas. It could well be one of the Cape's coolest vine-growing areas. The first wines have been made in the La Motte cellar where Hein Koegelenberg, one of the of the partners, is managing director. Vines planted include the classics: Cabernet Sauvignon, Merlot, Sauvignon Blanc and Sémillon. Earliest wines show potential.

## LANDSKROON ESTATE
### Paarl

In 1689 Jacques de Villiers and his family arrived from Holland with a letter of recommendation for their wine-making skills from the Here XVII. In 1872 the De Villiers family purchased Landskroon, situated on the southern slopes of the Paarl mountain. They soon acquired considerably more land and then developed the wine-making side of the farm. With a strong sense of dynastic continuity, all the eldest sons have been named Paul. At present, Landskroon is owned by Paul and Hugo de Villiers. Ninth-generation Paul Junior is the winemaker and Hugo is responsible for the 270 hectares of vineyard. Five white wines and seven red are currently bottled, but the estate is known for its port which won the Diners Club 'Winemaker of the Year' award in 2000 for the port category. Due to demand, port production has been increased from 25 000 to 30 000 bottles a year.

## LANDZICHT WINERY
### Jacobsdal – Free State

The Landzicht Winery was formerly known as Jacobsdal Co-op. It was established in 1974 and pressed its first grapes in 1977. The winemaker is Ian Sieg, who successfully made wine in a summer-rainfall area in Zimbabwe for six years. Production has now grown to almost 250 000 cases. Some 30 000 are marketed under the Landzicht label from the 325 hectares of

vineyards owned by 45 members, including Patrick Lekota. Year by year, Ian Sieg upgrades the cellar and ensures growers are doing the same in the vineyards in order to continually improve the quality of the wine. Landzicht is the only 'non-Cape' winery to gather a Gold at Veritas and also at Michelangelo.

## LANGVERWACHT CO-OP
### Bonnievale – Robertson

Formerly known as the Boesmansrivier Co-op, this co-op pressed its first grapes in 1956. Although the 30 members deliver nearly 10 000 tons of grapes, only a few thousand cases are bottled under its own label. The balance is delivered in bulk to merchants or for brandy distillation. The co-op produces consistently good Colombar. The importance of red wine has been recognised and a new red wine production cellar has been commissioned. The first red, Ruby Cabernet, has been released.

## LANZERAC FARM AND CELLAR
### Stellenbosch

The original farm, named Schoongezicht, was granted by Simon van der Stel in 1692 to Isaak Schrijver. The farm changed hands many times and the historic homestead, cellar and outbuildings were built by Coenraad Fick in the early 1800s. In 1914 the farm was bought by Elizabeth Katerina English, and she changed the name from Schoongezicht to Lanzerac. She made extensive alterations to the house and the farm buildings, and was the first to produce wines of quality which were sold in bulk. Mrs English also made brandy which she exported to Egypt. In 1929 the farm was bought by Johannes Tribbelhorn, who became a member of the Cape Quality Wine Growers' Association. By 1936 he had established what was then one of the most modern wine cellars in the Cape. In 1941 the farm was purchased by Angus Buchanan, who enlarged and improved the cellars. In 1947 the first wines were bottled under the Lanzerac label. His exceptional Cabernet Sauvignon won a perpetual floating trophy for eight successive years at the South African National Young Wine Show. He also won the white wine trophy for three successive years. During this period sherry and brandy were produced at Lanzerac and sold in bulk. Angus introduced fermentation tanks of Algerian design which were the only ones of their kind in South Africa. He also developed a unique system of keeping the grape husks in constant contact with the fermenting must when making red wine. The Rawdons purchased Lanzerac in 1958 and transformed it into a luxury country hotel. The vineyards were managed by SFW. In 1959 SFW launched Lanzerac Rosé, the first wine in the range. Two years later SFW launched the world's first Pinotage with a 1959 vintage. These wines were made with some grapes from Lanzerac until the late 1970s when the farm stopped cultivating vineyards. Older vintages of Pinotage continue to fetch high prices at the Nederburg International Auction. A case of the 1968 Lanzerac Pinotage was the first lot at the 1997 Nederburg International Auction and the 1969 Lanzerac Pinotage was the last lot. In 1991 Christo Wiese bought the property, along with two adjoining farms. He embarked on an extensive replanting programme. Currently 50 hectares are planted mainly to Cabernet Sauvignon, Merlot, Chardonnay and Shiraz, and a new generation of wines is now being produced on this historic property. The Lanzerac Rosé and Pinotage will continue to be made by SFW. All other wines will be produced at Lanzerac by winemaker Wynand Hamman in close association with SFW.

## LE BONHEUR ESTATE
### Stellenbosch

This farm was first granted to Jurgen Hanekom in 1715. Since 1999 it has been owned by Lusan Holdings. Michael Woodhead had bought this property in 1972 and changed the name to Le Bonheur. He completely reworked the soils and planted selected vines. As an early member of the Bergkelder scheme, his first wines were bottled in 1982. A modern cellar was built and the first grapes were crushed in 1990. After Michael Woodhead retired, the Bergkelder completed replanting and restored the homestead and surrounds. Sakkie Kotzé has been winemaker since 1993. Le Bonheur markets two reds, a Merlot and a Cabernet Sauvignon, and two whites, a Chardonnay and a Sauvignon Blanc.

## LE GRAND CHASSEUR ESTATE
Robertson

The name means 'the great hunter' and could well be taken from the African fish eagles that are resident on this Breede River estate. The property is owned by Albertus de Wet, whose grandfather built the cellar in 1929. The 240-hectare vineyard produces some 60 per cent white, 37 per cent red and three per cent rosé. The cellar produces considerable quantities for merchants and for export, but has ever-increasing quantities under its own label. The range's name, Laughing Waters, comes from a spring that appeared after the 1969 earthquake.

## LE RICHE WINES
Stellenbosch

Etienne le Riche was winemaker at Rustenberg for over 20 years before becoming one of the Cape's newest *négociants*. Etienne only makes red wine, and his methods are traditional as he uses open fermentation tanks. Grapes are sourced from the Stellenbosch district and Muldersvlei. Total production is 6000 cases made up of Cabernet Sauvignon and Merlot. Most of the wine is marketed under the Le Riche label and a small amount is bottled as Leef Op Hoop.

*Vineyards near Robertson in the Klein Karoo.*

## LEIDERSBERG VINEYARD
Paarl

The farm is situated right on the boundary of Paarl and Stellenbosch near Elsenburg Agricultural College. Entrepreneur Jan du Preez has a syndicate of overseas investors for this 18-hectare vineyard that is now planted to a third red with the balance white. This will change with new plantings. A maturation cellar with sales and tasting facilities is being built and wines will be made in nearby cellars until it is completed.

## LEMBERG ESTATE
Tulbagh

In 1994 this farm was purchased by Klaus Schindler who built a cellar and did considerable replanting. He had early success when the German publication, *Alles über Wein*, placed his Sauvignon Blanc fifth out of 74 entries of Sauvignon Blanc and Sémillon wines from the southern hemisphere. With time one gets the impression the guest house, picnics and country walks become more important than the small, 1000-case production of mainly white wine. The names Sensual Red and Laughing Duck are labels certainly more attractive than the actual wines. The wines are not certified, so carry no vintage dates.

## LIEVLAND ESTATE
Stellenbosch

The first recorded bottling of wine at Lievland was by Baroness Hendrike von Stiernhelm. In the early 1930s her husband, Baron Karl von Stiernhelm, came to South Africa from Lievland, a small eastern European state situated on the Baltic Sea. The farm was bought by the Benadé family in 1974, and they replanted the vineyards with classic varieties. Cape Wine Master Paul Benadé was one of the first to plant Merlot, and he built an underground vaulted cellar. He had an interest in Shiraz and by the early 1990s Lievland became one

of the Cape's foremost producers of 'new style' Shiraz. Sixty-two hectares are planted to vines, with an additional 10 hectares to come. The main varieties planted are Shiraz followed by Cabernet Sauvignon, Cinsaut, Ruby Cabernet and Merlot. Grenache will be included in the new plantings. Winemaker Jaun (Pine) Pienaar and consultant James Farquharson, who was previously the full-time winemaker at Lievland, vinify Shiraz, a structured Bordeaux-style blend and a particularly good dry Weisse Reisling.

## LINTON PARK WINES
Wellington – Paarl

Linton Park and Capell's Court wines are produced on Slangrivier Farm located in the foothills of the Groenberg mountain near Wellington. The farm and wine-making operation is owned by Linton Park plc, a London-listed company with extensive agricultural and horticultural interests throughout the world, including the production of tea, coffee, citrus, nuts, avocados and grapes. Linton Park is also the largest importer of caviar into the United Kingdom. The property was purchased in 1995. Vineyards were replanted, a new cellar built and the 1809 homestead restored. Winemaker Ian Naude has made some stunning wines from the 180 or so hectares of vineyard on the 285-hectare property. The Shiraz is an absolute cracker and the Cabernet up with the best. The various ranges have wines from all the classic varieties.

## LONG MOUNTAIN WINES
Stellenbosch

The French Groupe Pernod Ricard has moved into local production under international wine developer Robin Day. He eventually sourced the desired grapes from the Langeberg, hence the brand name Long Mountain. The wines enjoyed immediate success in Great Britain, Ireland and Western Europe. Managing winemaker is Jaques Kruger, who works closely with

local winery partners and their growers to produce the fruit and wines required by this highly successful international operation. Ranges include Long Mountain, Gecko Ridge and La Fontein.

## LOOPSPRUIT ESTATE
Bronkhorstspruit – Gauteng

This estate is the first registered wine estate north of the Orange River, and is situated on the banks of the Loopspruit River about 35 kilometres from Bronkhorstspruit. It was established in 1969 from bushveld by Eric Oliver, and the winemaker is Boet Myburgh. More than 20 hectares of vineyard are in full production and include varieties such as Cabernet Sauvignon, Chardonnay, Chenin Blanc, Colombar and now Ruby Cabernet. A full range of dry wines, sparkling and fortifieds is produced and sold mostly at the cellar. Loopspruit also has its own pot still and produces witblitz and mampoer.

## LOST HORIZON WINES

This is a venture between US and French companies that have their wines made in a number of local cellars. They also buy wine from others. It is a highly successful export company with quantities now close to 200 000 cases. Local success has come with a blue one-litre bottle containing a carbonated Chenin/Sauvignon blend under the Quantum label.

## LOUIESENHOF
Stellenbosch

This property is a subdivision of Koopmanskloof and is owned by winemaker Stefan Smit, who for many years made wine at his family's property Koopmanskloof. He produced his first grapes for wine making on Louiesenhof in 1995, and farms as naturally as possible. Stefan's wines are elegantly labelled and bottled. His Cape Late Bottled Port is made in the traditional Portuguese style, and his pot-still brandy is called Marbonne. One hundred and twenty hectares are planted to vineyards, with a further 40 hectares in development. Pinotage is the most planted variety, followed by Cabernet Sauvignon, Merlot, Chardonnay and Sauvignon Blanc. Three whites and three reds are bottled under the Louisenhof label.

## LOUISVALE
Devon valley – Stellenbosch

Hans Froehling and Leon Stemmert have owned Louisvale since 1988. The farm originally specialised in Chardonnay, and has been successful with every vintage. More recently Hans and Leon have branched out into the production of red wines. At present 13 hectares are planted to Chardonnay. Cabernet Sauvignon, Merlot and Pinotage are bought in from the Stellenbosch area. Three whites and six reds are bottled. Louisvale Chardonnay has always been the flagship and in more recent years it has been joined by a Bordeaux-style wine named Dominique. Louisvale has recently been purchased by Michael Johnston.

## LOUWSHOEK-VOORSORG CO-OP
Rawsonville – Worcester

For many years this co-op has produced fortified Hanepoot and dry Sémillon for merchants in bulk. The co-op is well known for its Necta de Provision, a wine fortified with five-year-old brandy made from Colombar. Most of the wineries in this area are moving their focus from sweet fortified to dry natural white and red wines. The current trend towards Sémillon is good for Louwshoek, as it has been a long-time producer of large volumes of this variety for SFW's Graça blend. The 34 members deliver 14 000 tons.

## LUDDITE
Walker Bay – Overberg

This label belongs to Niels Verbrug and Hillie Meyer. Niels is better known as the winemaker at Beaumont Wines in Bot River, where the first Luddite wine was made. His first vintage was a 2000 Shiraz made from grapes specially selected in the Stellenbosch area. Only 500 cases were made, but by 2000 Luddite anticipates bottling 5000 cases. Only Shiraz will be produced. Two hectares of Shiraz are currently planted on this Bot River property and the vineyard will be increased to 10 hectares over the next few years.

## LUSAN PREMIUM WINES (PTY) LTD
Stellenbosch

In July 1999, Distillers Corporation (South African Distillers and Wines) joined forces with the international financier Hans-Joachim Schreiber (Hygrace) to form a new company, Lusan Holdings (Pty) Ltd. Based on a foundation of five superb wine properties, the expertise of well-established winemakers, and the marketing clout of Distillers, this merger took place to give its partners access to a wider range of quality wines for national and international markets. The operating company of this joint venture is Lusan Premium Wines (Pty) Ltd. Lusan is responsible for the farming activities and the production of wine from the following Stellenbosch properties: Le Bonheur Estate, Uitkyk Estate, Stellenbosch Vineyards, Alto Estate and Neethlingshof Estate. The name, Lusan, contains the first letter of each of the five properties. Towards the end of 2000, Distillers Corporation, in turn, merged with Stellenbosch Farmers' Winery to form Distell – a new giant in the wine industry. Lusan focuses exclusively on the production of quality wines and an estate brandy, while Distell handles the local and international marketing and sales of the company's products.

## LUSHOF
Helderberg – Stellenbosch

On the slopes of the Helderberg, this 14-hectare property was purchased by chemical industry businessman, Hennie Steyn. The 12.5 hectares of vineyard are being replanted with classic varieties. A compact cellar was in operation for the 2000 vintage, with its first release being a Sauvignon Blanc.

## LUTZVILLE VINEYARDS
Olifants River

Lutzville Vineyards was founded in 1962 as a co-op. It is now a company with 106 shareholders. Lutzville crushes some 42 000 tons, making it one of the biggest cellars in South Africa. Red grapes have almost doubled to around five per cent of production in the past few years. The cellar has been enlarged to cater for red wine making. The main brand is Fleermuisklip, named after a massive overhanging rock, now declared a national monument, that is home to millions of bats.

## LYNGROVE
Stellenbosch

Lyngrove is a beautiful country house with 76 hectares of well-established vineyards planted mainly to reds. The property is owned by Hollander 'Sip' Baarsma and the vineyards and wine making are looked after by Danie Zeeman. A cellar is planned, but in the meantime the wines are custom-made in a selected cellar. Some 5000 cases from its own production plus 10 million litres of wine are exported mainly to Europe. These wines are selected by Danie in cellars in Worcester and Robertson and blended to requirement.

## MASTERS PORT
Calitzdorp

Three Cape Wine Masters, Carel Nel of Boplaas, Boets Nel of Die Krans and Tony Mossop of Axe Hill, have combined to create an equal-parts blend for this Cape Vintage Reserve Port. Only two vintages, one in 1997 and the second in 1998, have been produced with Souzão, Tinta Barocca and Touriga Naçional.

## McGREGOR WINERY
McGregor – Robertson

This co-op was established in 1948 and produced its first wines in 1950. It has now converted to a company with 41 owners. Some 680 hectares of vineyards deliver close to 10 000 tons. More than 90 per cent is still white, but there are increasing quantities of red. First bottling was in 1975. Today some 25 000 cases are bottled and the balance is dispatched in bulk.

## MEERENDAL ESTATE
Durbanville

Meerendal is one of the oldest farms in the Cape and vines were recorded there as early as 1716. William Starke bought the farm in 1929 and produced wine for delivery to the KWV. In 1948 Koosie joined his father. He took over operations in 1952 and joined the Bergkelder's marketing scheme. In 1991, after Koosie's death, grandson William took over the management of the 200-hectare estate. The estate, however, is still owned by the J.C.F. Starke Trust. Meerendal is known for its Shiraz and Pinotage. Now a good Cabernet Sauvignon is bottled and an exciting 1998 Bordeaux-style blend named Cabochen has been added to the range, which includes five red and four white wines.

## MEERLUST ESTATE
Stellenbosch

This architectural gem in the Cape winelands has a fascinating history dating back 300 years. The farm was originally purchased in 1756 by Johannes Albertus Myburgh and Hannes Myburgh is the eighth-generation Myburgh to farm Meerlust. The recent resurgence of Meerlust can be dated to 1950 after Nicolaas (Nico) Myburgh took over. He set about restoring the buildings to their former glory. He also began a replanting programme, introducing noble varieties and in time a range of extremely fine red wines of exceptional quality. One of Italy's most valuable exports to the Cape has been Giorgio Dalla Cia. He has been responsible for making Meerlust wines the icons that they are today. Meerlust Rubicon, a Bordeaux-style blend, remains the flagship, followed by Merlot, a Pinot Noir Reserve and a huge Chardonnay that has been backed by 13 years of experimentation.

## MEERHOF CELLARS
Swartland

A novel claim to being different is that this is the only cellar on the Swartland Wine Route that will have a view of Table Mountain. Gert Kotzé is delighted about building this new cellar situated in the Bosmanskloof Pass. The first release, made by Frikkie Botes, will be a Shiraz. The wines will be labelled Meerhof de la Caille, named after a Frenchman who was the Cape's first Land Surveyor during Jan van Riebeeck's tenure as commander of the Cape of Good Hope.

## MEINERT WINES
Stellenbosch.

Martin Meinert owns Devon Crest vineyards. He purchased the farm in 1987 at the top end of the Devon valley. His 600-hectolitre winery was completed in 1991. Some 13 hectares of vineyard comprises Cabernet Sauvignon, Merlot, Pinotage and some Cabernet Franc. First wines under his own label only emerged from the 1997 vintage. Prior to that, the cellar was utilised by various winemakers to custom-make various wines. Martin makes his own label and produces for Ken Forrester, Sylvanvale and Woolworths.

## MELLASAT
Paarl

Mellasat is owned by British farmers Stephen and Alison Richardson who purchased the property in 1996. They have replanted the 13-hectare vineyard to about 60 per cent red varieties comprising Cabernet Sauvignon, Shiraz and Pinotage. Wines will be exported to the United Kingdom.

## PAUL CLUVER WINES
Elgin – Overberg

In 1875 De Rust was granted to Christiaan Krynauw. On the original title deed it was described as a cattle station. In 1813 De Rust belonged to Nicolaas Swart, one of only eight farms on the plateau now known as Elgin. Today there are more than 100 farms in the Elgin area. Present owner Dr Paul Cluver is the great-grandson of Matthys de Villiers, who bought the farm in 1896. Today the 2000-hectare farm is one of the few original farms in the district. Dr Paul Cluver took over from his father in 1976. Paul was assisted by Nederburg in his efforts to pioneer Elgin's outstanding potential for top wines. His Weisser Riesling won Double Gold for three successive years in the Veritas Awards, as well as a Silver in the 1994 International Wine and Spirit Competition. Elgin's uniquely cool climate makes it suitable for Chardonnay and Pinot Noir. Comparative studies have shown that this region has interesting similarities with Burgundy, the home of these two classic grape varieties. Günter Brözel saw the potential of this area and Paul agreed to accept the challenge to diversify his farming operation. The first vineyards were established on De Rust in 1986 under the guidance of Ernst le Roux, and in 1990 its first wines were made by Nederburg under the Paul Cluver label. In 1996 Paul then established a cellar on De Rust, and the first grapes to come into the cellar in 1997 were Gewürztraminer. Winemaker Andries Burger has been with the cellar since its inception and in time will produce 100 000 litres. Dr Paul Cluver developed the Lebanon Project, an empowering process, six years ago. Together with the South African Forestry Co. Limited (SAFCOL) and the Anglican Society Development Institute, this project found land so that the forestry workers' village would become a beacon in the new South Africa. They formed the Lebanon Fruit Trust, now known as Thandi Farms.

## PERDEBERG CO-OP
Paarl

Perdeberg and the now retired Joseph Huskisson are synonymous with Chenin Blanc. Joseph was one of the early co-op winemakers who served his apprenticeship at Nederburg under Arnold Graue. The co-op was established in 1941 and pressed its first vintage in 1942. Membership has always been about 50 and tonnage has grown to 18 000 tons. The co-op is geared to take in 1000 tons a day. Wines are supplied mainly to merchants in bulk, but it is famous for Pinotage, Chenin and an unusual Cinsaut liqueur wine. The new, small-scale production has yielded an upbeat, modern-styled Shiraz.

## PLAISIR DE MERLE
Franschhoek – Paarl

This farm is owned by Stellenbosch Farmers' Winery. The buildings were restored and the vineyards replanted with classic varieties. The magnificent new cellar is surrounded by a moat. Gargoyles and a frieze depicting the history of the farm decorate the building. Winemaker Neil Bester spent time working at Château Margaux with Paul Pontallier before his first vintage at Plaisir de Merle. Neil's maiden 1993 vintage Cabernet Sauvignon was hailed as a new direction for Cape wine. The regular range includes Cabernet Sauvignon, Merlot, Chardonnay and Sauvignon Blanc. An outstanding Shiraz might not be repeated as it is now included in a Cape red blend. Experimental wines from Petit Verdot and Sangiovese are showing great promise.

## PORTERVILLE CO-OP
Piketberg – Swartland

This is the only co-op in the Piketberg area. It has recently been upgraded and its capacity increased from 14 000 to 20 000 tons. The co-op was established in 1941, and it now has 110 members. A small amount of wine has been bottled since the early 1980s, but most of the wine still leaves the cellar in bulk. Whites have been dominant, but plans are to deliver 20 per cent red by 2005.

## POST HOUSE CELLAR
Helderberg – Stellenbosch

The Post House Cellar takes its name from the Post Office which used to serve the local missionary community of Raithby. It is now the owner's residence and also contains the winery office with its bright red post box outside. The rustic cellar produces close to 1000 cases under colourful labels. The owner, winemaker and farmer is Nicholas Gerber.

## PROSPECT 1870
Robertson

The farm is situated in the Robertson District near the confluence of the Cogmanskloof and Breede rivers. Immediate neighbours are Zandvliet, Excelsior and De Wetshof. Owned by even more De Wets, the brothers Chris and Nic are fifth-generation farmers of the land. Vines were first planted in 1870 and in recent times delivered mainly to a co-op cellar. For the past four years, Shiraz, Cabernet Sauvignon, Merlot and Pinotage have been planted on selected sites. The current 20 hectares will be increased with further plantings of Cabernet as well as Chardonnay. Until their own grapes come on stream, wine has been bought in. The Prospect brand has been launched in the USA with a 1998 Cabernet Sauvignon and a 2000 Merlot.

## RADFORD DALE
Stellenbosch

The owners are Ben Radford, the winemaker for Winecorp, and Alex Dale, who was the previous marketing man at Longridge. Ben Radford makes the wine, while Dale, with many years of French experience, handles the exports. Sourcing grapes from top-quality vineyards and hiring space in local cellars, they produce some 3000 cases at present.
Current production is about two thirds red with the balance white. So far they have produced absolutely top-class Merlot, Chardonnay and Shiraz.

## REMHOOGTE ESTATE.
Simonsberg – Stellenbosch

Murray Boustred has adapted quickly and easily to the wine scene with help from wine guru Jean Daneel and vineyard consultant Johan Pienaar. Remhoogte was recently registered as an estate and 30 hectares are planted to Cabernet Sauvignon, Merlot, Chenin Blanc and Pinotage. Murray intends to make red wines and the cellar has been enlarged to accommodate increased production each year. Currently three red wines are bottled and they are all wood matured for two years. The 1998 Merlot has already received special accolades after being placed in the Top 10 by *Wine* magazine.

## REYNEKE WINES
Stellenbosch

Situated on the slopes of the Polkadraai hills, this property has 20 hectares planted to Cabernet Sauvignon, Merlot, Shiraz, Sauvignon Blanc and Chardonnay. Reyneke is owned by the Reyneke Family Trust, together with James Farquharson who has been winemaker since 1998. To qualify for this position James had to learn to surf, a sport that Johan Reyneke is very good at. Cleavers and other hand tools dating from the Early Stone Age have been found in the vineyards of the farm. These beautifully crafted implements are depicted on the wine labels. Reyneke wines are exported to the United Kingdom and Germany. The farm workers have shares in the business, making for a motivated team.

## RHEBOKSKLOOF ESTATE
Paarl

Rhebokskloof was granted to Dirk van Schalkwyk in 1692, but the early history of the farm is not known. Mervyn Key restored this 450-hectare property in the 1980s and made it one of the Paarl District's show farms, with export fruit, an Ile de France sheep stud and wine grapes. Mervyn built a large wine cellar, two restaurants and conference facilities. In 1994,

Rhebokskloof was bought by Keith Jenkins, whose daughter, Tracey, is senior estate manager. There are 90 hectares planted to vineyards which will be increased by 11 hectares over the next three years. The five most planted varieties are Chardonnay followed by Cabernet Sauvignon, Pinotage, Merlot and Sauvignon Blanc. There are 13 wines in the range, seven whites and six reds. A particularly opulent Chardonnay Sur Lie is produced. The 1998 vintage of this wine and the Grand Reserve of the same year received recognition at the International Wine and Spirit Competition. In the June 1999 edition, *Decanter* magazine's Buying Guide chose the 1995 Rhebokskloof Estate Cabernet Sauvignon as one of their two recommended wines for the month.

## RICKETY BRIDGE VINEYARDS
Franschhoek – Paarl

The property was originally granted to Paulina de Villiers in 1797 and named Paulinas Dal. The new name was given by one-time owner, Dr Nigel McNaught. However, the bridge is no longer rickety, as Deborah Idiens and Robin Singer rebuilt it during their brief ownership. They also significantly upgraded the cellar and restored the homestead. After purchasing Rickety Bridge from Deborah and Robin, Alan Tolkin built a new cellar. The farm changed hands when Duncan Spence purchased the farm from Alan Tolkin. It has recently been put up for sale yet again. Butch McEwen is currently manager of the property. Approximately 16 hectares are planted to vines, producing four reds and three whites.

## RIEBEEK CELLARS
Swartland

This cellar was established during the Second World War because a cellar was essential to accept the grapes of the area. Despite shortages of building materials and equipment, the co-op crushed its first crop in 1942 from 20 members. In the early 1980s tonnage rose to 16 000 tons from 70 members. The co-op has now converted to a company with 63 shareholders who deliver 18 000 tons. The range includes reds from classic varieties and a Chardonnay with a single vineyard designation. Labels include A Few Good Men, Cape Table and Riebeek.

## RIETRIVIER CO-OP
Klein Karoo

Rietrivier is a 45-member co-op 20 kilometres outside Montagu. Its 5000 tons are made mainly into wine for brandy distillation, although some wines are bottled for sale. In 1978 the cellar produced its first wine for bottling. Most was consumed by the 45 members, but it is now moving cautiously into public sales.
The co-op crushes some 6000 tons and the top wine is a Montagu Muscadel. It also bottles brandy, distilled by the KWV from rebate wine made at the cellar.

## RIETVALLEI ESTATE
Robertson

Rietvallei is situated east of Robertson, and has been in the Burger family since 1864. The farm produced wine until the end of the Second World War. Muscadel was produced in the old farm cellar. Johnny Burger started to work on the farm in 1968 and learnt how to make Red Muscadel from the original recipe which had been written out and tacked behind the cellar door so as not to be forgotten. In 1974 he produced South Africa's champion Muscadel. In 1981 he built a modern cellar capable of producing natural dry wines and in 1989 launched a wooded Chardonnay. Rooi Muscadel remains the estate's most sought-after wine and the grapes for this wine are grown from cuttings of the original muscadel vines planted in 1908. The wines are marketed by the Bergkelder. Known for its fortified wines, this lovely estate has 170 hectares planted to vineyards with a further 30 hectares on the drawing board. Sauvignon Blanc is the most planted variety, followed by Chardonnay.

## RIJK'S PRIVATE CELLAR
Tulbagh

Rijk's arrived on the scene with a spectacular debut at the 2000 Young Wine Show, garnering a bunch of Gold Medals. All of a sudden, traditionally white Tulbagh had award-winning red wines. At Veritas in the same year Rijk's won a Double Gold for a Sauvignon Blanc. The release of the ground-breaking reds is eagerly awaited. Rijk's is owned by Neville Dorrington. He has planted 31 hectares of vineyard from scratch where it was previously considered vines would not succeed. Vines now bearing include Cabernet Sauvignon, Shiraz, Merlot, Pinotage, Chardonnay, Sauvignon Blanc, Sémillon and Chenin Blanc. Production is planned for 15 000 cases in a cleverly designed, purpose-built cellar heavily influenced by *supremo* Brözel.

## ROBERTSON WINERY
Robertson

The co-op was founded in 1941 with 41 members and pressed its first grapes with Pon van Zyl as first winemaker. He held this post through to his retirement in 1985. In 1968 Pon was so taken by the aromas coming off some Colombar being fermented for brandy distillation that he decided to pursue its production as a natural wine. Today the co-op has 42 members and crushes 25 000 tons. Robertson Co-op began to bottle some of its production in 1969 and eventually bottled its entire production. Bottling might be the wrong word, since wine is also packaged in Vinipaks, which are aseptic wine cartons. The present winemaker, Bowen Botha, has been in charge since 1984. His aim is to make friendly, drinkable wines at affordable prices. The cellar has collected many accolades and awards. Pernod Ricard bases the production of its Long Mountain range at this cellar. A R10-million red wine production facility is now in operation to handle the expected move to about 8000 tons of red grapes by 2005. The cellar is also dipping into brandy production, with its first release expected in about 2004 or 2005.

## ROBUSTO WINES
Stellenbosch

Teddy Hall left a thriving business in Pretoria, bringing his family to the Cape, to enable him to attend Stellenbosch University to learn about wine making. He now heads up the wine making at Kanu. For his own account, he has a three-hectare vineyard with about a 50/50 split between red and white grapes. He also manages a Chenin vineyard at Koelenhof. With these grapes he made the oak-aged Robusto Chenin runner-up to his winning Kanu 1999 Chenin at *Wine* magazine's Chenin challenge. It's a gutsy wine appropriately named after a gutsy cigar. Teddy is chairman of the Chenin Study Group.

## ROMANSRIVIER WINERY
Worcester

Romansrivier was founded as a co-op with 18 members. It pressed its first grapes in 1950. When Olla Olivier was winemaker from 1974 to 1996, it developed a reputation of developing fine young winemakers such as Eben Sadie, now at Spice Route, and Bartho Eksteen. Today 43 members own the operation, which crushes about 7500 tons. It produces some 6000 cases under its own label, drawing grapes from far afield, including Ceres where the farm Koelfontein is situated. It is noted for its Chardonnay.

## ROODEZANDT CO-OP
Robertson

Roodezandt gets its name from the original farm where the town of Robertson is built. Roodezandt Co-op was formed by 14 members in 1953. Early production was for brandy and spirit distillation. Winemaker Robbie Roberts joined the cellar in 1966 and put Roodezandt on the map. During the devastating floods of 1981, Robbie, always one to make the best of any situation, produced a remarkable Noble Late Harvest from salvaged grapes. He marketed it as Le Grand Deluge. Today there are 53 members. Tonnage can vary from 23 000 to 27 000 tons, depending on the vintage and new plantings coming on stream. Red plantings will move the current crop from seven per cent to close to 15 per cent of tonnage by 2005. Winemaker Christie Steytler will be receiving mostly Cabernet Sauvignon, Ruby Cabernet, Chardonnay, Sauvignon Blanc and Colombar in the cellar.

## ROOIBERG CO-OP
Robertson

Rooiberg was established just outside Robertson in 1964 by 11 farmers. Now it has 35 owner/members who collectively have some 720 hectares of vineyard. They deliver about 12 000 tons on average. The red percentage is already at 15 per cent and growing. Rooiberg was the domain of Dassie Smith for 25 years and now is in the capable hands of Tommy Loftus. Rooiberg consistently receives many awards, which has helped in the success of its export drive.

## ROZENDAL FARM
Stellenbosch

Kurt Amman bought Rozendal, originally part of Lanzerac, in 1981. The original homestead and wine cellar were built in 1864, and wine was made there until 1955. Kurt's first vintage, a Cabernet Sauvignon/Cinsaut blend, was made in 1983. The wine was sold at the Cape Independent Winemakers' Guild Auction in 1985 and won a Silver Medal at the International Wine and Spirit Competition in 1989. Kurt has now changed his Rozendal blend predominantly to Merlot with some Cabernet Sauvignon. Production runs to 2000 to 3000 cases.

## RUITERBOSCH MOUNTAIN VINEYARDS
Ruiterbosch

Ruiterbosch is in the Outeniqua mountains overlooking Mossel Bay. After buying the land in 1985, Carel Nel and his late father developed the vineyards. Ruiterbosch experiences some of the coolest average temperatures in the Cape and this ensures slow ripening. The first wine produced was a 1989 Sauvignon Blanc. The range of wines under the Ruiterbosch label includes a Sauvignon Blanc, a Chardonnay and a sparkling Pinot Noir. The grapes are vinified at the Boplaas winery.

## RUITERSVLEI ESTATE
Paarl

The Faure family have long been producers of fine fortified wines, which were delivered to local merchants. In 1996 there was a dramatic change because John Faure's four daughters took over. They have moved this 300-hectare estate into a top-quality producer of some 50 000 cases with excellent export results and good local demand. Currently the estate is planted 50/50 red and white, but recent red plantings will change this significantly in the next few years. The ranges include Ruitersvlei, Ruitersberg, Four Sisters and John Faure, and they include a stunning Cabernet Sauvignon, a Merlot and a blend of both. The Cinsaut/Cabernet blend makes for great regular wine.

## RUPERT & ROTHSCHILD VIGNERONS
Franschhoek – Paarl

Rupert & Rothschild Vignerons is a partnership between Anthonij Rupert and Benjamin de Rothschild at the historic French Huguenot farm called Fredericksburg. The farm, situated on the slopes of the Simonsberg mountain between Paarl and Franschhoek, was founded in 1690 by the brothers Jean and Daniel Nortier. Michel Rolland, world-renowned oenologist, is consulting with winemaker Schalk-Willem Joubert. They produce a range including Baroness Nadine, a 100 per cent barrel-fermented Chardonnay, and Baron Edmund and Classique, both red blends made from noble varieties.

## RUST EN VREDE ESTATE
Stellenbosch

Granted by Simon van der Stel in 1694, this large property's first owner was Willem van der Wêreld. Rust en Vrede was part of the original property formerly called Bonterivier. Vines were planted at Bonterivier in 1730 and the old wine cellar was built in 1790. The Rust en Vrede homestead was built in 1825. Bonterivier was subdivided in the mid-1850s and one of the portions became Rust en Vrede. Jannie Engelbrecht purchased Rust en Vrede in 1978. Chenin Blanc and four red varieties were then planted on the farm. Jannie built a new cellar for his first vintage in 1979. Small wood was introduced quite recently and Jannie was one of the first to use new French oak barriques for all the red wine he produced in 1979. Kevin Arnold was winemaker from 1988 to 1997. The estate's flagship wine is labelled Rust en Vrede Estate Wine and is a blend of Cabernet Sauvignon, Shiraz and Merlot. Its other successful wine is the Rust en Vrede Shiraz. A good Cabernet Sauvignon and Merlot are also bottled. In 1998 Louis Strydom, who was assistant winemaker at Saxenburg, took over the wine making from Kevin Arnold. Forty hectares are planted to Cabernet Sauvignon, Shiraz and Merlot, with small plantings of Mourvèdre. Five red wines are bottled. The estate's flagship remains the Rust en Vrede Estate Wine, which is predominantly Cabernet Sauvignon, with Shiraz and Merlot. The 1996 vintage of this wine was awarded 92 points in *Wine Spectator*.

## RUSTENBERG
Stellenbosch

The land was originally granted to Roelof Pasman by Governor Simon van der Stel, and the history of Rustenberg has remained indelibly intertwined with the neighbouring farm, Schoongezicht, even though the two farms were separated in 1810. In the first quarter of the 19th century these two farms were very successful. Peter and Pam Barlow bought Rustenberg in 1940. Five years later they purchased Schoongezicht, the other half of the original farm, thus reuniting the properties. Rustenberg was one of the few wine farms to market its own wines before the First World War, and after the Barlows bought Schoongezicht they replanted the old vineyards and rebuilt the cellar. The winemaker, Reg Nicholson, continued to make wine until 1974, when his former assistant Etienne le Riche took over. Until 1987, the red wines were labelled Rustenberg and the white wines Schoongezicht. In 1988 the Barlows bottled a Chardonnay under the Rustenberg label, and since then they have discontinued the Schoongezicht label. In 1992 Rustenberg had a double celebration, the founding of the estate 310 years before and a century of uninterrupted bottling. In the past 20 years Rustenberg has had an impressive record of local and international awards. Etienne, only the third winemaker in more than 100 years, left after the vintage in 1995. Simon Barlow took over from his mother in 1988, and with the advice of 'flying' winemaker and consultant Kym Milne, he made a completely fresh start in 1996. Adi Badenhorst is now making the wine in the new wine cellar. This new cellar is built within the old cow byre to maintain the historical atmosphere, as most of the buildings on the estate are national monuments. Simon plans to produce 1000 cases annually of his top wine, labelled Rustenberg, which will be the best red wine of each vintage and could vary from year to year. A wine labelled Rustenberg Peter Barlow, in honour of his late father, is a Bordeaux-style blend. The estate's second label, Brampton, sources grapes from Nooitgedacht, where Simon and his family live. A Sauvignon Blanc, a Chardonnay, a Chardonnay Reserve, a Cabernet Sauvignon/Merlot blend and possibly a port will be bottled under the Brampton label.

## SAXENBURG
### Stellenbosch

Saxenburg was granted to a German named Sax in 1693. The original homestead was built in 1702. The De Villiers family lived on Saxenburg early in the 20th century and there is mention of them making wine. The Saxenburg homestead was destroyed by fire in 1945 and was rebuilt on the same site into the traditional H-shape. Fortunately the inner doors made of stinkwood and yellowwood, and a built-in cupboard, the oldest of its type in South Africa, were saved. Nothing of note happened in the next 40 years, and the vineyards and buildings became neglected. Adrian Bührer bought Saxenburg in 1989 and restored the homestead, farm buildings and garden. Nico van der Merwe joined Saxenburg as winemaker in 1991. Nico's 1991 Cabernet Sauvignon won the South African National Young Wine Show Champion Red Wine Trophy in 1992. In spite of this success, he predicted that Saxenburg was going to become best known for its Shiraz. By 1992 a third of the vineyards had been replanted. At the 1993 Championship Bottled Wine Show, Saxenburg's wines swept the boards as a private cellar, winning five Double Gold Veritas Awards, three for red wines and two for white wines. Nico uses French and American oak to age his Shiraz and Pinotage. The 1991 Saxenburg Shiraz was judged the best red wine at the 1994 Cape/Australian Taste-Off held in Sydney. With Saxenburg's many successes and growing recognition, a new pressing cellar has been built and the barrel maturation area has increased. The Bührers bought Château Capion in the Languedoc region of France in 1996. Nico thus finds himself making two vintages every year – one in South Africa and one in France – a first for a South African winemaker. Assistant winemaker Koos Thiart looks after Saxenburg wines during his absences. Seventy hectares are currently planted to vines, with another 30 hectares on the way. The most planted grape variety is Shiraz, Saxenburg's flagship wine. These plantings are followed by Cabernet Sauvignon, Sauvignon Blanc, Merlot and Pinotage. In the extensive range, there are four white wines and 10 reds. Among these, a popular white and popular red wine are blends of Château Capion and Saxenburg wines. A limited release of the 1997 Saxenburg Shiraz Select, one of the few five-star wines in *John Platter South African Wines*, became available in mid-2001.

## SCALI
### Paarl

For years Willie and Tania de Waal supplied grapes from their 90-hectare vineyards on their Perdeberg farm to Boland Wine Cellar. They now keep back 10 tons of their grapes and have started making Pinotage in an old, but renovated stone cellar.

## SIEDELBERG ESTATE
### Paarl

It is said that history repeats itself. The new owner of one of Paarl's oldest farms, Roland Siegel, is from Hamburg, Germany. The first owner of the same farm in 1691 was also German. Vast sums of money have been spent on re-establishing Siedelberg Estate, situated between Landskroon and Fairview. The estate, 420 hectares in extent, has 85 hectares planted to vines and another 35 hectares should still be established. The most planted red variety is Cabernet Sauvignon, followed by Merlot, Pinotage and Shiraz. White varieties in order of importance are Chardonnay, Sauvignon Blanc and Viognier. Three different ranges of wines are bottled: Rolands Reserve, Siedelberg and De Leuwen Jagt. Winemaker and manager Nicolaas Rust has ambitions to develop Siedelberg into one of Paarl's top properties.

## SIGNAL HILL
### Stellenbosch

Jean-Vincent Ridon is making wine in hired cellar space and sourcing grapes from selected sites while he develops his own four-hectare vineyard on the Simonsberg slopes. He is a prime mover behind the Air France-Préteux Bourgeois competition. His own wines, mainly for export, are all individually styled and his dessert wines are usually outstanding.

## SIMONSIG ESTATE
### Stellenbosch

Frans Malan, the patriarch of the Malan family, has always been an energetic innovator. He was not only elected as a director of the KWV, but is also one of the three founding members of the Stellenbosch Wine Route. Simonsig, with 240 hectares planted to vines, is one of the largest estates, and comprises three farms, Morgenster, Simonsig and De Hoop where the cellar is situated. De Hoop was already registered as a name, so Frans decided on Simonsig as his trade name. Frans Malan was the first producer to introduce a sparkling wine made by the traditional *méthode champenoise* in 1971. He originally made his Kaapse Vonkel from Chenin Blanc, but some years ago changed to a blend of Pinot Noir and Chardonnay. The 1992 vintage scored a triumph in the UK *Wine* magazine's 1995 International Wine Challenge, winning the trophy for the Sparkling Wine of the Year against international competition. Frans's three sons are actively involved. Johan is the highly talented winemaker, Francois is the viticulturist, and Pieter is in charge of marketing. Simonsig produces 160 000 cases of wine, and bottles special ranges of wines for restaurants and supermarkets. Simonsig wines include a Bordeaux-style blend, Tiara, the Frans Malan Reserve Pinotage/Cabernet Sauvignon/Merlot blend which is unique in South Africa. Simonsig bottles eight white wines, including its Cap Classique, and seven reds. Most of the red wines are of special quality and the estate is also known for its Chardonnay, which did very well at the Chardonnay du Monde competition in France. New plantings in the last few years include Pinot Meunier for the Méthode Cap Classique wines, Petit Verdot for the Tiara Bordeaux-style blend and also Sémillon.

## SIMONSVLEI INTERNATIONAL
### Paarl

Simonsvlei was founded in 1945 with 45 members. Sarel Rossouw was appointed the first winemaker in 1946, holding the position for 40 years. Simonsvlei was one of the first co-ops to use 'flying' winemakers, and during each vintage a number of overseas winemakers are employed to bring their experience to the cellar. Cellar expansion has continually taken place to keep pace with export demand. Simonsvlei also produces Lost Horizon wines in distinctive blue bottles. The co-op became a company in 1996. Managing director Kobus Louw jokingly remarked that if a Veritas Double Gold, the ultimate at the South African Bottled Wine Show, were awarded to one of Simonsvlei's wines 'he would sit on the roof'. The 1997 Hercules Paragon Shiraz recently won this prestigious award. Kobus did exactly what he promised he would do and no doubt would sit on the roof again for the same reason. Simonsvlei bottles 12 whites and 10 reds. It has been successful at the International Wine Challenge and the Michelangelo 2000. Moreover, it won the President's Award for Export Achievement in 1994 and 1995, and was named one of *Wine* magazine's 'Best Value Cellars' in 1994 and 2000. Production at Simonsvlei is 220 000 cases from 1400 hectares. Winemaker Francois van Zyl makes 80 per cent white and 20 per cent red.

## SINNYA VALLEY
### Stellenbosch

Vinimark has had a long association with the Robertson Co-op, and has now embarked on a unique scheme with the Robertson Valley Wine Trust to market a regional wine brand. Production has grown from 17 000 cases in 1995 to 60 000 in 1996, and is now targeted at 200 000. Sinnya is a San word and the label depicts the famous rock painting of the White Lady of Brandberg with a wine glass in her hand; the bowl is half an ostrich shell.

## SIYABONGA
### Wellington – Paarl

Siyabonga, meaning 'we give thanks', is owned by Graham Knox. Numerous wine marketing successes over a long period have now culminated in this farm, where a life skills and economic empowerment programme is in full stream. The farm is funded by the South African Wine Industry Trust and the University of the Western Cape runs the programme. Wine making is done by Frenchman Etienne Charrier, with inspiration from Graham's partner, Alan Mouiex. First offerings show an excellent Pinotage and a complex multi-varietal white blend. Much more is planned for the future.

## SLALEY VINEYARDS
### Stellenbosch

Slaley Vineyards, a registered estate, is owned by Lindsay Hunting. In a short period of about four years Slaley has become one of the top young cellars. Set well on course by winemaker Ben Radford, Christopher van Dieren has been winemaker since 1998. Christopher learnt his skills at Château Giscour in the Haut-Médoc. The history of the Hunting family is depicted on the wine labels because Lindsay is a descendant of a ship-building dynasty. The Hunting family was also involved in aeronautical manufacturing and played an important role for England in the Second World War. Eighty-four hectares are planted to vineyards with a further 20 still in the planning stage. The most planted variety is Cabernet Sauvignon, followed by Shiraz, Pinotage, Merlot and Sauvignon Blanc. Three white wines are bottled and seven reds. Two vintages of Slaley Shiraz have really hit the headlines. The 1997 Shiraz won Veritas Double Gold locally and an award at the International Wine and Spirit Competition. The 1998 Shiraz won gold at Michelangelo and an award for 'Shiraz Excellence' at the 2000 Australia World Series of Wine in Sydney. The latest release, a 1999 Shiraz, won the Grand Prix D'Honneur at the Hamburg Wein Salon 2000. Under Slaley's second label, Broken Stone, a 1999 Cabernet Sauvignon/Shiraz blend won a Grand Prix at the same competition, as did the Broken Stone Sauvignon Blanc.

## SLANGHOEK WINERY
### Slanghoek – Worcester

This co-op, near Goudini, was established in 1951 and crushed its first crop in 1952. Today 25 members deliver 23 000 tons from some 1600 hectares, which are made into wine under the guidance of Kobus Rossouw. The cellar was upgraded in 1996 to cope with exports and now boasts a barrel-fermented Chardonnay, a Chardonnay/Sauvignon Blanc blend, a fascinating Sémillon/Riesling and a sweet Hanepoot. Recent plantings by members include more Cabernet Sauvignon, Cabernet Franc and Ruby Cabernet. The vineyard has been considerably updated over the years and now uses state-of-the-art technology.

## SOMERBOSCH
### Stellenbosch

The Roux family has owned the farm Die Fonteine since 1959. For many years the grapes were all delivered to the Helderberg Co-op. The farm buildings were converted into a cellar, but due to the pressure of production a new cellar has been pressed into service for the 2001 vintage. Production will remain at 6000 cases, although the 82 hectares of vineyard are capable of producing much more. A good Cabernet Sauvignon is made, as well as three other red wines and four white wines. A new addition to the Somerbosch range is a Ruby port-style wine. Marius and Japie Roux are both responsible for the wine making, and Marius also for the vineyards. Seven hundred tons of grapes are harvested but only 250 tons are used for own-label wines.

## SONOP WINERY
Paarl

This venture began in 1991 with a single farm named Windmeul in Paarl, specifically to produce wine for export. It has now expanded with a cellar in Stellenbosch and hired space in many cellars scattered around the winelands, and has a number of long-term contracts with growers. Winemaker Graham Weerts jokes: 'Talk of flying winemakers... I'm a driving winemaker!' Colossal quantities are now being produced, close to 150 000 cases under the names African Legend, Bredasdorp, Cape Levant, Sonop, Cape Soleil, Winds of Change, Out of Africa and others. Sonop also markets wines for Cilmor, Diemersdal and others. Its own state-of-the-art cellar is planned. The 'Winds of Change' programme for the Sonop staff is an empowerment programme whereby employees benefit from the sale of wines under that label. It's all part of the Swiss-based multi-national *négociant* business of Jacques Germanier known locally as SAVISA.

## SOUTHERN RIGHT CELLARS
Walker Bay – Overberg

Anthony Hamilton Russell and Kevin Grant launched this venture in 1995 to market a new range that included Pinotage and Sauvignon Blanc. Although grapes are still bought in, 113 hectares in the Hemel en Aarde valley are currently under development. This venture is completely separate from Hamilton Russell Vineyards. Fifteen thousand cases are made at Hamilton Russell Vineyards until the new 30 000-case winery and maturation cellar are opened. Building will start in 2002. The goal of Southern Right is to specialise in Pinotage grown on sites within the

Walker Bay area and its owners have committed themselves to donating R1.00 for every bottle sold to the Southern Right Whale Conservation Fund in Walker Bay. With the sale of the 1995 vintage, R12 000 was raised, which will sponsor the annual whale survey in Walker Bay. In 1996 R35 000 was raised and the amount continues to grow annually.

## SPICE ROUTE WINE COMPANY
Swartland

One of Charles Back's new ventures, Spice Route is an innovative new cellar in the Swartland specialising in Rhône-style blends and varietals under winemaker Eben Sadie. One hundred and forty hectares are planted to Shiraz, Merlot, Pinotage, Mourvèdre, Carignan, Grenache and Viognier, with a further 60 hectares to come. Two whites and seven reds are bottled. The wines have made a huge splash on both the local and international markets.

## SPIER HOME FARM
Stellenbosch

The farm was granted to Arnout Tamboer Janz in 1692 by Simon van der Stel. It was sold in 1712 to Hans Hendrik Hattingh who came from Speyer in Germany, and it was he who named it Spier. There were numerous owners until it was sold to Dick Enthoven. Spier is situated on the Eerste River and includes three restaurants, an amphitheatre, conference centre, farm stall and equestrian centre. A country hotel and an 18-hole golf course are planned for the future. A large winery was built in 1995 and the winemaker is Frans Smit. Spier's wine centre was established by Jabulani Ntshangase, who returned to South Africa after a career in the New York wine trade. Spier has over 57 hectares planted to vines, and plantings will be increased over the next few years. Spier Home Farm markets under the Spears label; a IV Spears Sauvignon Blanc and a blend, Spears Symphony, have been released. A Cabernet Sauvignon and Chardonnay are planned for the future. Since July 2001 Spier may once again use the Spier name for its wines.

## SPIER WINES/GOEDGELOOF
Stellenbosch

Robert Maingard bought the farm Goedgeloof in 1996. He later sold off portions of the farm, and the section with the homestead and wine cellar was bought by Hydro Holdings (Pty) Ltd. The 1997 vintage was sold in bulk in order to facilitate the reorganisation of the cellar.

## SPRINGFIELD ESTATE
Robertson

Springfield Estate is the registered name of the old farm Klipdrif on the banks of the Breede River. It was bought by the Bruwer family from Dr Hamph in 1902. After the Second World War, when there was a major shift from private producers to co-operatives, the Bruwers stayed on their own and built up a tremendous reputation for the quality of the wines they provided to the merchant wholesalers in bulk. They launched their own wines onto the market in 1995 under the Springfield label. Abrie and his father, Piet, are experienced winemakers, and they have modernised the cellar. In 1996 Springfield won a Veritas Double Gold for its Sauvignon Blanc Special Cuvée. Part of the reason for the Springfield success was the move to grow vines on a part of the farm that for many years was considered too rocky. The farm is cooled by late afternoon sea breezes, and harvesting is done in the cool of early morning. Low yields and low temperatures give high-quality wines, and the Cabernet Sauvignon, Chardonnay and Sauvignon Blanc are commendable. Abrie is both winemaker and viticulturist at Springfield.

## SPRUITDRIFT CO-OP
Spruitdrift – Olifants River

Founded in 1968 with 77 members, the cellar was completed in time for the 1970 crop. The co-op initially received Steen and Hanepoot for dry white production, Sultana and Palomino for brandy, and some Grenache, which was considered only good enough for spirit distillation. The cellar was run by Giel Swiegers before Johan Rossouw took over in 1978. In turn wine making became the charge of Erik Schlunz in 1996. The 85 members deliver some 30 000 tons to the cellar, where easy-drinking wines have an ever-increasing number of reds in their ranges.

## ST CLEMENT
Paarl

St Clement is owned by international golfer David Frost and his brother Michael. Jason Fischer, who hails from California, is consultant winemaker. Presently St Clement markets Chardonnay, Cabernet Sauvignon and Merlot in the USA, and the Frosts are considering a second label for local consumption. St Clement's grapes are crushed at Boland Co-op and the wine is matured at St Clement. The Frosts intend to build their own crushing cellar in the future.

## STEENBERG
Constantia

Steenberg is the oldest wine farm in the Cape Peninsula and was granted to Catherine Ustings Ras by Governor Simon van der Stel in 1682. Her husband was no doubt in the employ of the Dutch East India Company and not officially allowed to own land. This was three years before Simon van der Stel acquired the property of Groot Constantia. The Louw family, who had owned Steenberg for a number of generations, sold it to Johnnies Industrial Corporation (Johnnic) in 1990. Steenberg is 203 hectares in extent, with 68 hectares planted to vines. It is interesting to note that Steenberg has planted Nebbiolo, which produces some of the greatest wines of the world in north-western Italy. The winery was completed in January 1996. Nicky Versfeld was appointed winemaker and Herman Hanekom is the viticulturist. Production is 38 000 cases, and this will eventually climb to 50 000 cases. Johnnic has restored the 1740 manor house, the *jonkershuis* and the original wine cellar. The main gable of the house is the

only surviving example of its type in the Cape Peninsula. The Steenberg range includes a Sauvignon Blanc, Chardonnay, Sémillon, Cabernet Sauvignon and Merlot. Steenberg produces another range under the Motif label with a horticultural theme, and this range consists of a Dry White, Dry Red and Dry Rosé. A Cap Classique is planned for the future. Christa von la Chevallerie assists with the wine making. Steenberg has certainly made the headlines with its wines. The 1998 Merlot was judged best South African Red Wine and Best Merlot Entered Worldwide at the International Wine and Spirit Competition in Tokyo. Steenberg also won the South African Airways Floating Trophy for its 1999 Sauvignon Blanc Reserve. John Loubser has recently replaced Nicky Versveld as winemaker.

## STELLEKAYA
Helderberg – Stellenbosch

A portion of the old Stuttaford farm is being redeveloped by computer whiz Dave Lello with farming help from Peet le Roux. Lello purchased two properties in 1998 and combined them into one 110-hectare farm. Although there were vines on the property, complete replanting is underway, with plans for five hectares per year until 50 hectares of top-quality Cabernet and Merlot are in production. Stellekaya's first wine, a Merlot with a touch of Cabernet Sauvignon, was made at a neighbouring cellar. A small cellar is now operational. Inspired by Tuscany, Lello aims to produce only the best-quality wines reflecting a Tuscan feel. Stellekaya, meaning 'home of the stars' is a name combining Italian and the local language.

## STELLENBOSCH FARMERS' WINERY
Stellenbosch

La Gratitude, the former home of SFW's founder, Charles Winshaw, inspired the name of a famous dry white wine which, unfortunately, is no longer available. The famous house on Dorp Street in Stellenbosch has been sold to an overseas *hôtelier*. The wine's red partner, Château Libertas, was one of the earliest wines to have the historical figure of Adam Tas featured in its name. The site where SFW developed was once part of the Tas farm, Libertas. Other wines to carry the Tas name are the popular dry red, Tassenberg, known as 'Tassies'; Tasheimer, one of the pioneering semi-sweet wines in South Africa and still an old favourite; Oom Tas, one of the largest brands over time; Taskelder; Vinotas, the country's first 'light' wine; and Libertas, an export range. After the Wine of Origin laws were introduced in 1973, SFW launched the first Wine of Origin range under the name Oude Libertas, which introduced the variety Tinta Barocca to the wine drinkers of South Africa. In 1930 SFW introduced Grand Mousseux, a tank-produced sparkling wine that for years dominated the market. SFW also has the prestigious Zonnebloem range dating back to the 1930s, and the Lanzerac range from the late 1950s. This range gave the world the first-ever Pinotage from the 1959 vintage. SFW was also responsible for well-known, affordable wines like Kellerprinz, Autumn Harvest, Capenheimer, Honey Blossom, Overmeer, Roodendal, Golden Alibama and Virginia, the single biggest selling wine in South African history. SFW created the modern wine market with Lieberstein, a semi-sweet white wine closed with a screw cap that was launched in 1959. Lieberstein brought about the need for colossal amounts of fruity white wine, requiring large-scale plantings of Chenin Blanc which rapidly grew to be a third of all grapes planted for wine making in the Cape. Co-ops had to produce vast volumes of the wine as SFW could not produce the quantities the market demanded. Large stainless steel tanks, road and rail tankers, and bottling equipment had to be upgraded to cope with the Lieberstein demand. This brought about considerable innovation on the production side, which at the time made South Africa a leader in wine-making technology. Sales of Lieberstein rocketed from 30 000 litres in

*(left) Wheat and vines near Riebeek Kasteel.*
*(right) Temperature-controlled steel tanks at Vergelegen.*

1959 to 31 million litres by 1964. Bill Winshaw and Ronnie Melck were the brains behind this phenomenal success, ably supported by a youthful and innovative production team. SFW was the original sponsor of the Cape Wine Academy, which is the only educational body of its kind in South Africa and has produced all the candidates who have made it to Cape Wine Master. The Academy today has a very important role in training wine industry staff. SFW also established the country's premier annual wine event, the Nederburg International Auction. This event is held and managed by Nederburg for the South African wine industry. In 1993 Dr Paul Pontalier of Château Margaux opened SFW's new cellar at Plaisir de Merle.

## STELLENBOSCH VINEYARDS LIMITED
Stellenbosch

In 1996 four Stellenbosch co-ops, Bottelary, Eersterivier, Helderberg and Welmoed, merged their operations. This joint venture linked 150 of the region's growers under one umbrella. The enterprise changed from a co-op to a company, with Hermann Bohmer as managing director and New Zealand-born Chris Kelly as group head winemaker. Dynamic is the only way this venture can be described. It has had major success with a large-volume white in litre bottles. At the other end of the spectrum, there is the top-quality Genesis range of excellent Cabernet, Shiraz, Chardonnay and Sauvignon Blanc. There is also a sparkling Shiraz named Infiniti that has potential. Stellenbosch Vineyards produces wine under various labels, with Kumkani being another premium range. The wine-making team includes experienced Mike Graham and Elizabeth Augustyn. Grape quality is all-important and a leading Australian viticulturist, Di Davidson, is playing a vital role in vineyard improvement and the change to more red grapes. The Bottelary cellar is all but closed and a modern, hi-tech, economic, highly efficient cellar has been designed and only awaits planning approval to be built.

## STELLENZICHT VINEYARDS
Stellenbosch

This property was bought by Hans-Joachim Schreiber in 1981. The label was put firmly on the wine map by André van Rensburg. His successor, Guy Webber, has slid into André's shoes with confidence and ease. One hundred and thirty-nine hectares are planted to Cabernet Sauvignon, Shiraz, Chardonnay, Merlot and Sauvignon Blanc. A further two will still be established. The range at Stellenzicht has changed completely. There are now three tiers: Founders Private Release range; Stellenbosch range; and the Golden Triangle range. All labels have changed except for the Syrah and the Sémillon. The Stellenzicht 1998 Sémillon Reserve has won the Cape Wine Academy Trophy for 'Best South African Dry White Wine' at the International Wine and Spirit Competition three years in a row. The Stellenbosch range draws on the combined strengths of the five well-known wine estates in the Lusan/Distillers group: Alto, Le Bonheur, Neethlingshof, Uitkyk and Stellenzicht. Guy Webber can now source grapes from 800 hectares of prime vineyards for these wines. The Golden Triangle range, however, will preserve the identity of the constituent wine estates.

## STONY BROOK
Franschhoek – Paarl

This is a new venture of Dr Nigel McNaught who purchased this small property in 1996. He is busy replacing the orchards with 14 hectares of vineyard and converting the fruit-packing shed into a cellar. A friend's comment, 'You must have rocks in your heads,' led to the name Stony Brook. Nigel and Joy McNaught are a completely hands-on team. Nigel makes the wine and both he and Joy care for the vines, with viticulturist Paul Wallace as consultant. Production numbers 3000 to 4000 cases, including three whites and four reds.

*(left) View of Rustenberg farm from the Simonsberg.*

## STONEWALL
Stellenbosch

The farm Happy Vale is a landmark between Stellenbosch and Somerset West because of the white stone wall that surrounds the Cape Dutch farmhouse. Happy Vale has 80 hectares of well-established vineyards and delivered grapes to other producers. This changed in 1997 after owner De Waal Koch crushed a portion of his crop in the farm's rejuvenated cellar. A series of talented winemakers have made the wine since the first vintage and now Ronell Wiid is consultant winemaker. Although winemaker at Hazendal, she has long lived on a cottage on Happy Vale. Stonewall was the choice of name for its export wines. About 90 per cent of production goes to the United Kingdom and Denmark.

## STORMBERG
Wellington – Paarl

Stormberg is the result of the ambition of one-time Nederburg assistant winemaker, Koos Jordaan, to have his 'own' wine. With a freshly planted 32-hectare vineyard in Wellington, Jordaan has bought in grapes for his initial production.

## SUMARIDGE
Walker Bay – Overberg

Architect and Cape Wine Master Greg de Bruyn has built a cellar that will eventually produce 40 000 cases in the Hemel en Aarde valley near Hermanus. With a lot of help from Mike Dobrovic and Bartho Eksteen and the use of the next-door Newton Johnson winery, the first release will be the 2000 vintage.

## SWARTLAND WINE CELLAR
Swartland

This cellar was established in 1948 by 15 Malmesbury farmers. By the time the winery opened in 1950, the membership had grown to 48 members who delivered 2500 tons. Today over 100 members deliver 25 000 tons of grapes. In the early 1970s, Swartland began bottling most of its production and it now bottles well over one million litres per annum. The cellar was also a pioneer in 'Own Label' production. At present Swartland produces about 75 per cent white, 20 per cent red, and some rosé. Red plantings now stand at 40 per cent and will grow to 50 per cent by 2005.

## SYLVANVALE VINEYARDS
Devon valley – Stellenbosch

David Nathan-Maister, computer boffin, classical music historian, and wine and spirit *aficionado* was looking for a small vineyard to produce his own wine. He found one, but it surrounded the Devon Valley Hotel. He bought the property and not only had to become a vintner but an *hôtelier* as well. Vineyards are cultured by Lorna Hughes and wine made by Martin Meinert. Pinotage and Chenin Blanc have gathered all kinds of accolades, while the dry rosé has become a favourite for many. The oddity is a Late Harvest from Pinotage.

## TEN FIFTY SIX WINERY
Franschhoek – Paarl

The first release was a 1996 vintage from bought-in Sauvignon Blanc grapes. Now the winery produces 3000 odd cases made by Gerda Willers. About three hectares are planted to an equal mix of red and white.

## THANDI WINES
Elgin – Overberg

Dr Paul Cluver, in conjunction with Tienie van Vuuren, conceived this scheme after forestry workers of the Lebanon village were threatened by privatisation. Trevor Steyn of the Anglican Social Development Institute organised the community and the Lebanon Fruit Farm Trust was born. The idea was to create forestry and fruit operations to maintain the social fabric of the community. With help from Stellenbosch Farmers' Winery, the venture moved into wine

production. A revamp resulted in the formation of Thandi Farms as a joint venture between the workers trust and Paul Cluver. Working from the Paul Cluver cellar, production now tops 100 000 litres and is sold by Tesco stores in the United Kingdom.

## THELEMA MOUNTAIN VINEYARDS
Stellenbosch

In less than two decades this property, situated at the top of the Helshoogte Pass, has become one of the Cape's top wine producers. Thelema was bought by the McClean Family Trust in 1983 after a long search by Gyles and Barbara Webb for a rare location where exceptional wines could be made. Thelema is 157 hectares in extent and the elevation ranges from 370 to 460 metres above sea level. As such, it is one of the highest and coolest wine farms in the Stellenbosch area. Currently 40 hectares are planted to classical varieties and another 4 hectares will be established over the next three years. Gyles also leases an additional 10 hectares nearby. The most planted variety at Thelema is Sauvignon Blanc, followed by Chardonnay, Cabernet Sauvignon, Shiraz and Merlot. Currently five white wines are being bottled and two reds. Gyles does not enter local or overseas competitions with one exception. He enters the Diners Club 'Winemaker of the Year' Competition when the relevant category for the year is suitable. He has won the competition in 1994 with Thelema's Bordeaux-style blend, a 1992 Cabernet Sauvignon/Merlot, and again in 1996 with a Thelema 1994 Cabernet Sauvignon.

## THEUNISKRAAL ESTATE
Tulbagh

Theuniskraal is owned by Rennie and Kobus Jordaan. Andries Jordaan has joined Kobus in the cellar. The estate has been known for its Cape Riesling for 50 years and now produces a Sémillon/Chardonnay blend and a Special Late Harvest made from Gewürztraminer and Chenin Blanc. The wines are marketed by the Bergkelder.

## TRAVINO
Olifants River

Travino was established in 1968 near Klawer. The co-op now has 46 members producing some 9000 tons. A portion of production is bottled, but most of it is sold in bulk. The winemaker, younger brother of Nico at Saxenburg, has the inappropriate name of 'Alkie' van der Merwe.

## TOKARA
Stellenbosch

G.T. Ferreira has established this farm with his neighbour, Gyles Webb of Thelema, as consultant cellarmaster, Miles Mossop as winemaker, and Eddie Smit as vineyard manager.

## TRAWAL WINE CELLAR
Olifants River Region

Sixteen members decided to build this co-op in 1967, but due to the delay in building, they could not deliver their grapes to the cellar until 1970. Winemaker Frank Meaker joined the co-op in 1991. He raised the standard of wines sufficiently to impress the British market. Until then, most of the production had been delivered to merchant wholesalers. From 1992 a small amount has been bottled for sale locally.

## TUKULU
Darling – Swartland

Tukulu is owned by SFW, Leopont 98 Properties and the Maluti Groenekloof Community Trust and it is certainly the largest black empowerment initiative in the wine industry. It is a huge, R32-million venture on a 975-hectare farm, Papkuilsfontein, on the West Coast. The wine is made at the Stellenbosch cellars of SFW. So far, 180 hectares have been planted and planting will continue until 330 hectares are in production. The name comes from the deep red

Tukulu soils on the farm. Tukulu's Pinotage was an ABSA Top Ten in 2000, which is a great pointer to future potential. Its Chenin Blanc has also received accolades locally and overseas. Leopont 98 Properties is a Gauteng-based black entrepreneur in the retail sector and will give a sales push to the wines.

## TULBAGH CO-OP
Tulbagh

One of the oldest co-ops in the Cape was formed by six farmers in 1906 and first called the Drostdy Co-op. In 1922 the co-op poured its wine down the drain as there was no market due to over-production and low prices. It survived, however, went on to bottle and market its own wine under the Witzenberg label. In 1933 the product was recognised by the KWV, which sold the wine on the export market. By 1937 the co-op was producing a sparkling wine, Winterhoek. In 1940 a sherry *solera* was developed to take up the excess wine that was caused by the shortage of bottles due to the Second World War. In 1964 Distillers Corporation took over the marketing of Witzenberg, as well as Drostdy sherries, and the co-op changed its name to the Tulbagh Co-op. Today it has 70 members who deliver 10 000 tons. Success on the export market has prompted the building of a new bottling plant three kilometres from the cellar, which is linked by a pipeline. A wide range of different types and styles is produced, with innovative packaging and most attractive labels.

## TWEE JONGE GEZELLEN ESTATE
Tulbagh

The 600-hectare estate was founded by two young bachelors – *twee jonge gezellen* – in 1710. There are presently 130 hectares under vines. Nicky Krone is the fifth generation on the estate, and over the years there have been many developments, including the early use of cold fermentation and the introduction of night harvesting. Nicky's father, 'NC', who had mainly been involved in sherry production, made the move to natural white wine. In the 1960s he introduced refrigeration to his fermentation and gave Twee Jonge Gezellen a head start with non-oxidised white wines. Twee Jonge Gezellen is widely known for its Krone Borealis Cap Classique sparkling wine. Tulbagh is very similar to Champagne, where it is not easy to make good natural wines, but because of the climate, it is possible to make great sparkling wines. Nicky planted Pinot Noir and Chardonnay, built a vaulted brick underground cellar and made his first sparkling wine in 1987. Bacchus, the Greek god of wine, fell in love with Ariadne, the daughter of the king of Crete, and in order to prove his love for her, he threw his golden crown, a circlet of gems, into the heavens. There it has remained forever as the constellation, Corona Borealis. *Corona* means crown, as does Krone, and Nicky's wife, Mary, thought there could not be a better name for a bubbly. Krone Borealis is matured for at least three and a half years on the lees in the bottle to achieve its rich, French-style character. In 1995 Nicky became the Diners Club 'Winemaker of the Year' with his 1993 Krone Borealis. Owner and winemaker, Nicky Krone, is starting a new range of varietal wines under the Krone label which will be released later in 2001. Red wine varieties have already been established, including Shiraz and Petit Verdot, together with Viognier, a white variety from the Rhône. Not surprisingly, the most planted variety is Chardonnay, followed by Pinot Noir for the Méthode Cap Classique.

## UITERWYK ESTATE
Stellenbosch

Dirk Coetzee settled on this property in 1682, but was only granted the land by Simon van der Stel in 1699. The Krige family built the homestead in 1791 and the wine cellar in 1798. Uiterwyk was bought by Jan Christoffel de Waal in 1864 and three brothers of the ninth generation of the De Waal family still farm Uiterwyk. Chris, who took over from his father in

1979, is in charge of white wine making; Pieter, who joined in 1984, is in charge of marketing; and Danie, who joined his two brothers in 1990, is in charge of red wine making. Uiterwyk wines were sold in bulk until 1972, when Danie bottled a proportion of the wine to sell under the Uiterwyk label. A new cellar was built in 1979. The original one is among the oldest cellars that have been in continuous use since it was built. The estate produces three white wines and five reds. The first blend of Pinotage, Merlot and 20 per cent Cabernet Sauvignon was an instant success on the UK market. Uiterwyk exports 20 per cent of its production under the Rosenburg label. In 1995 Uiterwyk received the State President's Award for its success in the export market. One of the larger farms in the Stellenbosch Kloof area, Uiterwyk has 113 hectares planted to vines and a further five hectares are being planted annually. Sauvignon Blanc is the most planted variety and the estate is marketing Viognier. Of the reds, Pinotage is the most planted variety, followed by Cabernet Sauvignon, Merlot and Shiraz. The Uiterwyk 'Cape' blend has done particularly well both locally and internationally. It is predominantly made from Cabernet Sauvignon and 30 to 40 per cent Pinotage, depending on the vintage. Uiterwyk is also recognised for its Pinotage. In the October 2000 German *Wein* magazine, Uiterwyk 1997 Pinotage came second out of 33 Pinotage wines tasted.

## UITKYK ESTATE
Stellenbosch

The unusual house on Uitkyk was built by J.C. Herzendosch, who also built the Martin Melck House in Strand Street, Cape Town. Recent restoration has revealed a beautiful mural under 12 layers of paint. The doorway was carved by Anton Anreith and the design is repeated on all the inner doors. Originally granted in 1712, the estate is today owned by Lusan Holdings. The Bergkelder upgraded the vineyards and wine-making facilities; 200 of the 600 hectares are planted to vineyards. Uitkyk has had several interesting owners, including Martin Melck and, more recently, J.W. Sauer. Paul Sauer, his son, became the well-known senator and was a great promoter of red wine. In 1920 a Prussian owner, General Georg von Carlowitz, brought to Uitkyk a lifestyle that included dining by candlelight in full dress uniform. His son, also Georg, developed Uitkyk's reputation for fine wine with his red Carlonet and white Carlsheim. Uitkyk has a long record of producing great Shiraz and now boasts a Cabernet Sauvignon/Shiraz blend. Two white wines are bottled, as are three reds and an excellent 10-year-old Uitkyk Grand Reserve Estate Brandy. In 1998, at the International Wine Competition in Slovenia, the 1994 Uitkyk Sauvignon Blanc was named the champion wine of the competition, albeit that it was already three years old. Very approachable when young, it develops beautifully in bottle.

## UITVLUCHT WINERY
Montagu – Klein Karoo

This co-op was founded in 1941 as Cogmans Co-op, but changed its name in 1996 to the name of the farm on which the cellar is situated. The original building was constructed in 1941 and is now the reception and sales area. Production is 15 000 cases, predominantly white, and the balance includes fortified wine, with Cabernet Sauvignon, Merlot and Ruby Cabernet slowly coming into the picture.

## UPLAND ESTATE
Wellington – Paarl

Upland Estate is owned by Dr Edmund and Elsie Oettlé who opted out of their original careers when they purchased this 46-hectare property overlooking Wellington. Thirteen hectares produces 700 to 1000 cases of Cabernet Sauvignon and Merlot. Close to 10 hectares of Chenin and South African Riesling go to the distillation of grappa and a brandy due to be released in 2001.

## UVA MIRA
Helderberg – Stellenbosch

The man behind Uva Mira, retired mining engineer Des Weedon, died in 2000 before many of his ventures had come to fruition – new home, mountainside restaurant and cellar. His widow Denise is now firmly in control and will continue to see the bold venture, high on the Helderberg, to conclusion. Already streams and dams have been stocked with trout and some 850 olive trees have been planted. The first few vintages of wines have been made by Jan Boland Coetzee in his Vriesenhof cellar until the Uva Mira cellar is completed. The initial production of 5000 cases comprised 80 per cent white and 20 per cent red, but by 2004 this will change to a 70/30 mix. The 2000 vintage saw the first harvest of Roobernet, which will be blended with Merlot to produce a unique red wine.

## VAALHARTS CO-OP
Vaalharts – Kimberley

This area is entirely dependent on irrigation. In 1933 an irrigation scheme was built and work began on the farm Andalusia, 80 kilometres north of Kimberley. An agricultural co-op was formed in 1944 and in 1974 the co-op agreed to add wine to its range of produce. In 1977 148 tons of grapes were crushed in a temporary installation. Today the cellar handles 4000 tons from 40 members. Easy-drinking wines are sold under the Overvaal and Andalusia labels. Ruby Cabernet and Pinotage now feature and a Californian clone of Chardonnay that thrives in warmer climes has also been planted.

## VAN LOVEREN
Robertson

The Retief family have owned this property since 1937. It had produced sweet fortified wines which were supplied to wholesalers, but this changed in 1972 with the installation of cooling. This allowed the production of dry white natural wine, and in 1980 the Retiefs bottled a portion of their production under the Van Loveren label. The Retief brothers, viticulturist Nico and winemaker Wynand, have run the operation since the death of their father in 1982, and have now handed over the reins to their sons. Adjoining farms have been added to the property and today four farms make up Van Loveren, with 150 hectares under vineyards. The modern cellar has a capacity of 3000 tons and production is currently around 150 000 cases. Van Loveren pioneered certain varieties and was already bottling a perlé from Fernão Pires before many were even planting this variety. Its Blanc de Noirs from Shiraz and Red Muscadel are unique, and new plantings include Cabernet Sauvignon, Merlot and Ruby Cabernet. Van Loveren has a record of producing a wide variety of wines at reasonable prices.

## VAN ZYLSHOF ESTATE
Robertson

Van Zylshof is one of Robertson's smallest estates. Three generations of Van Zyls have farmed at Vanzylshof and their 30 hectares of white grapes have supplied merchant cellars since 1940. In 1994 winemaker Andri van Zyl, together with his father Chris, bottled some wine under their own label for export. Their intention is to remain small, only bottle their best, and continue to provide bulk to the merchants. They produce fine, slightly wooded Chardonnay and Riverain, a Chardonnay that is all fruit with absolutely no wood. Four white wines and a Cabernet Sauvignon are due to be released. Currently Van Zylshof Sauvignon Blanc is served on KLM's Business and First Class international flights.

## VEENWOUDEN
Paarl

Deon van der Walt, an internationally acclaimed operatic tenor, bought this farm in 1988. It was originally named Ebenaezer. Deon's brother Marcel is the winemaker. Deon changed the farm's name to

Veenwouden, as the first Van der Walt to land at the Cape came from Veenwouden in Friesland. Veenwouden is a boutique winery planted to noble grape varieties. Yields are limited to a maximum of five tons per hectare, ensuring that the wine will be of the best possible quality. The first harvest in 1993 was handled by French winemaker Laure Ambroise who spent a year at Veenwouden. There are four wines in its range: an excellent Chardonnay, a fine Merlot, a good Bordeaux-style blend, Veenwouden Classic, and Vivat Bacchus, which is made for earlier drinking.

## VENDOME WINES
Paarl

Vendome is owned by Jannie le Roux, chairman of Boland Cellars and deputy chairman of the KWV. Wine making is done by Jannie Junior who is the 10th generation of Le Rouxs to farm the property. Forty hectares produce a mix of 60 per cent red and 40 per cent white.

## VERA CRUZ ESTATE
Stellenbosch

The estate is owned by Delheim owners Hans Hoheisen and Spatz Sperling. At present, it bottles two white wines and three reds under the Vera Cruz label. The 1998 Vera Cruz Shiraz won a Gold Medal at the 2000 International Wine and Spirit Competition.

## VERDUN ESTATE
Stellenbosch

This estate was originally part of Vredenburg, a large farm which together with Vlottenburg farm was bought by Paul Roux in 1792. His descendant Johann Roux divided Vredenburg between his three grandsons. The land 'across the road', which Kosie Roux inherited, had no name. The name he chose had a ring of destiny because the First World War battle of Verdun was raging at the time. Roux's nephew ironically remarked that his uncle's battle with this undeveloped land might be on the same scale. Picking up the implicit challenge, Roux named his new farm Verdun. Kosie Roux established the basic working structure of his farm on a red wine basis, gradually improving the quality of the varieties planted. His most important step was probably the introduction of Gamay. A relatively prolific bearer in its Burgundy homelands, on the gravelly and granitic soils of Verdun the Gamay developed slowly, producing good-quality grapes. In time it was marketed under its varietal name as the only Gamay to be bottled in the Cape. A renaissance started at Verdun when Francois Tolken purchased Verdun in 1995. The re-development of Verdun in the short period of five years has been absolutely phenomenal. Francois built a modern cellar, retaining some of the historic walls with special facilities to handle single-vineyard varietals. He also planted the vineyards, which are now 80 hectares in extent, with more classic varietals. Among those planted are Petit Verdot, Cabernet Franc and Sémillon. Winemaker Jan van Rooyen is making both red and white Bordeaux-style blends and certainly a Sauvignon Blanc/Sémillon blend is long overdue in South Africa. Although Francois and his wife Colleen have enjoyed the lifestyle of the farm, they have decided to retire. Verdun was purchased in February 2001 by Markus Rahmann, a German businessman based in Hong Kong.

## VERGELEGEN
Helderberg – Stellenbosch

This was the estate of Willem Adriaan van der Stel, a governor of the Cape Colony. His rise and fall in less than a decade adds an interesting note of villainy to the historical record of those early days of the Cape. He was thoroughly disliked by the colonists who felt he was an administrative martinet and overwhelmingly arrogant. Willem Adriaan, however, was an intelligent man and more at home with the theory of agriculture. He tested a wide range of stock and crops both European and Asian. Vines were planted in 1700 and

within six years 500 000 vines were in production. The treatment of his vines under local conditions is recorded with precision in *The Gardener's Almanac*, which makes fascinating reading. Vergelegen passed through a succession of owners following Willem Adriaan's demise and sadly became progressively more run-down. In 1798 the Theunissen family acquired the property and it remained in the family for a full century. Once again the vineyards flourished and a new wine cellar was built. The estate again fell into disrepair until Sir Lionel and Lady Florence Phillips purchased it in 1917. Lady Phillips immediately set about restoring and improving the buildings, garden and eventually the entire property. After Sir Lionel and Lady Phillips died, their heirs decided to sell Vergelegen and it was bought by Charles 'Punch' Barlow and his wife Cynthia. Finally, Anglo American Farms bought Vergelegen in 1987 and immediately started developing the vineyards. Martin Meinert moved into the new, impressive underground cellar, crushing his maiden vintage in 1992. In 1998 André van Rensburg took over as winemaker. There are currently 100 hectares of bearing vines planted to Cabernet Sauvignon, Merlot, Sauvignon Blanc, Chardonnay and Sémillon. There are also small plantings of Sangiovese and 9.5 hectares of young Shiraz. An additional 20 hectares of vineyard will be established over the next three years. The range contains five whites and five reds. Vergelegen's Schaapenberg Sauvignon Blanc Reserve is the Premium label, an amazing wine and in such demand that the first vintage was sold out by word of mouth.

## VERGENOEGD ESTATE
Stellenbosch

This property was granted to Pieter de Vos in 1696. Johannes Colijn built the most attractive gable onto the existing house in 1773, and wine was made at Vergenoegd during the 18th century. Johannes Faure bought the farm in 1820. Vergenoegd has 95 hectares planted to vines, and over the years the vineyards have been upgraded to more noble varieties. When John Faure died in 1969, his two sons took over. Jac made the wine and Brand was in charge of the vineyards. In 1990 Jac's son, John, became the winemaker. Vergenoegd won the General Smuts Trophy for the Best Red Wine at the South African National Young Wine Show for three successive years in the early 1970s with its Cabernet Sauvignon. At a special tasting of wines of older vintages, held earlier in 1997, the 1972 Cabernet Sauvignon still showed exceptionally well. Vergenoegd Reserve, introduced in 1990, improves with every vintage. A delightful Cinsaut/Merlot blend is extremely popular. Vergenoegd does not bottle any white wines. The most planted variety is Shiraz, followed by Cabernet Sauvignon, Merlot and Tinta Barocca. Vergenoegd only bottles four red wines and a really good port-style wine.

## VILJOENSDRIFT WINES AND CRUISES
Robertson

Seems an odd combination, but if you look at the name you will appreciate that the farm lies on the Breede River. The innovative Viljoen family have a double-decker boat named *Uncle Ben* that cruises along a navigable portion of the Breede. You can sip their wine and just enjoy or make a decision on what to buy. In 1818 the Viljoens made fortified wine and distilled brandy. Since the 1970s their grapes went to local cellar. In 1998 Fred and Manie Viljoen restored the old cellar and went back into production with a more or less 50/50 red and white split. The 300-hectare farm has 60 hectares planted to Cabernet Sauvignon, Pinotage, Sémillon, Chenin Blanc and Colombar.

## VILLIERA
Paarl

Villiera got its name from J.W.S. de Villiers who purchased this 120-hectare property in the 1930s. Until 1941 his grapes, mainly Cinsaut and Chenin

Blanc, were sold to merchants. Since 1983, the estate has been owned by the Griers. The winemaker is Jeff Grier, his sister Cathy looks after marketing, and cousin Simon is the viticulturist. Jeff and Cathy are the only brother-and-sister combination of Cape Wine Masters. In 1983 French Champagne-maker Jean-Louis Denois brought his skills to Villiera, and as a result Tradition Carte Rouge was launched in 1984. Villiera is known not only for its excellent Cap Classique sparkling wines, but also for its Cru Monro, a blend of Cabernet Sauvignon and Merlot. Merlot at Villiera is considered one of the best in the Cape, and its Sauvignon Blanc, first released in 1995, is made from bush vines. Villiera is also one of the best producers of Rhine Riesling, Gewürztraminer and Chenin Blanc. The estate has received a number of awards, including many Veritas Double Golds, regular SAA 'Wine of the Month' selections and is three times winner of SAA trophies, once for its Blanc Fumé and twice for the Tradition Carte d'Or Brut. Villiera has moved away from traditional oak bark corks to plastic 'corq' closures for its Blue Ridge range. Jeff Grier is a member of the Cape Independent Winemakers' Guild and annually selects a wine for its auction. He is also a regular participant at the Nederburg International Auction.

## VILLIERSDORP CO-OP
Overberg

The co-op was originally formed in 1922 to produce *moskonfyt* (concentrated grape juice jam), and named Villiersdorp Moskonfyt and Fruit Co-operative. Fruit drying was started during the Depression in the 1930s, and even wheat was received on behalf of the wheat board, but the co-op was forever financially troubled. Sugar shortages in the Second World War resulted in a great demand for *moskonfyt* and by 1947 finances had improved dramatically. A pressing cellar was added for the production of distilling wine, and in 1974 natural wine was produced and delivered to wholesalers with small quantities being bottled for sale to the public in 1976. In 1980 the name was changed to Villiersdorp Co-op. Grapes are sourced from Worcester to Swellendam, and Hermanus on the coast. Included in the range is a Chardonnay of note and prices are very affordable. Growers have planted Cabernet Sauvignon, Pinotage, Sauvignon Blanc and some port varieties, and 70 members deliver 7000 tons.

## VINFRUCO
Stellenbosch

Vinfruco was established in 1993 by Unifruco with the specific aim of exporting Cape wine by using its fruit marketing links. It originally exported Stellenbosch-sourced wines, but now has suppliers throughout the winelands in an effort to meet demand. Vinfruco brought in 'flying' winemakers such as Kym Milne to produce quality wines for British and European tastes. Lynne Sherriff, Cape Wine Master and the first South African to become a Master of Wine, handled the sales in Britain and Europe. She took the sales to 500 000 cases under the brand name of Oak Village and many others.

## VINUM
Helderberg – Stellenbosch

This is another Alex Dale inspiration, this time with partners Martin Gerbers, French Cooper, Christophe Durand and French winemaker Edouard Labreye. Eleven hectares of grapes are under cultivation while more are bought in. The wine is made at Onderkloof winery. Current production is all red and close to 2000 cases are all exported.

## VLOTTENBURG CO-OP
Stellenbosch

This is the only Stellenbosch co-op that has not joined the Stellenbosch Vineyards Company. It has 22 members and crushes 8000 tons from some of the prime areas of the country. The co-op was established in 1945 primarily because the farmers were totally

frustrated by having to spend many hours waiting in line to deliver their grapes to the KWV's Stellenbosch distillery. In 1976 a new cellar was built to improve the production of white wine. The cellar underwent a further upgrade in 2000. The members visited Australia as a group and now are fired up to produce even better wines. The cellar's Limited Release wines should become more available, even though the bulk of its production will still be delivered to SFW. Kowie du Toit has been the winemaker since 1973. The co-op produces particularly good Cabernet Sauvignon, Merlot and Pinotage, as well as several popular whites.

## VON ORTLOFF
Franschhoek – Paarl

Georg Schlichtman bought Von Ortloff in 1992. The Schlichtmans had no experience in wine farming, and as they wanted to learn every aspect, helped with all the manual labour from cultivating to harvesting the grapes. The experience ensured the highest quality, which has been proved in their wines. Georg's wife, Evi, with her architectural talents, has restored the homestead and cellar. The vineyards now exceed 15 hectares and plans to extend farther up the Dassenberg mountain are well underway. A state-of-the-art cellar was completed in 1999. Three thousand cases are produced and volume will be increased with new plantings, which will have more emphasis on reds. The name of the farm was originally Dassenberg, but since it sounded similar to another popular red wine, it was changed to Von Ortloff, Evi's maiden name. Von Ortloff's wines have been acclaimed in the German press, and the cellar produces a good Cabernet Sauvignon/Merlot blend. In 1995 Von Ortloff bottled a Merlot which is being labelled Quintessence No. 7 Merlot.

## VREDENDAL WINERY
Olifants River

This co-op was established in 1948 as the Olifantsrivier Co-op to handle mainly white wines. It produces 80 000 tons, which is more wine than the entire production of New Zealand. Cellarmaster Gielie Swiegers, now at the KWV, was responsible for putting this remote cellar on the map. He introduced the San language label, Goiya Kgeisje, in 1988 for his nouveau-style wine which carries a different San painting with each vintage. The exception was in 1994, when he flooded the supermarket shelves in the United Kingdom with a label depicting the Peace Dove to celebrate the pending inauguration of President Nelson Mandela. It was a marketing coup that few budgets could have afforded. In 1994 the co-op dramatically entered the world of red wine by winning the General Smuts Trophy for the Best South African Wine with a Ruby Cabernet. Members grow Cabernet Sauvignon, Merlot and Pinotage and its Maskam is a Cabernet Sauvignon/Merlot blend. The cellar underwent a R23-million upgrade in 1995, and now handles a staggering 2000 tons of grapes a day. Vredendal is certainly South Africa's largest cellar and biggest single exporter.

## VREDENHEIM
Stellenbosch

This historic estate is owned by the Bezuidenhout family. The homestead's baroque gable is best seen in winter when the oak trees have lost their leaves. Elsabé Bezuidenhout is the winemaker and her first vintage, with the assistance of wine-making friends, was in 1987. The farm is gradually being planted to more red varieties. The Vredenheim range consists of four red wines.

## VRIESENHOF AND TALANA HILL
Stellenbosch

Vriesenhof is situated on the outskirts of Stellenbosch. Jan (Boland) Coetzee bought this 25-hectare farm in 1980 and this purchase represented Jan's strong desire to strike out on his own. This move was not surprising because Jan had been winemaker at Kanonkop for 10 years. On arrival, Jan first built housing for his labourers, the vineyards were continuously upgraded

and after a few years he sorted out the cellar. Finally, after 10 years, he restored the gracious old homestead, built at the beginning of the 19th century. Jan's reputation at Kanonkop was built on wines of robust quality. This has changed as the macro-climate at Vriesenhof is considerably cooler. There are two reasons for this: the influence of the cooling breezes off the Indian Ocean as well as the beneficial effect of the relatively fewer sunshine-hours at the foot of the Stellenbosch mountains. As a result, Vriesenhof wines are both elegant and complex in character and made in Jan's definitive Cape style. One of Jan's final ambitions is to make Pinot Noir from Dijon clones. He did so in 2000, yet there is still no talk of a release date.

## WABOOMSRIVIER CO-OP
Worcester

The co-op was established in 1949 and pressed its first 4000 tons of grapes in 1950. The 22 founding members set out from the start to make quality wine as opposed to distilling wine. As electricity was not affordable, members took turns using their tractors to power the machinery in the cellars. The first winemaker was M.J.M. Cloete, who in 1956 designed and built a drainer that gave a higher yield of free-run juice. By 1958 he had installed 12 of these drainers, and the Cloete drainer/separator was also being used by other cellars. Electricity was installed, and the new pressing cellar, built in 1969, included several Cloete-designed pieces of equipment, including his 'quick' fermenter for distilling wine. Cloete also designed and built a special tank for fermenting quality red wine. The cellar has sold some of its production from as early as 1983 under the Wagenboom label, depicting *Protea nitida*, whose hard wood was used for wagon building. The current membership of 50 deliver about 12 000 tons. To date only two per cent of production has been bottled under the co-op's own label, but this is changing. The co-op is currently bottling 60 per cent white and 40 per cent red, but this will change with new plantings of Ruby Cabernet, Cabernet Sauvignon, Sangiovese, Petit Verdot and Malbec.

## WAMAKERSVALLEI WINERY
Wellington – Paarl

This co-op was formed out of the frustration of farmers waiting to deliver grapes to a distillery. In 1941 two farmers rallied together 45 others and they set about starting their own co-op. They bought a partly constructed cellar and pressed 2000 tons in 1942. Today 45 members deliver 12 000 tons from areas around Wellington, Hermon and Riebeek West. Vineyard improvement schemes have upgraded the quality of grapes and the cellar has also undergone recent modernisation, resulting in a good range of quality wines. Wine is custom-made for various *négociants,* including Ashwood and SA Dried Fruit. Red plantings have grown from less than five per cent at the start of the 1990s to nearly 40 per cent.

## WARWICK ESTATE
Stellenbosch

Warwick has been bottling its production since 1957. Stan Ratcliffe returned to the wine farm in 1972 after marrying Norma. She is a self-taught winemaker and began by producing some experimental wines which were well received by friends. She then went to Bordeaux for a season's cellar experience, only to have the French winemaker break his leg. Norma was thrown into the deep end, and made wine following his sick-bed instructions. The initial launch at Warwick was in 1985, and by 1995 the cellar had been extended twice. The Warwick range includes Cabernet Sauvignon, Cabernet Franc, Merlot and a traditional bush vine Pinotage. The flagship Trilogy is a Bordeaux-style blend. There is also a Chardonnay. Norma was the first female member of the Cape Independent Winemakers' Guild and has served as its chairperson. In 1996 Warwick was a recipient of the State

President's Award for Export Excellence, and in 1997 its Cabernet Franc was judged the Best South African Red Wine at the International Wine and Spirit Competition. There are 50 hectares under vines with a further six in the pipeline. Production is 10 000 cases. Norma was not sure whether she should continue with her Chardonnay. She then won the 2000 Cowra Tri-Nations Chardonnay Challenge with her 1999 Warwick Chardonnay, beating all the Australian and New Zealand Chardonnay competitors – a major upset for those 'Down Under', as the prize was a return ticket to Burgundy for the winemaker of the winning wine, and the ticket had been booked from Sydney. Warwick was also the first cellar to make a really exciting Cabernet Franc varietal wine in the early 1990s.

## WATERFORD
Helderberg – Stellenbosch

Jeremy Ord is better known for his association with information technology. Now he is very much part of the Cape winelands after purchasing Waterford on the slopes of the Helderberg. Kevin Arnold was appointed winemaker and the combination of Jeremy's financial muscle and Kevin's special talent makes this an assured winning combination. Kevin first made a name for himself 20 years ago when he was at Delheim. He was South African Champion Winemaker in 1986. When he joined Rust en Vrede, where he was winemaker for 10 years, his ambition was to make this property one of the top red wine producers. In joining Waterford at its inception, Kevin has been fully involved in the working design of the cellar and the building operations. Waterford is refreshingly different and certainly a beautiful cellar. Kevin describes it as Mediterranean in style. Thirty-nine hectares are planted to vines and another 11 hectares will be established over the next three years. The most planted variety is Cabernet Sauvignon, followed by Shiraz, Chardonnay, Merlot and Mourvèdre. Barbera, Malbec and Petit Verdot have also been planted and Tempranillo and Grenache are still to come. There are three white wines in the range, including a Pecan Stream second label, and two Waterford red wines.

## WEBERSBERG
Stellenbosch

In 1996 Fred Weber bought Groenrivier farm on the slopes of the Helderberg. Forty hectares are planted to Cabernet Sauvignon and Merlot. With Giorgio Dalla Cia as consultant, it is not surprising that the wines are outstanding.

## WELGEGUND WINES
Wellington – Paarl

Alex and Sheila Camerer bought their 50-hectare Wellington property in the late 1980s. The small planting of old, shy-bearing Carignan grapes were delivered to Bovlei Co-op only to disappear into its production. In 1997 they decided to have the grapes vinified separately and they bottled the wine as a Carignan. Close to 30 hectares of vineyard also produce excellent Cinsaut which is delivered to Bovlei.

## WELGEMEEND ESTATE
Paarl

Billy Hofmeyr bought this farm called Monte Video in 1974. He changed the name to Welgemeend because the Hofmeyr family had owned the last working vineyard within Cape Town's city boundaries. Welgemeend is a specialist boutique winery producing a limited range of red wines. For several years Ursula Hofmeyr was solely in charge of the farm, with Billy taking leave from work during the vintages. Professor Joel van Wyk, then head of the Oenology faculty at Stellenbosch University, worked closely with Billy for Welgemeend's earlier vintages. The first wines were released in 1979 and immediately developed a faithful following. Billy was a pioneer of the Cape's Bordeaux-style blends, and in 1987 he consolidated Welgemeend's range, producing only four blended

*(previous page) Vineyards below the Hottentots Holland mountains in Somerset West.*

wines. Billy's daughter, Louise, took over as winemaker when Billy became seriously ill in the early 1990s. Like her late father, she believes in as little interference with her wines as possible and only does a light egg-white fining. She is also experimenting with spontaneous fermentation. Louise Hofmeyr has always had a natural talent for wine making. This is mirrored in the 1997 and 1998 Welgemeend Estate Reserve, South Africa's first classic Bordeaux-style blend. They are rich, complex, elegant wines and received high praise from *Decanter*.

## WELLINGTON WYNKELDER
### Wellington – Paarl

This cellar is one of the original co-ops founded with Government assistance in 1906, and was then called the Wellington Co-operative Winery. This was dissolved in 1936 and replaced with the Wellington Wynboere Koöperatiewe, now known as the Wellington Wynkelder. It receives grapes from new plantings of Merlot, Pinotage and Cinsaut from the slopes of Groenberg and these produce fresh, fruity wines. Gert Boerssen has been the winemaker since 1980, and the winery receives 12 000 tons from 50 members. The red portion of the crush now comprises almost two thirds of total production. Most of the production is custom-made for other labels, but an increasing amount is being sold under the co-op's own label on the export market.

## WELMOED WINES
### Stellenbosch

The Welmoed Co-op was previously the distillery of Castle Wine and Brandy Company, which closed the plant in 1940. The affected farmers decided to take over the cellar and formed the Welmoed Co-op Wine Cellars in 1941, having purchased the operation from Castle Wine and Brandy. In 1942 eight members delivered 500 tons. By 1966 the tonnage rose to 4200 tons. Winemaker Jassie Coetzee introduced cold fermentation while still working in the old cellar. In the early 1980s, Kobus Rossouw improved the cellar facilities. Under winemaker Nicky Versfeld major upgrades took place in the cellars and new ranges were introduced. Christo Roux is now the winemaker. Welmoed is a founder member of the Stellenbosch Vineyards Company. It produces some fine wines under the Reserve Range and very drinkable wines under the Selection Range.

## WELTEVREDE ESTATE
### Robertson

In 1976 Lourens Jonker was the first producer in the Robertson area to bottle his own wines and sell direct to the public. Lourens qualified as a pilot in the South African Air Force and became a squadron leader. An only son, he decided to follow in his father's footsteps and studied Viticulture and Oenology at Stellenbosch University, graduating in 1961. He did his graduate studies at the University of California at Davis and in late 1962 started farming with his father. He bought adjoining property and Weltevrede now has 100 hectares planted to vines. Lourens was appointed as a director of the KWV and in 1995 elected chairman. Weltevrede Estate is known for its white wines and excellent dessert wines. A premium range, Oude Weltevreden, consists of a Chardonnay and a Merlot/Cabernet Sauvignon blend. Lourens' son Philip has been winemaker since the 2000 vintage.

## WELVANPAS WINES
### Wellington – Paarl

Welvanpas is the birthplace of Piet Retief and is owned by direct descendants, who have refurbished the 100-year-old cellar. Dan Retief Junior is the winemaker. There are 45 hectares of vineyards, some of which have been replanted and new sites have been developed. Plantings are strictly in accordance with what varieties suit the site and soil, and not according to fashion. Early wines have been very encouraging, with the 1994 Cabernet Sauvignon showing great charm and

good development potential. Current production is about 2000 cases but could increase.

## WESKUS WINES
### Swartland

Winkelshoek Wynkelder, the marketer of Weskus wines, is something of a local legend and well marketed by Hennie Hanekom. Although there are vineyards in the vicinity, the wines are made at the Swartland Co-op. The brandies and fortified wines have remarkable reputations and the fun labels add to the attraction of very drinkable products.

## WEST PEAK WINES
### Stellenbosch

West Peak wines are made on Simon Barlow's Nooitgedacht farm from 44 hectares of vines. The West Peak label is a creation of Simon Barlow and merchant vintners in the United Kingdom.

## WESTERN WINES

Wines are made in various wineland cellars for this United Kingdom company under the direction of Kiwi winemaker Rhyan Wardman. Volumes now exceed half a million cases, with the best-known label being Kumala.

## WHALEHAVEN
### Walker Bay – Overberg

Owner and winemaker Storm Kreusch is a *négociant* and buys in her grapes from Oak Valley, Villiersdorp, and a nearby farm, where she has employed a vineyard consultant. Storm's winery was built at Whalehaven in only two months, but when her first load of grapes arrived for the 1995 vintage the floor was still being laid and the electricity had yet to be connected. Storm, however, still managed to make her wine, producing successful Pinot Noir, Cabernet Sauvignon, Sauvignon Blanc and Chardonnay. Also in her range for earlier drinking is a red blend of predominantly Shiraz with Merlot, named Baleine Noir. The 1996 vintage was three times the size of the previous year, and the 1996 vintage Whalehaven Pinot Noir was made entirely from a Burgundian Pinot Noir clone. Storm is now considered one of the leading Pinot Noir producers after receiving high ratings from *Wine* magazine and leading writers abroad.

## WILDEKRANS CELLARS
### Overberg

Currently owned by Bruce Elkin and E.K. Green, Wildekrans lies below Houw Hoek Pass in the Bot River valley. The cellar was installed in 1992 under the guidance of winemaker Bartho Eksteen. Eventually 60 hectares of a number of varieties are envisaged and there is always the option to buy in. Bartho Eksteen made excellent Sauvignon Blanc and Pinotage. In 1996 his Cabernet Sauvignon was awarded the General Smuts Trophy for the Best Wine at the South African National Young Wine Show. No wonder that *Decanter*, in its 21st birthday edition, rated Wildekrans as one of the hot properties for the new millennium, one of only two from South Africa. Bartho Eksteen left Wildekrans to produce wines under his own label and Jacques Fourie has been winemaker since 1997. Forty hectares are planted to vines and a further five hectares will be planted over the next three years. The most planted variety is Pinotage, the flagship wine, followed by Merlot, Cabernet Franc, Cabernet Sauvignon and Sauvignon Blanc.

## WILHELMSHOF
### Stellenbosch

Nico van der Merwe, current winemaker at Saxenburg, has finally produced his own label. The grapes are sourced from the Olifants River region, but plans are already on the drawing board to develop land and a cellar at Bot River. The first release 1999 Robert Alexander Shiraz has confirmed Nico's status as the icon Shiraz exponent in the Cape. The first vintage of

Mas Nicolas, a 1999 Shiraz/Cabernet Sauvignon blend, is still awaiting release.

## WINDFALL
### Robertson

The ebullient Eddie Barlow purchased this farm in the Agterkliphoogte area. Existing varieties have been grubbed out and replanted with Pinotage, Ruby Cabernet, Merlot and Viognier. Despite Eddie suffering a stroke, his first production is scheduled for bottling in 2001.

## WINDMEUL CO-OP
### Paarl

The co-op gets its name from the windmill in Agter Paarl, and was established in 1944 when a group of export table grape producers needed an outlet for grapes that were not up to export standard. Their quantities were not enough to make a co-op viable so they involved several wine grape growers, and in 1946 the 23-member co-op pressed its first grapes. Today close to 10 000 tons are crushed from 54 members, but only minute quantities are bottled. The Cabernet Sauvignon and Cabernet/Merlot blend are both stunning.

## WINECORP SA LTD.

In 1999 the interests of Longridge, Savanha and Spier Cellars were merged into Winecorp Ltd. Brands have been streamlined into Longridge, Savanha, Spier and Capelands. One large facility for blending, stabilising, bottling and warehousing has been established at the upgraded Simondium site in Paarl. Winecorp is listed on the JSE and Spier Resort owns approximately 62 per cent of the shares, while 32 per cent is owned by the public. The farming operation will be carried out by Afrika Vineyards (Pty) Ltd headed by Gerrie Wagener. Winecorp has a wide network of 35 contract growers and long-term contracts with a dozen core growers. Ben Radford, born and bred in Barossa valley, Australia, is Winecorp's group winemaker, leading all the wine-making teams in the three different cellars. Naledi (Cabernet Sauvignon) and Sejana (Merlot) are made from grapes drawn from premium vineyards in Stellenbosch and Durbanville by Frenchman Stephane de Saint Salvy with consultancy from Alain Mouiex. Savanha, founded in 1994, has wines that reflect the essential soul of Africa: Sémillon, Chardonnay and Sauvignon Blanc in white; Cabernet Sauvignon, Merlot and Shiraz in red. Longridge and Bay View are wines from the Helderberg cellar where Ben Radford has produced world-recognised Chardonnays under the Longridge label. Bay View are fruit-driven, New World wines that are very accessible for early drinking. Longridge was founded by Johann Laubser in 1993. Spier Cellars have wines made by Frans Smit who has a deft touch in producing excellent Noble Late Harvest wines as well as fine varietal wines from all the classics. Capelands is a stylish, modern and easy-drinking wine sold only in litre bottles.

## WITHOEK WINERY
### Calitzdorp – Klein Karoo

Withoek lies next door to Axe Hill. It is owned by the Geyser family who are in the construction business. A son, Fanie, is studying wine making and viticulture at Stellenbosch University. At present, some seven tons are pressed. The first port was produced in 1998. Now port, muscadel and dry red wines are made.

## YONDER HILL
### Helderberg – Stellenbosch

This cellar was built by Rob Mundell, who crushed his first vintage in 1993 with the assistance of Jan Coetzee. Unfortunately, for health reasons Rob had to sell the farm early in 1997. Yonder Hill is now owned by the Naudé family and David Lockley has been winemaker since 1998. Ten hectares are presently planted to vineyards with a further two to come. The most planted variety is Merlot, followed by Cabernet

Sauvignon, Cabernet Franc, Petit Verdot and Chardonnay. One white wine and three reds are bottled. David Lockley's ambition is to make one of South Africa's best Merlots. Yonder Hill iNanda 1995 was rated among the top 100 wines in *Decanter*.

### ZANDDRIFT VINEYARDS
Paarl

The cellar and a chapel were built by Italian prisoners during the Second World War when Professor Ronnie Belcher owned this property. Hennie le Roux bought the farm from Professor Belcher in 1995. Since then wine quality has been steadily improved under Yvonne le Roux, with assistance from Mark Carmichael-Green. Twenty-nine hectares produce 90 per cent white and 10 per cent red.

### ZANDVLIET ESTATE
Ashton – Robertson

Paul de Wet, long-time partner with the Bergkelder, has gone independent. The Zandvliet label is still the premium label. The estate is 1000 hectares in extent, with 175 hectares under vines; the balance is devoted to the thoroughbred racehorse stud run by Paul's brother Dan. Zandvliet has traditionally been a red wine producer, even though the area is known for white varieties. Paul now has plantings of Sauvignon Blanc and Chardonnay. The first wine bottled under the Zandvliet label was a 1975 Shiraz, which made a name for Zandvliet in the wine world. In 1984 the first Cabernet Sauvignon was made. Paul and Dan have achieved a great deal over the years. More recently they have injected considerable capital into the estate, updating their cellar. They have also appointed California viticulturist Dr Phil Freese as a consultant. He and Dan have been developing new vineyards over the last three years. Zandvliet is blessed with rich lime deposits in its soils and new vineyards are gradually being planted on the hills. The new plantings include Mourvèdre, Grenache, Rousanne, Marsanne and Viognier. Johan van Wyk has been winemaker since 2000.

### ZEVENWACHT ESTATE
Stellenbosch

This estate comprises two farms, Langverwacht and Zevenfontein. Jean le Roux was granted the land in 1712 and called it Langverwacht. In 1793 the adjoining property Zevenfontein was granted to Daniel Bosman. Pieter de Waal, owner of Langverwacht from 1798, then purchased Zevenfontein, but the properties were divided again when he sold Langverwacht to his son Adriaan. Zevenfontein was purchased by Petrus Heibner in 1799 and a year later he converted the existing house into the more traditional T-shape, adding the attractive neo-classical front gable. In time the house was changed to the traditional H-shape. In 1979 Gilbert Colyn purchased Zevenfontein and Langverwacht and called the combined properties Zevenwacht. Colyn designed and built his new cellar at Zevenwacht and restored the homestead. Neil Ellis was the first winemaker. Zevenwacht was bought in 1992 by Harold Johnson, who has made a great number of changes and improvements at Zevenwacht. An additional adjoining property with prime vineyards was purchased a couple of years ago. Zevenwacht is now 200 hectares in extent. The most planted variety is Cabernet Sauvignon, followed by Sauvignon Blanc, Chenin Blanc, Chardonnay and Shiraz. Ten whites and 10 reds are made by winemaker Raymond Greyling.

### ZORGVLIET
Stellenbosch

Since Peter Rymer purchased this 1000-hectare property, it has been totally revitalised. The original home dates back to 1692. The property comprises three farms with an 80-ton cellar on Springrove already in production.

*Cellar at Vriesenhof.*

# INDEX